ADVANCE PRAISE FOR

GETTING TO WHERE WE *MEANT* TO BE

"If you'd like to see public education thrive, here is a book to bolster your arguments. Down to earth writing and excellent choice of content allow vitally important concepts about schooling in contemporary America to be analyzed and easily comprehended. It is one of the clearest discussions I've read about curriculum and other key policy issues, including their meaning and their importance for our administrators, teachers, schools, parents—and yes, for our nation as well. Every decision about these issues is a decision that will shape the knowledge base, skills and dispositions of tomorrow's citizens. This insightful and highly readable book explains why such decisions should never be made lightly."

David C. Berliner
Regents' Professor Emeritus, Arizona State University

"Education is plagued with good intentions gone awry, particularly when the follow-through is framed by commonsensical assumptions that lack a sound research basis. Hinchey and Konkol paint a compelling and nuanced picture of exactly how this is happening in many core areas of schooling, and then offer concrete tools for reframing and reimagining. In this moment when too many so-called reforms are taking advantage of seductive rhetoric, educators and policy makers alike who are fortunate enough to pick up this book will find themselves at once enraptured, unsettled, and more hopeful."

Kevin Kumashiro
Author of *Bad Teacher!: How Blaming Teachers Distorts the Bigger Picture*

"In this provocative and compelling book, Pat Hinchey and Pamela Konkol challenge us to rethink assumptions about teaching, learning, and curriculum. Their powerful text details assumptions currently dominating neoliberal education reform as well as alternative perspectives, illuminating complexities in critical issues that often go unexamined. Those who care about public education and the imperative of its deep potential need to read, contemplate, and take purposeful action prompted in *Getting to Where We* Meant *to Be*."

Brian D. Schultz
Professor and Chair of Teacher Education at Miami University
Author of *Teaching in the Cracks: Openings and Opportunities for Student-Centered, Action-Focused Curriculum*

GETTING TO WHERE WE *MEANT* TO BE

GETTING TO WHERE WE *MEANT* TO BE

 Working Toward the Educational World We Imagine/d

PATRICIA H. HINCHEY

PAMELA J. KONKOL

Myers Education Press

Gorham, Maine

Copyright © 2018 | Myers Education Press, LLC

Published by Myers Education Press, LLC
P.O. Box 424
Gorham, ME 04038

Myers Education Press is an academic publisher specializing in books, e-books and digital content in the field of education. All of our books are subjected to a rigorous peer review process and produced in compliance with the standards of the Council on Library and Information Resources.

Library of Congress Cataloging-in-Publication Data available from Library of Congress.

13-digit ISBN **978-1-9755-0001-6** (paperback)
13-digit ISBN **978-1-9755-0000-9** (hard cover)
13-digit ISBN **978-1-9755-0002-3** (library networkable e-edition)
13-digit ISBN **978-1-9755-0003-0** (consumer e-edition)

Printed in the United States of America.

All first editions printed on acid-free paper that meets the American National Standards Institute Z39-48 standard.

Books published by Myers Education Press may be purchased at special quantity discount rates for groups, workshops, training organizations and classroom usage. Please call our customer service department at 1-800-232-0223 for details.

Cover design by Sophie Appel

Visit us on the web at **www.myersedpress.com** to browse our complete list of titles.

Contents

THREE   Whither and Whence Curriculum?   52

While it seems obvious that curriculum consists of the academic subjects taught in a school, thinking about it instead as everything students learn in and from their school environment expands curricular boundaries considerably. For example, rules tell students how much they are trusted—if at all. Abusive or deceitful adults teach that people with more power don't need to treat those with less power ethically. This chapter pokes into the many parts of school that teach students lessons—intentionally or not.

FOUR   What Does It Mean to Educate for Citizenship?   90

Most people would agree that yes, public schools should teach citizenship. But things get difficult when it turns out that different people define concepts like "patriotism" differently. Does a patriot support all government policies without questioning them, trusting political leaders' judgment? Or monitor government activity and speak out when policy may be unjust or immoral? Do schools teach all history—or avoid unflattering events?

FIVE   How Much Control Does a (Student) Body Need?   123

Schools must maintain an orderly environment conducive to learning, but how much control of students is appropriate? This chapter explores issues ranging from appearance to classroom pedagogy and disciplinary systems. It's known that zero tolerance policies have had damaging results for a wide range of K-12 students, especially students of color and with special needs. And, damage from restraint and seclusion policies have included even student suicide. How much control is too much?

SIX   **Reform? By Whom and for What?**   159

Since at least 1983, politicians and many others have been arguing that American education is failing and needs significant reform. The results of the push for reform include an emphasis on standardized testing to hold teachers and schools responsible for student learning, school choice policies, the vast expansion of charter schools, and recent growth in for-profit and online schools. Do American schools need reform? And if they do, are these the reforms they need?

SEVEN   **The Way Forward . . .**   194

This book invites readers to think deeply about their own intentions and to consider whether their actions are leading toward or away from their original goals—and to follow up with action. Those who feel encouraged because they seem to be on the right path might consider trying to persuade others to come along. Those who feel the need for a course correction might consider possible changes. No matter any individual's specifically intended destination, no step in the right direction is too small to be worth the effort.

A Message from the Publisher

The book that you are holding in your hand (or reading on your device) is unique and important for a variety of reasons. Selfishly, there is the fact that it is the first book from this fledgling publishing company. If every subsequent title produced by Myers Education Press matches the quality of *Getting to Where We Meant to Be*, this will be a successful venture.

But of even greater significance, it is my hope that you will recognize the real, unique, down-to-earth viewpoints presented by the authors at a time when we are inundated with so many opposing viewpoints about what is right and wrong with our schools. There is no question that public education is under assault, and not always by the bad guy (however an individual may define "bad guy"). Often, good intentions can do as much damage to public education as budget cuts and the loss of talented teachers. One of the major themes of this book is that incorrect assumptions and preconceived notions about public schools distort the picture of what happens inside them.

These assumptions do not exist in a vacuum; they live in the real world. I am reminded of a situation that a young teacher I know encountered several years ago. Armed with a master's in education, she began her career teaching second grade in a charter school in an idyllic setting: a new school building, a pastoral landscape, and a fairly affluent student body prepared to learn each day. In her fifth year of teaching, circumstances led her to take a new position teaching first grade in an urban school district at an underresourced school with a high incidence of poverty and homelessness. It doesn't matter where in the country this took place, since it is the unfortunate truth that we have an ample supply of schools that could be characterized in this way.

Bringing her previous experience to her new classroom, she set about decorating the space in preparation for the new school year. Anticipating that many students would lack basic supplies, she stocked the classroom's closet with pencils, notebooks, and other school materials. Her pleasure in this preparation, however, turned into something very different on the first day of classes. She discovered that almost half of her students were either homeless or on the verge of becoming so. To her horror, she realized that instead of markers and paper, what her children needed most was food: many of them came to school hungry because they hadn't had breakfast that morning or dinner the night before. So the classroom closet became a pantry, so that she could feed any child who asked for something to eat. Her previous experience in a wealthier school led her to do the "right things" preparing a classroom in a different setting, but hunger, poverty, and homelessness forced her to face a different reality.

Recognizing this dichotomy, the authors of this book present a balanced, rational view of public education today, discussing pros and cons in a sensible, nonconfrontational way. And they certainly have the talent and experience to conduct this conversation.

In my previous position as director of another academic publishing house, where I edited the education list, I had the distinct pleasure of working with Pat Hinchey on two excellent titles, *Finding Freedom in the Classroom: A Practical Introduction to Critical Theory* (which at the time of this writing is in its second edition and seventh printing, no small feat) and *Becoming a Critical Educator: Defining a Classroom Identity, Designing a Critical Pedagogy* (in a mere third printing), both of which went on to rank among the best-selling titles on the education list. Those two experiences allowed me to get to know Pat as a scholar, a teacher, and a friend. In publishing, we talk about books having "long tails" if they stand the test of time, selling as well on the backlist as they did as new titles. Pat's two books sell year after year, becoming more relevant with each passing semester. Before we sell a single copy of the present book, *Getting to Where We Meant to Be* will exceed anything else she's written, if the high quality of the text is any predictor of its success. I have always admired the eloquence of her writing and the clarity of her thinking. But the real proof of the impact of her books comes from students and pre-service teachers. Many of them write to her to discuss cogent concepts and to thank her for her passion for public education.

My association with Pamela Konkol is of a more recent vintage. I have had the pleasure of working with her through the American Educational Studies Association for the last couple of years. As of this writing, Pam is an officer in the organization and there is no doubt that she will run that show soon. Pam brought a rich teaching background in a variety of settings to the table, which is evident in her concise observations about classroom settings and her passion for children. Many of the examples given in the book originate from her public school classroom experiences, both good and bad.

When the three of us first started discussing the plan for the book, we set up to a few ground rules. First, Pat and Pam made clear that they wanted the freedom to say what they wanted to say. That was an easy decision based on the outline they proposed. Second, we agreed that the content needed to speak to undergraduates preparing for professional roles in education as well as to graduate students in such areas as curriculum, administration and pedagogy, avoiding the jargon that alienates the people who need a clear understanding of the topics discussed in the book. Finally, from my side, I asked that they write this book as quickly as possible and adhere to tight deadlines in return for my promise that it would be the first book published by the company. And here you have it.

At the start of the process, we decided to recruit an expert in the field to help with the vetting of the text. Karen Cadiero-Kaplan graciously assumed this role, and the final content of the book has been greatly enhanced because of her efforts. She even cooperated with our insane deadlines to keep the production calendar on track. Words can't express how grateful we are for her assistance.

So that is the brief tale of bringing this book into existence. I am deeply humbled by the confidence that Pat and Pam have put into this new venture, I am delighted with the results of their efforts, and I hope you are too.

Chris Myers
Gorham, Maine

Preface

As our good friend Karen Cadiero-Kaplan noted when she did us the favor of commenting on our manuscript, readers like to know where they're headed as they begin reading. Context is important, and so we provide some here.

First, the authors are both longtime teachers and teacher educators, and this book comes out of our experience working with undergraduate and graduate students as well as with a wide variety of education professionals in K-12 schools and higher education institutions. More specifically, it comes from our concern for both students and educators in U.S. public schools as we've watched an era of reform shift control farther away from communities and schools to distant politicians and corporations. Too often, the effects have been devastating for the people in those communities and schools. Students face narrower and narrower curriculum, more and more alien to their own interests and goals, while teachers and administrators find themselves increasingly pressured to impose things on kids they know in their hearts are harmful. To be blunt, the suffering we've seen makes us crazy—as does the fact we know that the suffering is strongest in schools serving poor communities, where students may be rich in intelligence and ambition but poorly served by underresourced schools that can't afford even toilet paper, let alone engaging and relevant curricular materials.

Second, we are terribly worried by the despair too often expressed by experienced teachers—who themselves are so upset by the policies tying their hands—that more and more of them are choosing to leave the classroom at the very time when their professionalism and commitment are most needed. No one knows better than teachers and administrators working in a specific school what students in that school need, and losing the wisdom of their experience impoverishes a school in unimaginable ways. Kids can't afford to keep losing the efforts of the most experienced and committed education professionals.

Third, we have long believed that if the well-financed, powerful corporate effort to privatize public schools and turn them into profit centers is to be resisted, it will be education professionals—teachers, administrators, support staff—who turn the tide. Unfortunately, the same forces that are promoting privatization are also trying to stifle professional education programs, pushing for various kinds of accountability that tend to squeeze theoretical considerations and critical questioning out of higher education curricula. This makes us as crazy as the other policies we oppose. How are educators to choose among alternatives if they don't know alternatives exist? And how are they to know about alternatives if education programs focus exclusively on "This is how you do it" rather than "What is it you hope to do for your students?"

And so this text explicitly lays out alternatives. We invite readers to think through common assumptions and consider whether and how to respond to the questions we pose in areas we believe are critical to improving conditions in schools. What goals should schools pursue? What type of curriculum would target those goals? What kind of citizen should public schools educate? How much control of students is appropriate? Which reforms might make things better for students, and which worse?

And most importantly: in light of individual answers to those questions, what can individual education professionals *do* to make things better for students in U.S. public schools, despite the agendas and efforts of corporate and philanthropic titans?

Where we hope this text leads readers, then, is to carefully consider the many aspects of schools that have critical implications not just for life *in* the classroom but for life *after* the classroom. To state the obvious: the goals in a for-profit school—and many already exist—will not and cannot be the same as the goals in a public school charged with serving important democratic functions. And as they say: "If you're not part of the solution, you're part of the problem." We hope this text not only empowers readers to understand some problems in current conditions but also inspires them to enthusiastically tackle those problems and work toward better conditions tomorrow.

GETTING TO WHERE WE *MEANT* TO BE

ONE

∾ "You Have Arrived at Your Destination." Oh, Really?

Think of story as a mnemonic device for complex ideas.
—*Annette Simmons*

W E BEGIN WITH THE STORY of where and how this book began.

We were in Puerto Rico, our rental car temporarily parked along a string of brash beach bars and worn motels as we listened to that oh-so-annoying voice: *Your destination is on the right. . . . Destination . . . is on the right.*

But no: it wasn't. We were somewhere or other that looked a whole lot like the exact opposite of where we had planned to go.

Pat had promised Pam an enchanted oceanside resort. We were taking a twenty-four-hour detour from our travels to a conference to carve out some time together in a serene and inspirational setting where we could focus, could think deeply about whether we really had anything useful to say to people investing their best efforts on behalf of students. We had suffered hours of crushing traffic and miles (or kilometers) of twisting one-and-a-half lane roads winding through apparently uninhabited jungle, and we had taken our trusty rental into brave (or naive) plunges into roadwide stands of water that might have been three (or thirty) inches deep. In, we might add, a proverbial ink-black night.

No. The doorways blaring rock and the tired motels were not our destination at all. And Pam noticed why: Pat had put the name of the resort into a mapping system, printed out the resulting directions after a quick glance at them, and handed them off to Pam, who as navigator simply checked what she'd been given against an electronic map. Neither of us thought to check whether the directions were in fact to the place we actually intended to go.

And they weren't.

Somehow, the electronic mapping system provided correct directions to the place we found ourselves—but it was not at all where we intended to be. Asked for directions to one place, the mapping program somehow changed the destination and provided directions to somewhere else. It was our own fault, of course. One of us assumed she got what she asked for; the other assumed the person who set the destination got correct instructions to where they wanted to go. Both ended up lost on the way from here to there. And so it goes, ever and always, on and on.

We think we know where we're going and how to get there, we think we know what we want and how to get it, and we drive on through metaphorical nights following directions from faceless and nameless sources—and eventually find ourselves somewhere we don't recognize, somewhere we never intended to go, asking ourselves *How in the world did we get here?*

The Many Ways We Lose Our Way

We've all been lost, both physically and metaphorically, and we've all thought about what wrong turns we might have taken and why. Often, our analysis indicates that things started going wrong when we relied on an assumption to guide our actions—as when Pat assumed the computer gave her what she asked for and when Pam assumed the directions Pat handed over were trustworthy. When we make such a mistake—when we literally take the wrong road from here to there—it's not a particularly big deal. We can just recalculate, make a couple of U-turns, and get back on track after losing a bit of time. But in other situations, mistaken assumptions can put us on paths that not only lead away from our goals but cost much more than a little lost time.

For example, we assume that anyone we've accepted as a friend or lover is trustworthy—until we learn that someone we trust has lied or cheated, leaving us feeling deeply betrayed and wounded. And, we become wary of trusting again. Or, fully immersed in a consumer culture, we assume that having the latest electronic gadgets and clothes and cars will bring us happiness—until we find our wallets empty and our pleasure in purchases evaporating startlingly soon. And in this case, we are also stuck with the need to work and work and work in order to pay off the new clothes, the new phones, the new car.

But here we oversimplify: decisions are more complex than we've just made them sound. More specifically, there is usually not one assumption that leads us astray, but many. How we arrive at one place rather than another is often determined by a confused blur of routine assumptions about where we are, where we want to go, and which route will get us there:

- We think we know what we want or should want—so we head for the wrong place right from the start.
- We think we know more than we do—so we don't question our own plans, don't ask whether there just might be a better route to where we want to go.
- We think what is true for us is true for others—so we don't adapt our plans for differences in people and contexts.
- We think good intentions can be trusted to ensure good outcomes—so we don't ponder possible unintended consequences of our actions.
- We think some things will never change—and so we fail to act, ensuring nothing changes.

A perfect storm of such assumptions produced a family crisis when Pat was young and can illustrate how easily good intentions can nevertheless lead to unintended disaster.

Pat's dad, then a school director in the local district, once persuaded the high school's staff to fail her brother at the end of the year even though his low, low grades were high enough to pass—having tanked only after football season ended. Like most parents, he had good intentions: he wanted his son to have a dependable income, a successful life. He assumed that for his son, the best route to that goal would be to get into a good college, and he further assumed that being retained in grade for a year would mean better grades at college application time. But no: that wasn't the outcome. Instead, Pat's brother ran away from home to work at a dude ranch. He didn't return to his family or to high school until a horse stomped and broke his shoulder, and he never did go to college. Instead he became an operating engineer—and ironically, he also made a lot more money expertly running bulldozers and cranes than his nerdy sister ever made as a college professor.

For *some* people, college may be the best route to a successful life—but it's a mistake to assume that's true for everyone. It certainly wasn't true for a boy who was never happy indoors, who spent every waking hour he could outdoors and who had hated school from first grade. And, while punishment can make *some* people do (or stop doing) some things, it's a mistake to assume that punishment will automatically produce desired behavior in everyone. (Think for a minute: If punishment worked reliably, would we have repeat criminals?) Moreover, the assumption that college will automatically produce the highest salaries has not been true for a very long time (if ever): the guy on the crane can outearn the college professor. Although Pat's dad had the very, very best of intentions, the entire family suffered because of his several mistaken assumptions about the best goal for his son and best way to get there, given the specific people in the situation.

All humans make such miscalculations, and since educators are human, they too often suffer from missteps in goals and strategies. For example, some teachers try to create a happy classroom and some administrators try to create a collegial environment by encouraging students and coworkers to consider them a *friend*, assuming that *friendly* and *friend* are equivalent concepts. Instead, they often find themselves dismayed when chaos results in their kingdoms, since friends have no authority over friends and usually don't punish each other for bad behavior. Assuming their *friend* will understand and be forgiving, students and teachers alike begin missing deadlines for work, and then they are hurt when their *friends* in authority pull rank and punish or criticize them. On the flip side of that coin, others in authority who want cooperation from students or teachers they supervise become martinets, insisting that their authority be respected and their directives never be questioned. However, the autocrat's assumption that respect can be mandated is unreliable; rather than respect, the disappointing reaction is often resentment and resistance. What teacher has not faced the dilemma of being so friendly with students—or so authoritarian with students—that he or she ended up backed into an uncomfortable corner? What administrator has not been disappointed when being so friendly with teachers—or so authoritarian with them—that he or she ended up in some painful dilemma?

What makes the entire process of education so complex and challenging is the reality that in fact some assumptions will apply to some people . . . but not to others; some goals will be good for some people . . . but not for others;

and some strategies will be effective with some people . . . but not with others. And, ummm . . . the whole mess is made still messier when people act on their *unconscious* assumptions, which tend to be very nearly all of them. If we had to stop and examine every assumption we make every day (for example, the assumption in the United States that cars will stay on the right hand side of the road), we'd be paralyzed. So we develop assumptions somehow, somewhere, for some reason, and once we've fully internalized them we rarely look back to ask ourselves how well they are serving us.

And so: this book.

Our own assumption is that given the complexity of public education, decisions about goals and the best strategies to reach them have to be made by people in specific contexts, and the best way to make better decisions is to tease out assumptions guiding efforts and strategies, to consider how reliable and effective they've proven in a given context, to seek out and assess alternatives, and *then* to determine stances on issues and directions for practice and policy—in light of the many elements that shape their unique environment. As an obvious example, while students in a wealthy and highly educated community might be well-served by prioritizing the development of a junior year abroad program, students who come to school hungry every day would likely be better served by a breakfast program.

This is *not* to say that both groups should not have experiences that widen their exposure to other ways of being in the world; it *is* to say that priorities and specific experiences will sensibly differ in different contexts—as long as public schools are inequitably funded. Many educators are currently documenting and discussing what has become known as *the opportunity gap*[1] in schools caused by vastly inequitable resources, a condition exacerbated in recent years by growing constraints on and reductions to school funding. Ideally, all students should have access to both a healthful breakfast and travel abroad. But that is not the current reality, and no one knows that better than people now working in schools. Priorities must be determined. Choices must be made. Since that is the case, our efforts here are to help educators identify and think through their options as carefully as possible in order to accomplish as much as possible given existing constraints. That said, what *can* be accomplished at any given moment is *a lot*, if we are thoughtful and do our best. The fact that we're unlikely ever to live in a perfect world is no excuse for failing to try to make the existing world better.

Each of the following chapters intends to put an element of schooling under a microscope to examine its many parts—and possible permutations.
There is no argument for *this* being better than *that*. There is no effort to tell
anyone what they *should* choose or do. Such thinking is barren outside a specific context, and even potentially harmful. As an obvious example, consider
policymakers' assumption that one of the most important things right now
for every student in the country is to score well on standardized reading tests
as opposed to, say, learning English or music or having enough to eat and/or a
safe place (even *any* place) to do homework and to sleep. This book is both an
invitation and, we hope, an aid to educators who work through its chapters to
develop more thoughtful, nuanced and effective goals and strategies.

As a general introduction to the kind of thinking readers will find in subsequent chapters, the following is a brief illustration of how the kinds of mistaken
assumptions detailed earlier—in goals, in assuming we're on the best path, in
failing to seek out alternatives, in trusting good intentions to produce good
outcomes, in failing to believe every educator can make a difference—generally
undermine the hard work and unquestioned dedication of so many educators.

The Many Ways We Lose Our Way in Schools

Each of the following segments details examples of how the mistaken assumptions identified previously—however well-intentioned—have produced unintended, harmful outcomes.

Mistaken Goals

Beginning with the passage of the *No Child Left Behind Act,* the federal government has imposed ever-higher test scores as the dominant goal in public
schools. Much has already been written about the correlative damage this
mistaken goal has produced. Some has been academic: a stunningly narrowed
curriculum, for example, along with developmentally inappropriate tasks for
younger and younger children. Some has been physical: children being denied recess in the interest of more time for practice in filling in bubbles on
answer sheets, and children so anxious that they become physically ill on test
day, a phenomenon so common that publishers have included "vomit kits" in
test packages (more on this later). Yet other damage has been ethical, as when

"bubble kids" on the cusp of a higher score have received more attention and resources than children who need much more help, or when educators have cheated on the exams. Some has even been tragic: in New York City, an elementary school principal of a prestigious charter school died after throwing herself in front of a subway train when it was discovered that she'd cheated to raise disappointingly low test scores.[2] Undoubtedly, these outcomes were unintended—but they are nevertheless the results of policy that sets high test scores as a primary goal.

Educators, too, have set goals that have proven harmful to students: zero tolerance policy is a good example. The goal of eliminating absolutely, positively every trace of a weapon in schools has led to many students being suspended or expelled, which denies them instructional time for reasons that many people would consider absurd. Students have been suspended for simply drawing cartoon guns (even in a picture of a soldier), or for "shooting" from a finger or a breadstick. In one case, an eight-year-old was suspended after he took some bites from a Pop-Tart—and the remaining pastry had a gun-like shape.[3] In another, authorities sent a student who reported that a friend was suicidal to the friend's locker to retrieve the knife he intended to use—and then suspended the student who retrieved the knife for having a weapon in hand.[4] Similarly, the notion that *no* drug should ever be allowed in a school has also led to suspension for students carrying aspirin or other analgesics.

While it may be tempting to say these are extreme examples of misapplication of policy, the fact is that such occurrences are not rare. Moreover, some evidence suggests that application of policies seems discriminatory and that it also frequently drags children into the juvenile justice system for minor offenses formerly dispatched by principals.[5] Simply stated, specifying the wrong goals can easily wreak unintended havoc.

Assuming We Know What We're Doing

The case of high stakes testing also illustrates how often people who think they know what they're doing . . . don't. Underlying federal policy are the assumptions that standardized tests are the best measure of student learning and that threats are reliable means of spurring both students and teachers to better and better efforts.

As educators (not to mention the American Psychological Association)[6] have said from the beginning, absolute standardized test scores are inappropriate as high stake measures of student achievement. Learning is far too complex and a single test far too limited for standardized tests to serve as stand-alone and reliable evidence of student learning. In addition, experienced educators know it's laughable to think older students always try their best on standardized tests. Many do, of course, but many also consider the exams pointless and, when frustrated, begin making designs on the bubble sheet with their answers rather than trying to think them through.

Moreover, any first year student taking introductory educational psychology (or any parent with a truly stubborn child) knows that punishment is the weakest of motivators for many (perhaps most) people. Even in instances where potential punishment *is* an effective motivator, outcomes might be made worse rather than better. Children who are stressed and frightened may squander their energy and focus on being anxious and may also become physically ill—witness the "vomit kits" routinely packaged with test kits along with standard instructions for personnel about what to do when a child vomits on a test booklet.[7] As one New York principal reported:

> We know that many children cried during or after testing, and others vomited or lost control of their bowels or bladders. Others simply gave up. One teacher reported that a student kept banging his head on the desk, and wrote, "This is too hard," and "I can't do this," throughout his test booklet.[8]

And teachers and administrators who are frightened—or who fear for the health and the future of their school or their students—may feel they have no option but to cheat to protect them.

Generally, anyone who's been to school seems to believe she or he knows everything necessary to figure out how to make all schools better. This is pretty much the equivalent of suggesting that anyone who's taken aspirin or antibiotics could step into a pharmacy and take over. Few policymakers, philanthropists or business leaders seem to know, or admit, that about one in four or five children in the United States lives below the poverty line[9] (which is artificially low to begin with) or understands such issues as the impact of low birth weight on cognitive development.[10] None seem to understand that teachers are not primarily motivated by salary—or they wouldn't accept starting salaries in the $40,000 range; instead, they'd probably head for someplace like the computer field where assorted jobs tend to start somewhere around $60,000.

Of course, educators themselves may be too sure of their own preconceptions. Students are often told to get their priorities straight when they turn up without homework—but their priorities may *be* straight. Some students work 8–10 hours after school to help their families keep food on the table, an activity that outranks circling adjectives on a worksheet. A student may come to school with greasy hair and dirty clothes not because parents just don't care—as many adults in schools assume—but because the entire family is homeless and lacks access to showers and washing machines. In fact, when Whirlpool began donating washing machines to schools in low-income areas, the project resulted in significantly improved rates of student attendance and engagement.[11] Teachers typically come from middle class backgrounds where three meals a day and a bed to sleep in are taken from granted; for many students in public schools, however, regular meals and a bed every night are blessings to be prayed for. School personnel are both arrogant and perhaps nearly delusional when they tell students to "get their priorities straight" and make sure those adjectives get circled.

As folks as diverse as Paulo Freire and Bill Nye have pointed out, while we all know something others don't, all others know something *we* don't. If we all could remember that none of us knows everything, then we all might choose poor paths less often.

Failing to Seek Out Alternatives

The idea that anything worth doing is worth doing well somehow seems unable to coexist with strategies when budgets come into play. For example, many states have succumbed to federal budget incentives and mandated "value-added assessment" as part of schools' teacher evaluation systems. One motivation, surely for policymakers as well as many others, is that the student test scores necessary for value-added systems already exist. If existing data can be plugged into some new formula, costs will be minimal. Besides: numbers are easy to understand . . . and even if they're not exactly accurate, they're probably close enough to serve the purpose.

While this may be a cost effective strategy, it's a strategy that numerous research studies have already shown to produce estimates a million miles away from "close enough to serve the purpose"—as when a teacher's rank moves erratically year to year among the four quartiles, with some teachers being ranked in the top 25% one year and the lowest 25% the next. (We will stay off a soap box and refrain from discussing at length the additional consideration that the entire system rests on the additional assumption that 25% of all teachers are inept, an assumption based on zero evidence.)[12]

The validity of test scores as an ultimate indicator of student learning is hotly disputed, and the same is true of teacher assessment based on those test scores. That debate is beyond the scope of this discussion. However, what is not debatable is whether there are other viable means of teacher assessment that can yield better or more information about teacher performance. There are.

Researchers have worked for years to improve on such strategies as classroom observation and teaching portfolios, and much is known about how to execute such assessments well.[13] What gets in the way is that they tend to be time consuming—and expensive. For example, for classroom observation to be truly valuable, observers must be trained and also frequently retrained to ensure that the observer's understanding of standard criteria and evidence for meeting them doesn't erode over time. And of course it takes time to sit in on classes, to write up thoughtful evaluations based on specific evidence, and to have meaningful conversations with teachers about strategies for improvement. Checklists are inadequate to the task.

Done *well*, classroom observation not only provides detailed information on a teacher's classroom performance, but it also offers direction for improvement. Of course, done badly by a principal who barely has time to breathe, let alone to devote to sitting in classrooms for hours, it's useless or harmful, just as its critics charge. Because it takes time and money to do observation well, it is costly. The practical result is most often a default to the cheapest measure, imperfect as it may be.

Though better alternatives might be found to this-or-that policy, if they will mean new costs, rarely do efforts target how to make them work despite the cost. With budgets already stressed to the maximum in so many organizations and so many people asked to do with less, little energy goes into trying to reallocate resources from one area to another or to finding new revenue streams to allow for more ambitious systems or practices. And that is understandable. However, settling for what seems easiest and cheapest, or perhaps for what seems self-evidently a solution, has its costs as well. Some of these are not only wasteful and misguided but can literally be tragic.

A good case in point here is the widespread use of restraints and seclusion rooms in schools as a response to student behavior deemed uncooperative or out of control. Theoretically, such measures are to be used in the rare cases where student behavior poses immediate danger to the student involved and/or others. A 2014 report from the U.S. Senate, however, found 66,000 reported instances of restraints and seclusion being implemented, a figure deemed low because many schools did not report their use.[14] Students can be restrained many ways, including handcuffs, bungee cords, and being pinned to the floor by one or more adults; seclusion rooms are typically small padded cells lacking light. And, in this environment, abuses (such as using duct tape to silence a student, or using beanbags to pin a student to the floor) make a bad situation worse. Damage to students has included not only mental anguish, ranging from the embarrassment of urinating on oneself to post-traumatic stress syndrome, but also a wide range of physical damages—ranging from bruises . . . to death. Attempted and successful suicide attempts are also known outcomes.[15]

Teachers and other school personnel are not to be blamed. When as many as 30 or 40 students are crammed into a classroom, teachers have their hands full trying to teach effectively; immediate control of any disruption is an understandable response to it. And, while there *are* alternatives, few educators have received sufficient—if any—training, and procedures require both time and patience to implement. But when the costs of the default solution for difficult students includes their deaths, the easiest and cheapest solution is far too expensive in the long run.

Of course no one *means* to inflict any type of damage to anyone when they choose what appears to be a readily available strategy to address an issue, especially in the face of severe economic restraints. Still, the unintended consequences of not seriously considering possible alternatives and seeking ways to employ them are often higher than anyone would want.

Trusting Good Intentions

Pat's experience offers a good example of how nonproductive it can be to keep thinking that trying hard and having good intentions is enough to make something good happen. She tells this story:

> At one time I was teaching basic writing at a university, and a Korean woman entered the class to learn to improve her writing. I worked and worked and worked with her to explain what a thesis is, what topic sentences are and how they control a piece of writing. I knew she was intelligent and I could not figure out why, no matter how well she seemed to understand what I was saying, she continued to write in a fashion I judged rambling and disjointed.
>
> It was not until years later that I discovered that in Korean and other Asian cultures, politeness requires indirectness in speech. There is a line in a novel by Amy Tan that goes something like this: "In this matter you need not concern yourself on my behalf." In contrast, an American would likely phrase the same message like this: "Mind your own business." My Korean student's culture not only insisted that she be indirect in her language, but it also mandated that she be always respectful of authority figures—including college professors, like me.
>
> So there I was, an American in the habit of saying plainly what I mean, blithely instructing her to be rude and disrespectful to me—something that she simply not could not bring herself to do. She was too polite, too gentle, far too lovely a human being to contradict or disrespect me. To this day I am chagrined by my own failure, even my own stupidity, in my encounter with her. She deserved much better.[16]

Obviously, this issue is also related to the failure to seek alternatives (remember, we've said problems often come from a "blur of assumptions"). But we too often believe that if we just try really, really hard, somehow that will be enough to make what we want to happen actually happen. It seems appropriate to note here that according to some definitions, doing the same thing over and over and expecting different results is the definition of *insanity*. And yet, how many of us do that all the time?

Having good intentions and working hard are no guarantee of finding an effective way forward. Policymakers didn't set out to make children vomit. School personnel using restraints and seclusion didn't anticipate student deaths. If we trust our intentions as sufficient for getting where we want to go, we set ourselves up for failure, and we end up mourning the wasted effort and collateral damage too often inflicted on those we most intended to serve.

Failing to Believe We Can Make a Difference

Between us, the two authors of this book have several decades of working with teachers and other school personnel, and countless experiences trying to introduce new ideas to them. It is not work for the faint-hearted or easily discouraged. A common refrain, and a justifiable one, is "Look, I've been through this reform business at least a dozen times before. It's just been one fad after another, with barely time for us to figure one out before the next is on its way down the pike and our throats. Me? I'm just gonna wait until this train passes by, too, because I know another one will be along directly." Like exhausted American voters, they stop believing that anything they do can make a difference because power lies far beyond them and no one seems much interested in what *they* have to say. And, believing what they do has no effect, they stop doing much of anything except rolling with whatever punches come their way.

And we confess: it is that attitude that serves as our primary motivation for writing this book. We believe, and we think there's evidence to support our belief, that dedicated practitioners can make a difference. If they genuinely consider alternatives and choose carefully among them, they can effect real change. We insist they can. And, we further insist that they can effect change that is good not only for students but also for them and for their communities. And, we dare to hope, even for democracy.

We find evidence in several disparate places. First, the battle to take control of schools away from distant policymakers and to tailor reform to context has been joined by various allies. A good example here is the organized resistance to standardized testing that has exploded in recent years, with coalitions of school personnel, parents and others moving against extreme testing policy. These have included teachers, among them teachers who have sought sane test policies during contract negotiations in widely publicized strikes in Chicago and Seattle. And several states, including New York, New Jersey,

California and Florida, have seen steadily increasing numbers of parents join-
ing the resistance and opting their children out of state exams. In 2015, the
New York Times reported that some 20% of students in its state did not take
the exams. Rather than an anomaly, it's clear that the New York numbers are
indicative of a powerful growing trend. FairTest reported:

> In the spring of 2015, more than 620,000 students refused to take
> state standardized exams. The numbers were stunning in some places:
> 240,000 in New York; 110,000 in New Jersey; 100,000 in Colorado;
> 50,000 in Washington; 44,000 in Illinois; 20,000 in Oregon and Florida;
> 10,000 each in New Mexico and Rhode Island. Statewide, the New York
> opt-out rate reached 20%, topping 70% in some districts. Washington's
> numbers represented half the grade 11 class. In several other states, high
> school refusals reached 15%.
>
> These numbers are a huge leap over 2014, when the Opt Out
> movement first began to have an impact. New York quadrupled, while
> New Jersey increased a hundred-fold. Overall, the numbers went from
> probably under 100,000 to closing in on three quarters of a million.[17]

States have begun changing policy as a response, and opponents of excessive
and inappropriate testing have been accumulating a steadily growing number
of victories as states and districts begin retreating from oppressive policies.[18]
Despite the heavy-handedness of federal policy, a wide variety of alliances
has been succeeding in rolling back a movement that has done much harm to
children and schools.

Nor is standardized testing the only front on which opponents of strong,
federally supported reforms are succeeding. Opposition to charter schools,
especially for-profit charter schools, has also been having some effect. Because
states have rarely imposed the same accountability mandates on charters as
on traditional public schools, the failure of many charters to produce the
promised gains in student achievement has been increasingly recognized and
publicized, even by charter school advocates.

The expected opposition to charters of public school personnel and organizations has been amplified by parents and a public increasingly aware that
tax dollars are being diverted into private pockets while students are cheated
of a meaningful educational experience. Victory on this front, while perhaps

currently modest in relation to the testing wins, has still been remarkable. For example, in the 2016 fall election, voters in Massachusetts overwhelmingly rejected expansion of charter schools in a heated election season that drew national attention. Several states are beginning to take seriously the need for new regulations of charter schools in the interest of accountability. And, when a for-profit charter school billionaire was nominated for Secretary of Education, public outrage, outcry and demonstrations resulted, based on the widely publicized dismal record of her charter schools in Detroit—further energizing public opposition. Federal enthusiasm for any and all charter schools is one thing; state policy quite another.

Things *can* change. But it takes clear thinking, strong alliances, faith, smart strategizing . . . and a lot of hard work.

Where Do You Want to Go . . . and How Will You Get There?

People who become educational professionals typically take that path because they think kids and kids' education matter. They know today's children will be tomorrow's workers and parents and voters. That they will help build strong communities . . . or not. That they will be ethical and innovative workers . . . or not. That they will understand, live and promote core American values . . . or not. That they will understand civic responsibility, will think critically about candidates, and will vote their conscience . . . or perhaps not vote at all.

While it may sound hyperbolic to say that public education is an indispensable pillar of democracy, that is nevertheless the truth. The role of public education in maintaining a free and democratic society is one Thomas Jefferson realized and articulated as he argued for mandating public education:

> Of all the views of this law, none is more important, none more legitimate, than that of rendering the people safe as they are the ultimate guardians of their own liberty.[19]

Ignorant people are not free, but captive to their own inability to craft their individual destinies through critical thinking and self-directed choices. Without education, no one can be truly free, and the nation will be vulnerable to manipulation by clever rhetoric rather than rational analyses.

You are free. You are free to think through the best interests of the multiple citizen groups in your school. You are free to think through how best to lead them to a carefully thought-through goal in the interest of every group, or at the very least to promote the most good while imposing least harm. You are free to act in good conscience and to join others who see the world as you do and pursue the same goals.

Whatever role you do play or plan to play in schools as an education professional, we hope this book helps you to articulate your goals with confidence, to plot a well-considered route to them, and to resolve to *act* to help realize the improvements you envision. We firmly believe that significant hope for a better tomorrow lies literally in the hands of public educators, who will shape tomorrow's citizens, workers and community members.

Things to Think About

1. This chapter makes several claims about why things go wrong in schools and for students despite good intentions. Which of them ring true to you? What experiences have you had that lend them credibility? Try to identify and explain at least three.
2. Which of the claims in this chapter do *not* ring true to you? What experiences have you had that make you skeptical of them? Try to identify and explain at least three.
3. What are two or three examples of new information in this chapter that surprised you? Can you explain why you were surprised by each?

Things to Explore

Readings

Eisner, E. W. (2003). Questionable assumptions about schooling. *Phi Delta Kappan, 84*(9), 648–657.
This article, which should be readily available from many libraries, provides an extended look at our assertion that mistaken assumptions can wreak havoc in schools. He discusses some of the ideas we've included in the chapter, but also details several other taken-for-granted ideas about schools and schooling.

Rameriz, A. & Carpenter, D. (2005). Challenging assumptions about the achievement gap. *Phi Delta Kappan, 86*(8), 599–603.
This article, also likely readily available from many libraries, considers common—but mistaken—assumptions about the achievement gap. This piece can help readers assess what they think they know about that issue, especially in relation to Latino students.

Videos

Key and Peele, *The Substitute Teacher, Pt. 1.* (3 minutes) http://www.cc.com/video-clips/w5hxki/key-and-peele-substitute-teacher-pt--1
This brief and edgy video (which readers who object to coarse language may want to skip) offers a comic representation of how one teacher's culture and life experiences affected his assumptions about an unfamiliar group of students. A serious point lies underneath the comedy, however: Things can go seriously wrong in a classroom when a teacher makes wholly inappropriate assumptions about students from an unfamiliar culture. Perhaps this piece will spark some relevant thinking about other kinds of assumptions teachers make about students—often erroneously.

Emily Green, *How to Feed Children by Shedding Assumptions about School Lunches.* (TEDxNortheasternU). (20 minutes)
This video presents a kind of case study of our main point in this chapter—that assumptions about the way things are or must be often get in the way of improving less-than-perfect situations. Green first details where problems lie in school lunch programs (no surprise to anyone who has ever dumped a cafeteria tray of "mystery meat" and squishy lukewarm canned peas into a dumpster), and then she offers some thinking-outside-the-box ideas for how to improve things. We think this video illustrates the power of abandoning the assumption that some things will never change in favor of embracing the assumption that problematic situations surely should be, and can be, improved.

Notes

1. See, for example, Carter, P. L. and Welner, K. G. (Eds.) (2013). *Closing the opportunity gap: What America must do to give every child an even chance.* Oxford: Oxford University Press.

2. Toppo, G. (2015, July 28). NYC schools: Principal who committed suicide was subject of cheating probe. *USA Today.* Retrieved from *https://www.usatoday.com/ story/news/2015/07/28/new-york-principal-cheating/30800913/*

3. Chasmar, J. (2016, June 17). Pop-Tart gun suspension upheld by Maryland judge. *The Washington Times.* Retrieved from http://www.washingtontimes.com/ news/2016/jun/17/pop-tart-gun-suspension-upheld-by-maryland-judge/

4. Foster, J. (2001, May 20). Boy hero appeals suspension. *WND.* Retrieved from http://www.wnd.com/2001/05/9302/

5. See, for example, Ward, S. F. (2014, August 1). Schools start to rethink zero tolerance policies. *ABA Journal.* Retrieved from http://www.abajournal.com/ magazine/article/schools_start_to_rethink_zero_tolerance_policies

6. American Educational Research Association, American Psychological Association, and National Council on Measurement in Education. (1999). *Standards for educational and psychological testing.* Washington, DC: American Educational Research Association. Retrieved from http://www.apa.org/pubs/info/brochures/ testing.aspx

7. See, for example, section 6.7 of this PARCC manual: http://parcc-resouces. d105.net/modules/locker/files/get_group_file.phtml?fid= 27431693&gid=4915579

8. Strauss, V. (2013, November 21). N.Y. school principals write letter of concern about Common Core tests. [Web blog post]. Retrieved from https://www.washingtonpost.com/news/answer-sheet/wp/2013/11/21/n-y-school-principals-write-letter-of-concern-about-common-core-tests/?utm_term=.40662a373d4c

9. USDA. (2017, March 1). Poverty overview. Retrieved from https://www.ers.usda.gov/topics/rural-economy-population/rural-poverty-well-being/poverty-overview.aspx#childpoverty

10. See, for example: The Urban Child Institute. (2012, October 1). Prematurity and low birth weight. Retrieved from http://www.urbanchildinstitute.org/articles/ policy-briefs/prematurity-and-low-birth-weight

11. Weller, C. (2016, August 30). Whirlpool gave washers and dryers to 17 schools in Illinois and California and attendance rates shot up—here's why. *Business Insider.* Retrieved from http://www.businessinsider.com/washing-machines-solve-schools-big-problem-2016-8

12. For some insight on the teacher assessment issue, see Greg Michie's plainspoken blog post at http://www.huffingtonpost.com/gregory-michie/stupidity-and-valueadded-_b_6587352.html

13. Hinchey, P. H. (2010). *Getting teacher assessment right: What policymakers can learn from research.* Boulder, CO: National Education Policy Center. Retrieved from http://nepc.colorado.edu/publication/getting-teacher-assessment-right

14. Health, Education, Labor, and Pensions Committee. (2014). *Dangerous use of seclusion and restrains in schools remains widespread and difficult to remedy: A review of ten cases.* Washington, DC: United States Senate. Retrieved from https:// eric.ed.gov/?id=ED544755

15. Health, Education, Labor, and Pensions Committee. (2014). *Dangerous use of seclusion and restrains in schools remains widespread and difficult to remedy: A review of ten cases.* Washington, DC: United States Senate. Retrieved from https://eric.ed.gov/?id=ED544755

16. Hinchey, P. H. (1998). *Finding freedom in the classroom.* New York: Peter Lang.

17. Neil, M. (2016, March). The testing resistance and reform movement. *Monthly Review, 67*(10). Retrieved from http://monthlyreview.org/2016/03/01/the-testing-resistance-and-reform-movement/

18. Guisbond, L., Neill, M. & Schaeffer, B. (2015). *Testing reform victories 2015: Growing grassroots movement rolls back testing overkill.* Boston: FairTest. Retrieved from http://www.fairtest.org/sites/default/files/2015-Resistance-Wins-Report-Final.pdf

19. Thomas Jefferson: Notes on Virginia, 1782. Q.XIV.

TWO

What Are Schools for, Anyway?

What the best and wisest parent wants for his own child, that must the community want for all of its children. Any other ideal for our schools is narrow and unlovely; acted upon, it destroys our democracy.
—*John Dewey,* The School and Society

OUR STORY AT THE OPENING of Chapter 1 of how we lost our direction on the way to where we thought we were going seems an apt metaphor for the wisdom of double-checking our destination as educators. *What do we think schools should be doing?* And, it also suggests we should double check our route for getting there. *Is what we're doing creating the experiences and outcomes we intend for students?* Most stakeholders, from the youngest tot coloring circles in kindergarten to the seasoned legislator making school policy, operate much as we did in driving. We thought we were going someplace terrific and we relied on maps provided by others to get us there. But what exactly we mean by *there*, or how this or that school activity or requirement will get us *there* (wherever that may be) is far more often assumed than articulated. So let's begin at the beginning, with the destination, so that we have something to check our road map against. Just what are the unspoken assumptions about what schools should accomplish? Are they as clear and accurate as the address we typed into the GPS for our Puerto Rican resort? Or have our intended goals for schools, like our intended destination, been lost in translation?

Assumptions about the Goals of Public Schools

Public schools are so obviously necessary that the United States has always had them and counted on them to accomplish essential (if unspecified) goals.

Strangely, perhaps the first assumption we might check is that the goals of public schools are so obvious and self-evident there's no need to articulate them. Aren't schools required by law somewhere, like maybe in the Constitution?

Well, no . . . not in the Constitution. And in fact, the 1973 Supreme Court decision in *San Antonio Independent School District v. Rodriquez*[1] specifically held that "a free and public education" is *not* a "fundamental right" under the U.S. Constitution. Of course, some constitutional amendments, like the 14th (which provides equal protection under the law), do affect how schools operate. And other federal authorities have also influenced public education. Congress, for example, has enacted various laws (like the 2016 Every Student Succeeds Act), and the Supreme Court has also made highly influential decisions (like the famous 1954 *Brown v. Board of Education* decision that outlawed segregation). And *state* constitutions typically include some sort of provision.

But in fact, the United States has not always had a system of public education. The idea that every child should have the right to access a free, public, community-based K-12 education—now taken for granted—has actually matured over the last 200-plus years. The definition of who exactly is entitled to a "public" education has morphed many times. Once, for example, it seemed an "obvious" waste of money to try to educate various segments of the population, like females or African Americans or children with special needs. Through those years and even into the present, extended arguments have raged about why taxpayers should be compelled to support a universal public school system. And most contemporary efforts to raise school taxes trigger voter outrage, suggesting that many citizens still resent having to support public schools—even at a time when states themselves have been cutting back on their school funding.[2]

Indeed, rollback of funding and movement toward privatizing education (which we'll be discussing in Chapter 6) suggest that the current commitment to public schools and a free education for all U.S. children may actually be waning. For this reason, the Southern Education Foundation argued in the 2009 report *No Time to Lose: Why America Needs an Education Amendment*[3] that a constitutional amendment would not only clarify the role of the federal government in public education but would go far in ensuring that all children have equal access to quality schools and educational programs. Interestingly, U.S. schools often fare badly in international comparisons (which again, we'll be discussing in much more detail in Chapter 6), but the better performing school systems are often in countries with constitutions that *do* mandate free public education for their citizens. These include, for example, Finland and South Korea,[4] countries critics often hold up to the United States as having far more effective public schools.

Maybe, then, it's time for the United States as a nation to strengthen its commitment to public schools in one way or another. But that's unlikely to happen if we cannot say clearly what schools accomplish that is so critical that stronger national, or perhaps even constitutional—support is essential. But now we're back to where we started: what outcomes exactly are schools to produce, and how do those outcomes affect not only individual students' lives, but also U.S. social, political, economic and cultural life?

The purpose of education and the role of public schools in American society are obvious and agreed upon by everyone.

Hmmmm. It's time to tackle more directly this claim that at some level, there is universal agreement about at least some of the things we rely on schools to do. Both authors of this book have a lot of experience with university teaching at a various levels, and we both know a lot about students. One of the things we know is that students pretty much hold this assumption: there's no need to articulate what schools do because everyone knows what that is. When they are asked to specify what "everyone" knows schools are supposed to do and why that's important, they may have to take a minute or two to think, but then they typically have little trouble responding (especially if they are white, middle class, female teachers or teacher-wannabes, the largest demographic in many education courses).[5] The answers to our questions are obvious, they say. OF COURSE the purpose of education is to [do exactly what they think it should do given their personal experiences and social context]. OF COURSE an educated person knows [whatever it is they know or wish they knew] and can do [whatever they think is desirable]. OF COURSE they believe all students should be "successful" [by whatever standard they personally imagine success looks like]. And, OF COURSE schools are responsible for ensuring that every student is college and career ready [although they secretly think college is the right path to anywhere]. And, they are stunned when it turns out that other people in the room may have very different OF COURSE scenarios in their heads.

Moreover, when students are pressed for details, their "obvious" answers quickly fall apart. "Let's start off easy," we say. "What do you think is absolutely essential curriculum for all schools?" Some students will argue vehemently for whatever subject they themselves have been most successful in and against other areas they had less luck with (trigonometry but not pottery, grammar but not history, Shakespeare but not robotics). *Those* subjects they say—trig, grammar, Shakespeare—are absolutely essential, and they are stunned to find others arguing equally vehemently for pottery, history and robotics. Frustrated with good arguments being made for a wide variety of curricular elements, some classmates soon begin to argue that the specific academic program is somewhat beside the point anyway, because what is most wanted from schools is the development of good character (as they define it), while still others begin to argue that it's actually critical thinking that must be the heart of whatever schools do (never mind what exactly is to be thought *about*). The devil, as students in introductory foundations courses quickly learn, is in the proverbial details. As soon as we scratch the surface of assumptions about what schools should be doing, an avalanche of conflicting ideas appears.

It's hardly surprising that we have seen this in our classes year after year, since for millennia (yes, literally for thousands of years), philosophers, historians, sociologists, scholars, and reformers of all stripes have attempted to articulate *the* purpose of "education" and "schooling" for the masses. And although there are certainly threads of similarity in ideas offered by educational philosophers ranging from philosophers Socrates and John Dewey to reformer Ted Sizer and the politician Arne Duncan, the differences can be vast, and every attempt to reach a conclusion tends to result in still more debates and still (many) more questions. For example, the notion that schooling must communicate some sort of content and must contribute to the intellectual development of students is surely key to a school's goals . . . but what content exactly? And why? And what exactly does "intellectual development" look like? Students will become engineers and poets, retail clerks and hotel housekeepers, entrepreneurs and car salesmen. Do they all need to learn the same things? The same way? If they need to learn different things, or even the same things in different ways, who decides who learns what? And on what basis are students inserted into various curricular paths? Perhaps the most certain thing we can say here—that students currently are primarily "tracked" by zip code, since a student's school experience is shaped primarily by where he or she happens to reside—is hardly the most fair or most desirable way of matching students to school experiences (*if* we think different students should receive different educations in the first place).

Kevin Harris[6] does a nice job of representing a small sample of relatively modern competing conceptualizations,

> There is a common belief, significantly shared by many beginning formal tertiary studies in education, that 'education' has a fixed meaning, and distinct aims, which can be unveiled either by turning up a dictionary or by consulting a favoured authority. So, in the very first lecture of every course I give, I stress that 'education' is a changing, contested and often highly personalised, historically and politically constructed concept. To illustrate this I read a few dictionary definitions of 'education', as well as a selected set of stated 'aims of education'. When students hear that D. H. Lawrence claimed education should aim to 'lead out the individual nature in each man and woman to its true fullness', that for Rousseau the aim of education was 'to come into accord with the teaching of nature', that R. M. Hutchins saw the aim of education as 'cultivation of the intellect', that A. S. Neill believed the aim of education should be to 'make people happier, more secure, less neurotic, less prejudiced', and that John Locke claimed 'education must aim at virtue and teach man to deny his desires, inclinations and appetite, and follow as reason directs'; hopefully the penny has dropped. Just in case it hasn't I add in that while Pope Pius XI was declaring that the aim of education was to 'cooperate with divine grace in forming the true and perfect Christian', Sergei Shapovalenko insisted that education should aim 'to inculcate the materialist outlook and communist mentality'.

Do such varied positions really reflect contemporary reality? Yes.

We know that because lawyers from the Thomas More Law Center: The Sword and Shield for People of Faith—whose mission includes "preserv[ing] America's Judeo-Christian heritage" and defending "the religious freedom of Christians"[7]—regularly face off in court against lawyers from the American Civil Liberties Union (ACLU)—whose mission includes "defend[ing] and preserv[ing] the individual rights and liberties guaranteed by the Constitution and laws of the United States."[8] What do they face off about? Often, they argue about exactly what should and should not be allowed in the classroom, or even in the library, because different people have very different ideas about the influence schools should have on kids' experiences and character. Religious conservatives have objected to such readings as the Harry Potter series and the Captain Underpants series, while liberals have fought to protect the inclusion of evolution (known as "Darwinism" among conservatives) and to keep out the conservative-beloved book *Pandas and People* on the basis that it is creationism in disguise (and the Constitution bans religious teaching in public schools), while cheering on Harry and the bathroom humor of the Captain. Not everyone agrees on which "desires, inclinations and appetite" schools should help kids deny.

Other controversies abound. Right now, federal policymakers and many of their state counterparts agree that student "achievement" in certain subjects (notably English and math) is of paramount importance, while legions of educators and researchers argue vehemently against such a narrow vision of the purpose of schooling, noting the value of subjects like art and music that have been squeezed out of the curriculum in many schools. Parents have joined in the fray, forming a national movement against the current standardized testing frenzy by opting their children out of the tests.[9] No agreement whatsoever on this front. Indeed, we can't even agree whether "school" should be in a building, or whether students and teachers must ever meet face-to-face. A growing movement to place more and more of "schooling" online has reached the point where now even some five-year-olds in kindergarten interact regularly not with other kids around a sandbox or water table but with a computer screen.

For nearly two-and-a-half centuries, we have been trying very hard to perfect what David Tyack referred to as the "the one best system"[10] for U.S. public schools, with criticism of any contemporary status quo typically being loud and strong. The fact that we still don't agree doesn't mean we've failed. It means that the questions around what schools should be doing are complex, that perspectives on the issue are many and conflicting, and that education is widely understood to be critically important. If it weren't, no one would care what goes on in classrooms. In this contentious area, the best we can do is to help school personnel articulate a clear vision of what their specific school agrees it is striving for, and why, and how best to get there. Considering the following assumptions may provide some touchstones for that effort.

Because public schools must serve a widely varied population, the curriculum and other elements of schooling should be strictly neutral.

Earlier, we introduced the kinds of conflict that arise when one group of stakeholders in a school—say, devout Christian parents—finds something offensive that is valued by other stakeholders—say, passionate biologists. Those who believe that the Bible is literally true and that God created the world are deeply offended by the idea that humans have simian ancestors, as evolution holds. For these sincere and devout parents, teaching evolution undermines the belief system they consider essential to their children's spiritual health. But scientists see an enormous difference between religious belief and science, and they find physical evidence supporting evolutionary theory currently incontrovertible. As a result, the controversy over teaching evolution in schools has been sparking active battles at least since the Scopes Monkey Trial in 1925, when a high school science teacher was found guilty of teaching evolution (though the verdict was later overturned on a technicality).[11] As recently as January 2017, some states were introducing bills trying to undermine the teaching of evolution (and climate change) in public schools (more on this in Chapter 3).[12]

Our experience tells us that there are predictably two responses to information on this controversy and others like it: 1) so just teach both sides of the issue and let the kids decide which is right, and 2) so just don't teach evolution in biology class. Both of these suggestions are typically defended on the grounds that they put the school in the position of being neutral on the issue. But in fact, neither is neutral at all.

The job of a science teacher is to teach science . . . and religion is not science. The difference is that science depends on replicable, physical evidence to support its theories, and there are mountains of fossils and other evidence, including genetic evidence, to support evolution. Many opponents of evolution argue that they have evidence for creationism and say it is found in the Bible, which they consider absolute Truth. However, Biblical narratives are not subject to experimentation and they don't offer the physical evidence required in the domain of science. Rather, at the root of creationism (sometimes called intelligent design) is religious faith: faith that the Bible is literally true. There is no way to resolve the issue because a scientist will not teach something that is based on faith rather than physical evidence, and religious conservatives cannot tolerate children being told they have descended from animals. In addition, the U.S. Constitution forbids government institutions from favoring any particular religion, and teaching the Biblical story of creation in schools would amount to teaching religion. So, no: it is not possible to teach "both sides" of the issue in a *science* class because there are not two *scientific* sides.[13]

We've heard students suggest that teachers can avoid the whole issue by simply not teaching evolution at all. However, that would mean carving out of the biology curriculum one of the most important and influential theories in the field. It is a theory that has enormous implications for daily life:

Darwin's legacy has a direct bearing on how society makes public policy and even, at times, on how we choose to run our lives. Overfishing of mature adults selects for smaller fish (and higher prices at the supermarket), and excessive use of antibiotics leads, by natural selection, to drug resistance, all considerations for regulators and legislators. Many modern diseases—obesity, diabetes, and autoimmune disorders—come about, in part, because of the mismatch between our genes and an environment that changes more quickly than human genomes can evolve. Understanding this disparity may help convince a patient to make a change in diet to better conform to the demands of a genetic heritage that leaves us unable to accommodate excess, refined carbohydrates and saturated fats from a steady intake of linguine alfredo and the like.[14]

Presumably, schools teach science to help students to understand their world, to help them see how their actions as consumers and as voters who choose among policymakers directly affect the future for themselves, their families, and their country. To choose not to teach evolution—or global warming, or the impact of clear cutting forests—is to deny students information critical to their decision making as adults.

Here is the difficult reality: there *is* no such thing as a "neutral" education. Every decision about curriculum means bringing something in and leaving something out. Leaving out a topic like evolution is not neutral. Nor is banning Harry Potter or Captain Underpants from the library. Either schools filter curriculum through a religious lens, or they don't; either they embrace some standard of "proper" literature for schools and ban Captain Underpants, or they allow children to read silly and irreverent books because intrinsic interest promotes reading habits.

When it comes to curriculum, every choice becomes a stance. (More on curriculum in Chapter 3.) Anyone supporting the teaching of evolution and not of creationism takes a stance in opposition to those who believe the Bible is literal truth. Anyone supporting a wide variety of texts in classrooms and libraries takes a stance in opposition to those who think students must be protected from such topics as wizardry, bathroom humor and, very often, sexual issues. The impossibility of being neutral is also embedded in choices outside of curriculum—how to limit students' free speech inside and outside of schools, for example, or whether to endorse corporal punishment. (Yes, as of April 2017, 15 states still allowed paddling.[15] More on how schools treat students in Chapter 5). And while everyone thinks schools should teach citizenship, it's not clear whether that means schools should function as the proverbial melting pot, teaching all newcomers to the country to adopt the language, values and customs already in place, or whether it means teaching all students that diversity provides a cultural richness we can all benefit from. (More on this in Chapter 4.) Since so many elements of schooling involve a stance (acknowledged or not), it's best to think about *which* stance an educator or an entire school can support. While local school personnel do need to take community standards and mores into account, simply choosing a path by considering what routes are likely to offend the fewest parents evades the professional responsibility of making sound educational policy.

There is no such thing as a neutral or value-free school.

Schools should help develop productive members of a civil society.

In the United States, schools are the places where students are socialized into both their local communities and into American citizenry. By "socialized," we mean that students are taught the values and expectations that come with membership in those communities, and they are given practice in common behaviors: taking care of property, being honest, helping with communal tasks like cleanup and so on. Through such instruction and practice, the teachers and administrators and counselors and support staff work to cultivate an environment in which children can grow into the identity imagined for them as people inclined to live in communal harmony with others. The expectation is that the target identity will lead students in later life to perform roles that promote the public good and in doing so will somehow contribute to the welfare of all. John Dewey spelled out this goal pretty clearly back in 1899:

> When the school introduces and trains each child of society into membership within such a little community, saturating him with the spirit of service, and providing him with the instruments of effective self-direction, we shall have the deepest and best guaranty of a larger society which is worthy, lovely, and harmonious.[16]

Inspirational, right? Of course. Utopian even[17]—if only we could agree on values and expectations as well as on the definitions of "effective self-direction" and a "worthy, lovely, and harmonious" society.

But here's the rub. The conceptualization of what makes for a "productive member" of "a civil society" takes on different meanings depending on which segment of society is being discussed (the children of migrant workers or of technology entrepreneurs?) and on which stakeholder group is doing the talking (migrant workers or technology entrepreneurs?). Exactly what kinds of jobs should students be prepared for? Will society be better off if students are taught cooperation and sharing, or instilled with a fiercely competitive drive? Definitions of such lovely terms as "worthy" shift with perspective, and perspective shifts based on such factors as socioeconomic background, religious beliefs or lack thereof, prior experience with community initiatives and public service . . . and, importantly among other things, the historical and socio-cultural context.

For example, there was a time when the prevailing attitude held that join-
ing the military was a noble form of "service." Pam's father, and grandfather
in particular, talked often about volunteering for the Air Force and Marines,
respectively, as their "service" to the country; one served in the Middle East in
the late 1960s (her dad) and the other (her grandfather) in WWII, including
the Battle of Tulagi. Of course, those were different times, with the country
at war and a draft in place. Still, veterans of early times often felt proud of
serving the country. While that sense of service certainly exists for a segment
of more recent volunteers, the decision to enlist today typically has more to
do with self-improvement and less to do with service. Recruiters often entice
high school students, especially in working-class neighborhoods, to enlist by
actively "selling" the idea of military service as a form of first-job-after-high-
school (or viable long-term career), or on-the-job training, or a way to earn
money for college. Such pragmatic financial concerns come *first* for many
who enlist, and service to one's country becomes an almost accidental *secondary* by-product of the self-betterment the armed forces offer. Similarly,
many today would argue that individual involvement in politics is less of a
Mr. Smith Goes to Washington-like[18] notion of serving one's country or community through active participation in the democratic process, and more
of a professional aspiration involving the same kind of ladder climbing and
power-mongering as is common in the corporate world.

But maybe being a "productive" member doesn't require any kind of self-
sacrifice. Maybe "doing something" simply means agreeing to play by the
rules of the membership—like paying taxes and not robbing or mugging our
neighbors. And, of course, earning enough money so that we aren't a "drain"
on the community (hence the common focus on earning a living after high
school). But how do we maintain a democracy if no one contributes by voting or running for office? If no one values the health and welfare of the community and nation at least as much as individual personal health and welfare?
How do we knit an environment in which everyone can thrive if each citizen
doesn't feel some responsibility for the whole?

Schools are surely responsible for at least helping to communicate a set of
social values and behaviors, helping students learn attitudes and habits that
will help maintain and strengthen the greater good that is (or can be) life in
the United States. But how we conceptualize essential elements of a civil society is key. What is it that we want for our neighbors and ourselves? What do

we value, and how do we engage in our communities? And how do we find common ground when we bring a world of perspectives to the negotiation of answers to those questions? And if these questions aren't enough to keep us busy for a while, Chapter 4 will take up in detail the question of how to define *citizenship*, itself a term that shifts in similar ways depending on perspective.

Schools do provide all students with equal educational opportunity.

Again, there are terms in this assumption that beg to be defined. What exactly constitutes "equal opportunity"? There are multiple ways to come at this question. One of the most obvious—providing equitable resources for every child via funding—is a topic we're going to put off until Chapter 6, when we consider what kinds of reform American schools may need.[19] Suffice it to say here that for sure, Americans from any demographic, including average taxpayers and most politicians, have shown little or no will to provide equity in terms of financial support for schools in different communities. Schools for poor kids tend to be poor, while schools for rich kids tend to be rich. Despite that reality, many argue that schools do in fact provide equal opportunity, and they point to other areas to prove it. First, in legal terms, schools are bound to provide specific educational services to every child in a community for free. But if we take a closer philosophical look, we can see that opportunity can be defined in a variety of ways, all of which lead to different practical outcomes.

As a country, we've been aiming at the goal of having schools provide equal opportunity for all kids for decades. Still, the reality is that ongoing legislation illustrates that for a variety of reasons and in a variety of ways, the reality of schooling has been and remains far short of that goal. In recent decades, several pieces of federal legislation have tried to be more clear and direct in steering schools toward genuinely equal opportunity, and they have also implemented accountability systems to ensure progress. The Elementary and Secondary Education Act of 1965 (ESEA) and the Equal Educational Opportunities Act of 1974 (EEOA) were particularly important. They specifically emphasized that "educational opportunities" included a multitude of resources, such as quality teachers, adequate facilities, and support for parents; in addition, they prohibited school systems that were segregated on the basis of "race, color, sex, or national origin." In subsequent years, amendments were added to the ESEA to provide specific protections for vulnerable populations such as children with special needs and English language learn-ers. This history is one of steady inclusion, and while it documents earlier discrimination, it also demonstrates that at some level there is a national commitment to equal educational opportunity for all children.

As evidence of that ongoing commitment, the ESEA has been renewed every five years since 1965, undergoing numerous revisions, additions, and renaming. Frustrated by achievement gaps persisting among various student demographic groups, in 2001, federal politicians passed the No Child Left Behind Act (NCLB) that, among other things, essentially forced schools to define "equal opportunity" as translating to "equal achievement on some standardized tests" along with the right to be taught by "highly qualified teachers" and to receive paid tutoring if it appeared the schools weren't doing their purported job. This has been succeeded by the Every Student Succeeds Act (ESSA) of 2015, which tweaked the earlier provisions in light of the mas-sive failure of schools to meet the unrealistic NCLB targets—including, for example, 100% of all students (yes, including those with little skill in English and with severe learning issues) to attain proficiency on standardized tests in math and English. On January 23, 2017, HB610 was introduced to repeal the Elementary and Secondary Education Act of 1965. At the time of this writing, we are still waiting to see what this might mean for the long-standing goal of equal educational opportunity should it pass.

Such constant revision suggests (among other things) that the federal government has for some time recognized the many ways schools have in fact failed to provide the promised equal opportunity—for many reasons, and with many of those reasons far beyond the control of school person-nel. Inadequate funding is one; the ravages of poverty on student health and development are another. As noted earlier, we'll turn to those concerns more fully in Chapter 6. The point here is simply that there is a legislative history to demonstrate that over time, schools have not in fact served all children equally well and that to do so, special attention must be paid to some de-mographic groups of students (English language learners, children with spe-cial needs and others). The implication of *that* is crucial: any one-size-fits-all model of what a school provides to each student does *not* meet the standard of "equal opportunity" since students do not all need exactly the same things to succeed in schools. And here's another mess to ponder: how can "equal op-portunity" be provided if all students aren't treated equally?

On one level, this is a semantic quibble—but it has enormous implications. *Equal*, defined as exactly the same, does not mean equitable, defined as *fair*. For that reason it's even possible we should stop talking about "equal opportunity" altogether, as some have argued, and start talking about "equitable opportunity" instead:

> There is a common misconception that equity and equality mean the same thing—and that they can be used interchangeably, especially when talking about education. But the truth is they do not—and cannot. Yes, the two words are similar, but the difference between them is crucial. So please, don't talk about equality when you really mean equity. . . . Yes, making sure all students have equal access to resources is an important goal. All students should have the resources necessary for a high-quality education. But the truth remains that some students need more to get there. Here's where equity comes in.[20]

Here is also where a philosophical look at the question comes in, since what is *fair* or *just* can be answered in a variety of ways.

Social scientist Christopher Jencks identified ethical justification for various conceptions of equal educational opportunity across five philosophical perspectives, linking them to differences in practice.[21] He notes that our understanding of "equal opportunity" is linked to our concept of a good society. Because people have different ideas of whom schools should treat "equally," we naturally produce groups that can legitimately be treated "*un*equally."

> Everyone's conception of equal educational opportunity requires that educational institutions "treat equals equally." But we have dramatically different views about whom educational institutions should treat equally and whom they can legitimately treat unequally. Indeed, the enduring popularity of equal educational opportunity probably derives from the fact that we can all define it in different ways without realizing how profound our differences really are.

We've already pointed to the ways in which some students are treated "unequally" by receiving some services other students don't—say, aides for students with special needs, for example. Such services can be an advantage.

However, other ways in which different students are treated differently—such as in access to honors or advanced courses, especially math—clearly disadvantage some groups. By what rationale are different kinds of school experiences and opportunities justified in a system that purports to provide "equal opportunity"?

A look at how teachers rationalize the way they parcel out the valuable resources of their time and attention is instructive. Following are the five perspectives Jencks identifies that affect teachers' classroom behavior, and we've added some examples of our own to help clarify.

1. *Democratic equality* means everyone gets the same time and attention, regardless of how well they are currently doing, how deprived they have been in the past, what they want or need, or beneficence or detriment. Note Jencks' use of the term *equality* here: this is the one-size-fits-all approach of those who believe equality and equity are the same thing. In this classroom, the homeless student would be expected to turn in the same homework as completely and reliably as the student who goes home to a healthful snack and a mother hovering until homework is finished.[22] Same class, same expectations for every student; this teacher thinks that to do otherwise would be unequal and therefore unfair.

2. *Moralistic justice* means effort is rewarded with time and attention and everyone else is punished. Here we have those teachers who say, "If you can't be bothered to try as hard as you can, I'm not going to waste my time trying to help you." The homeless student is likely in trouble in this class as well if there is no place but under some bridge to sit and try to write—or no paper to write on. But this teacher believes that rewards must be earned and to do otherwise is simply to encourage passivity and even sloth.

3. *Weak humane justice* means that those who have been disadvantaged by *weaknesses in prior education* receive a disproportionately large share of time and attention. So, if a second grade teacher knows a struggling student was in the class of an incompetent teacher the year before, then the student would merit extra time and attention. But if the student was disadvantaged for noneducational reasons, then compensation is not in order. Education personnel are responsible for remedying educational

deficiencies and are not to be expected to overcome social, physical or familial disadvantages.

4. *Strong humane justice* means that those who have been disadvantaged in any way receive a disproportionately large share of time and attention. If the student is in the class, then the teacher does whatever it takes to help that particular student—time, attention, sometimes a sandwich shared at lunch, a home visit with the parents . . . whatever it takes to help the student suffering from poverty, or the death of a beloved grandparent, or a tumultuous home life, or the need to arrive late because of having to get younger siblings off to school. This teacher shrugs that "life happens" and helps the student stay on track rather than compounding the student's problems.

5. *Utilitarianism* means that access to time and attention is competitive and reserved for the best performers. Ask any student to tell you which of their teachers paid attention to the A students and ignored the C, D and F students: no matter who you ask, you'll get a ready response.

When we look at these rationales, we begin to see that there are apparently reasonable arguments for providing some students with more access and opportunity and some students with less—or none at all. That is a sobering thought for any educator.

Moreover, just as teachers determine for themselves what is "fair," schools and school systems mete out opportunities in ways that are inclusive for some and exclusive for others. This is only one illustration of the many ways there are to be inequitable in our pursuit of "equality." We hope readers will explore the many other nuances Jencks explores in the full article listed in suggested readings at the end of this chapter to develop a deeper understanding of this issue. We trust our summary here is essentially accurate. But, in simplifying an extended philosophical investigation, we've risked leaving out some key points. As a result we may have inadvertently misrepresented some of Jencks' points.

Here is the bottom line of this particular discussion: before the staff of a school can pull together toward the goal of "equal educational opportunity," everyone needs to be clear on what they believe that term means. While it's a philosophical question, it clearly has enormous implications for practice.

Schools should alleviate social problems.

It's not surprising, really, that schools should be expected to solve social problems, since it is schools that are expected to shape people into productive members of society. If there are problems, it is likely because some defect in the young isn't being adequately educated out of them in school. Or so the thinking of some people goes, anyway.

John Dewey emphasized the importance of the connections between the school and society and the school and community, but it was George S. Counts who was a tireless advocate of education as a force for building a good society through fostering both social change and social stability. As long ago as 1932, Counts wrote in *Dare the School Build a New Social Order,*[23]

> Like all simple and unsophisticated peoples we Americans have a sublime faith in education. Faced with any difficult problem of life we set our minds at rest sooner or later by the appeal of the school. We are convinced that education is the one unfailing remedy for every ill to which man is subject, whether it be vice, crime, war, poverty, riches, injustice, racketeering, political corruption, race hatred, class conflict, or just plain original sin. We even speak glibly and often about the general reconstruction of society through the schools. We cling to this faith in spite of the fact that the very period in which our troubles have multiplied so rapid has witnessed an unprecedented expansion of organized education. This would seem to suggest that our schools, instead of directing the course of change, are themselves driven by the very forces that are transforming the rest of the social order.

Counts' description of Americans' (superhuman?) expectations for schools is apt, and he is right in that changes in society drive the kinds of social change people want from schools. For example, as the liberating decades of the late twentieth century led to more youth engaging in more and more premarital sex—and generating more and more teenage pregnancies—schools suddenly found themselves responsible for "sex education." Of course, for some people that meant "teach these kids how to prevent unwanted pregnancy" while for others it meant "teach these kids that abstinence is the *only* sure method of birth control."

Whatever the social problem, schools are typically asked to fix it: addiction? Schools need drug programs. Youth obesity? Schools need nutrition and exercise programs. Sexting? Schools need Internet safety programs. Of course, schools need all this at the same time they currently need to focus full attention on standardized test scores. And equal opportunity for all. And . . . whatever problems turn up tomorrow.

One complexity in this area should already be clear: elements of programs to solve social ills are value-related. Parents who grew up smoking marijuana recreationally and never touched a hard drug want legalization—and drug programs that make a distinction between "weed" and "smack." Other parents want teachers to insist JUST SAY NO to everything that kids find pleasurable—no drugs, no booze, no sex. *Which* kinds of programs will "solve" the social problem *du jour*?

There's an actual name for the idea that schools can solve social problems by fixing people: social meliorism. That concept is implicit in efforts like the one that tries to change *people*, since *people* are seen as the root cause of the problem. Not surprisingly, there's another school of thought that looks at social problems from an entirely different perspective: if we want people to end antisocial behavior, or behavior that is self-destructive, then we'd better find out what is causing people to behave in those ways and change the social conditions that trigger the behavior. The real problem, in this view, lies outside rather than inside the person. This perspective also has a name: social reconstruction. For example, if there is a high incidence of drug trade and use in a given area, why is that so? Is it because there are no jobs available that offer a living wage? Because generations of poverty have made it all too clear that some people are not really meant to escape the life they were born into? Because, perhaps, a drug company dumped millions of opioids into the community, knowing that addiction will ensure their continued maximum profit?[24] Educators often try to do both by helping students understand the danger of something like drug addiction while also trying to encourage them to identify harmful social structures and trends and then try to change them.

Of course, that raises another question: *should* schools try to function as social change agents? Many would argue that teachers today are actively *discouraged* from taking any sort of political, or even advocacy, stances in the context of their professional work in the classroom, whether on behalf of individual students, teaching as a profession, or marginalized populations of the world. (There's that mistaken idea that schooling should be neutral again.)

Paulo Freire, noted Brazilian educator and activist, rejected the notion that teachers, and teaching, should be neutral (a point we will take up more extensively in relation to curriculum in Chapter 3): "The educator has the duty of not being neutral.... The educator as an intellectual has to intervene. He cannot be a mere facilitator".[25] In fact, Freire believed that social change required education to play a role in transforming societies into more just and healthful environments for all citizens:

> It is not possible to remake [a] country, to democratize it, humanize it, make it serious, as long as we have teenagers killing people for play and offending life, destroying the dream, and making love unviable. If education alone cannot transform society, without it society cannot change either.[26]

That educators should advocate for social change is a contested, and some would claim dangerous, notion in a time when test scores have been imposed on schools as *the* highest priority, elbowing out concern for the kind of world students will find themselves in outside the schoolhouse doors. As federal control has increased over schooling, educator autonomy has decreased. And yet, if improving society may depend heavily on students learning to question authority when authority needs questioning, then educators must be the conduits of that kind of thinking and encouragement.

Social control or social questioning? "Fixing" people or "fixing" society itself? Which is properly understood as the school's responsibility for alleviating social problems?

Schools should play an important role in U.S. economic health and global competitiveness.

From the earliest manifestations of public schooling in this country, the relationship between the work of the school and the economic health of the nation has been a concern. There is now much talk of twenty-first century skills, as industry and technology evolve at warp speed, and schools are frequently lectured on the need to teach students the knowledge and skills they will need in order to survive and thrive in a world that we can presently barely imagine. This is not a new phenomenon; other eras have seen other times of drastic change, and schools have been faced with similar challenges. In any era it's difficult to be sure *which* knowledge and skills will be useful tomorrow. For example, critics of public education often complain about the boredom of repetitive tasks that too often characterize schooling. However, that model at one time was useful in training students to endure the tedium of factory work. Two questions are relevant here. Is it possible to identify information and job skills that will see students through their work lives? And even if we can, should schools prioritize workforce training and the economic health of the country over the welfare and interests of the students themselves?

While most people might agree that schools absolutely must prepare students for their future work lives, that's actually not a self-evident truth. Neither educators nor anyone else can specifically prepare children for an unknown future—*because we don't know it*. If we don't know it, how do we teach it? Change is rapid, and what we know today is unlikely to be as sophisticated as what we will know tomorrow, or ten years from now, or fifty years from then. But we can prepare students to be able to figure out how to live in the future world, to develop the capacities to think through to the next development, by teaching them such things as problem-solving, flexibility and creativity—not always front and center in preparation for work, or at least not front and center for many students in many schools.

There's that thorny equality v. equity issue again. Woodrow Wilson once famously admitted, "We want one class of persons to have a liberal education, and we want another class of persons, a very much larger class of necessity in every society, to forgo the privilege of a liberal education and fit themselves to perform specific difficult manual tasks." This tends to be precisely the outcome of a workforce focus in schools. Typically, a robust liberal education is reserved for a relatively privileged few, while more rote instruction is designed to prepare students primarily for the large number of jobs that ask little of workers except for obedience and physical strength, as when they must carry heavy trays of food while waiting tables, or haul a vacuum cleaner on their backs while cleaning houses.[27]

Many strategies in schools implemented in the name of job preparation lead away from a challenging curriculum, no matter the rhetoric used to promote them. Currently, for example, many schools have been forced away from broad-based academic development in favor of limited offerings primarily stressing basic literacies and sometimes science, technology, engineering and math (STEM). Many have pointed out that these priorities have been to the detriment of study in such other areas as social studies, humanities, and arts, important elements of a substantively liberal education. And, such emphases have spawned a culture of testing, evaluation, and assessment in schools that often dominates the daily work of teachers and students. This isn't a modern phenomenon. We saw a similar national reaction to the 1957 launch of the Soviet Union's Sputnik satellite, and subsequent 1958 National Defense Education Act. We as a nation are terrified of "falling behind," and see our schools as one of the engines that drives our global positioning and power.

Actually, experience with the Sputnik response is instructive, since the emphasis on STEM was extremely successful in significantly increasing worker expertise in those areas. And as a result, an army of highly qualified scientists and engineers driving taxis evolved, because the supply of these kinds of workers far exceeded demand for them. Here's another point worth pondering as schools are driven to produce workers to the specifications of the work world: the greater the number of qualified workers for a given type of job, the lower wages will be. So, whose interest should schools be serving? Those of corporate managers, who need a steady supply of workers with specific skills, and preferably more workers than needed in order to depress wages? Or those of students, who might be educated in ways that develop their talents in a variety of areas, allowing them autonomy in determining how their interests and aptitudes might best be adapted to the future need to earn a living?

Yes, schooling has a role to play in supporting national economic prosperity and educating workers for a globally competitive environment. But the question of the degree to which schools should engage in specific kinds of workforce development is more complex.

Frameworks for Goal Setting

It should be painfully evident by now that it is no small task to flesh out a specific set of clearly-articulated and well-defined goals for a particular school in a particular community. While the typical public school has a mission statement and may have a list of goals as well, it is not unusual for school personnel to have never seen such a document—and it would be nearly miraculous if anyone paid attention to it or even faintly dreamed of checking to see how well stated goals were being met. Too many forms are required by too many bureaucracies that schools report to, annually detailing required and seemingly endless numbers of this-and-that. While some brilliant and self-sacrificing school leaders do actually manage to articulate local goals and work with staff to pursue them, they are exceptions to the rule of typically harried and overworked school leadership.

But there is no way to be sure of arriving at a desirable destination if some specific address isn't programmed into the GPS. If we don't even know where we want to arrive, what are the odds of our getting somewhere that makes us happy? The person living in the northeast United States who drives aimlessly south in pursuit of "a vacation" is going to be very unhappy to arrive in Florida if he absolutely hates beaches, bugs and humidity. As hard as it may be, we have to work through the options and be clear about where we want to go, where we want to take our students. As a starting point for figuring out where that might be for each reader, here are some frameworks others have put together that may help provoke some first thoughts.

From Researchers at the Economic Policy Institute

Rebecca Jacobsen and Richard Rothstein did an interesting study to determine where there are high levels of agreement about the goals of education (and we suggest you read the entire report, listed as suggested reading at the end of this chapter).[28] Essentially, they culled eight broad goals from over two centuries of education and asked a representative sampling of wide variety of stakeholders (including American adults as well as such policymakers as legislators and school superintendents) to rank the relative importance of common public school goals. Respondents had 100% of a school's effort to divide among the eight goals—so that a zero response for something irrelevant was possible. Here are the results, with interesting commonalities among different groups:

22%: *Basic skills and core subjects* (including reading, writing, math, science, and history)

18%: *Critical thinking and problem solving* (including using computers to develop knowledge and applying ideas to new situations)

12%: *Social skills and work ethic* (including personal responsibility and ability to get along with and work with others)

11%: *Citizenship and community responsibility* (including understanding government, voting, volunteering, and being active in the community)

10%: *Preparation for skilled work* (preparation for skilled work not requiring a college degree—or vocational, technical education)

9%: *Physical health* (including exercise habits and nutrition)

9%: *Emotional health* (self-confidence, respect, ability to resist peer pressure)

9%: *Arts and literature* (including ability to "appreciate" the arts and to love literature)

Perhaps the stress on basic skills is inevitable in the current environment, but it does seem that traditional academic preparation in the disciplines most often leading to college seems valued twice as much as preparation for skilled work (which may be why nearly any homeowner will complain about the difficulty and cost of hiring plumbers and electricians). An interesting question here is what this difference in emphasis suggests about the "equal educational opportunity" schools are intended to offer to *all* students. It's also interesting to ask how the low priority assigned to subjects that explore what it means to be human (arts and literature) suggests. Is it really nearly pointless to teach students to consider such things as what the term "quality of life" may mean to them individually? Equally interesting, we might ask how the low priority given to physical and emotional health affects the students' later ability to perform in a high-stress job while concurrently remaining physically and mentally healthy.

But this is just one framework.

From Two Classroom Teachers

How different goals may look from various perspectives in a single school is readily demonstrated by looking at what some classroom teachers have to say. It's not hard to imagine school leaders having in mind an agenda like the one just mentioned, while teachers in the school have a very different mind-set. Before defining what they term "the real goals of education," Dennis Littky and Samantha Grabelle cite John Dewey: "Education is not preparation for life; education is life itself."[29] They then say that their "real" goals for their students are to:

- be lifelong learners
- be passionate
- be ready to take risks
- be able to problem-solve and think critically
- be able to look at things differently
- be able to work independently and with others
- be creative
- care and want to give back to their community
- persevere
- have integrity and self-respect
- have moral courage
- be able to use the world around them well
- speak well, write well, read well, and work well with numbers
- **truly enjoy their life and their work.**

Here are some things perhaps notably missing from more standard laundry lists of goals:

- passion
- learning as a lifelong activity, not something confined within the schoolhouse walls (or its online equivalent)
- risk-taking
- **truly enjoy their life and work** (emphasis in the original)

Aren't these things we would all want for all students? Or are students really better off learning to color—and live—between the lines? And if we want such things, how do we explain the importance of something like "passion" in a time of test score tyranny? How do we persuade others it deserves a chunk of that 100% of the school's efforts?

From the National School Board Association (NSBA)

Technically, these are not goals for a specific school, or even for all schools. But, school boards set policy and develop district mission statements and goals, and NSBA is an influential actor at the district level. It offers on its website "sample" goals and strategies to help school boards determine goals for academic programs, for ensuring high quality teachers and administrators, for involving the community, and for cultivating excellence of the board itself. A single goal for each area is broken down into sub-goals. The sample overarching goal related to academics is stated as: "To offer high-quality student programming so that graduates are prepared to compete in a global society." Oh. Forget passion. Forget moral courage and enjoying life. Prepare "to compete in a global society." What exactly might schooling toward that goal involve? The organization offers fifteen subgoals. As you read, consider the difference in language between the teachers' list and this one:

1. Provide personalized learning for all students.
2. Support progression based on mastery of individual student goals.
3. Embrace a collaborative culture by leveraging and maximizing parent and community partnerships to support accelerated student success.
4. Create a parent scorecard for families and the community to increase transparency with regard to student and school performance.
5. Implement a plan to transition to student based budgeting, where funding is directly tied to students and their individual needs.
6. Require students to play a key role in setting their goals along with their teachers, advisers, counselors, and parents.
7. Provide student and families with choices and meaningful opportunities to improve their school experiences.
8. Ensure all classrooms are wired global places that encourage interactivity and learning by doing.
9. Provide a curriculum that balances individualization and vetted best practices.
10. Design classroom instruction to be a hybrid of face-to-face and online.

11. Design classroom instruction according to individual learning goals and assessment for competency.
12. Ensure all classrooms are using electronic tools for instruction.
13. Utilize digital textbooks.
14. Ensure that technology proficiency and digital citizenship literacy are part of the learning experience for each student.
15. Maximize all data sources to improve instruction for students.

Readers will have their own reactions, but we find something particularly striking about this list. That is, it reflects a shift from imagining education as a human process—as students interacting with adult instructors and mentors—to imagining education as a process in which "education" is delivered by technology rather than teachers (a topic we'll visit again in Chapter 6). First, teachers are mentioned only once, as part of a team of people helping students set individual goals. Their role otherwise seems to be to implement "vetted best practices." With the role of the teacher being minimized, that of technology is stressed: "classrooms are wired global places"; instruction is to be "a hybrid of face-to-face and online"; classrooms are to use "electronic tools for instruction" and "digital textbooks"; students are to develop "technology proficiency and digital citizenship literacy"; and, the instructional process is to include "assessment for competency" and be based on "all data sources," with a "parent scorecard" provided to parents to keep them informed about student progress.

Could the difference that goals make possibly be clearer than they are in these contrasting frameworks?

Choices for Educators

At this point, we return to the question with which we started this chapter: *What are schools for, anyway?* While the intrusion of the federal government and, increasingly, state governments into what schools are accountable for accomplishing is unavoidable, there are still choices to be made. As the frameworks suggest, school activities can be structured in a variety of ways that create astoundingly different environments with astoundingly different values, even as they all strive to teach basic reading, writing, and 'rithmetic. Will school personnel pursue equal educational opportunity—or equitable educational opportunity? Given that there is no such thing as a "neutral" school environment or curriculum, what values will guide choices and be endorsed for students? Are students to be educated to the specifications of business, or encouraged to pursue training for the most lucrative jobs, or to find life's work that they will personally find satisfying and fulfilling?

Without articulating answers to such questions, all of the efforts of school personnel are likely to remain as one prominent educator describes them: "contradictory and frequently counterproductive."[30]

Things to Think About

1. Consider your own K-12 experience. As you look back, what goals do you think your schools pursued? What do you remember experiencing that supports your analysis?

2. Drawing from all three of the frameworks just mentioned, identify 3-5 goals you feel strongly are the most important for any school, and 3-5 that you think could be minimized (or perhaps even banned). What is your rationale for each goal that you prioritize or minimize? If a goal is important, why and to whom? If it's not important, why not?

3. Which of Jencks' five concepts of equality/equity do you believe should be prioritized as a school tries to provide "equal educational opportunity" to its students? *Why?*

4. Do you agree that it is the responsibility of the school to "alleviate social problems?" Why or why not? If you do agree, do you think that goal involves trying to "fix" students by educating undesirable attitudes and behavior out of them, or educating them to identify and seek to remedy elements of society promoting the problem—or both? For example, if students routinely lie, should school personnel focus on getting them to stop lying, or should adults work with students to understand how the world around them might be promoting a tendency to lie?

5. Suppose you were a consultant asked to help design a process for school personnel to come together and design a set of schoolwide goals that had wide support from all stakeholders. What would be the first three or four steps in your recommended process? Who would you involve? How, and why?

6. In working with a school on the design process in question five, no doubt you would want to alert the school personnel you first worked with about difficulties likely to be encountered in the process. What are some of the difficulties you might anticipate?

Things to Explore

Readings

Jacobsen, R. and Rothstein, R. (2006). The goals of education. *Phi Delta Kappan 88*(4). Available from the Economic Policy Institute website, http://www.epi.org/publication/webfeatures_viewpoints_education_goals/
Along with detail on the goals that the researchers found to have widespread support, this piece contains a good bit of historical information. It traces trends over time and helps explain how we have arrived at where we now find ourselves in terms of expectations for public schools.

Jencks, C. (1988). Whom must we treat equally for educational opportunity to be equal? *Ethics, 98*(3), pp. 518–533. Available from the JSTOR database.
While the summary presented in this chapter offers an overview of Jencks' five conceptions, his original explanation offers much more detail and nuance that can deepen readers' understanding of the equality/equity issue.

Kober, N. (2007). *Why we still need public schools: Public education for the common good.* Washington, DC: Center on Education Policy (CEP) at The George Washington University. Available from http://files.eric.ed.gov/fulltext/ED503799.pdf
A bit more history, but more importantly another menu of goals for public schools well worth a look. This piece is especially clear about the relationship between public schools and a democratic society.

Labaree, D. F. (1997). Public goods, private goods: The American struggle over educational goals. *American Educational Research Journal 34*(1), 39-81. Available from https://web.stanford.edu/~dlabaree/publications/Public_Goods_Private_Goods.pdf
Still another framework, this one with three theoretical goals: democratic equality, social efficiency (i.e., education for the workforce), and social mobility. The article offers a close look at how these competing goals have led to an educational system "that is contradictory and frequently

counterproductive." This piece offers a particularly nuanced understanding of the current educational landscape.

Videos

Sir Ken Robinson. *Changing Education Paradigms.* (TED Talk). (12 minutes) https://www.youtube.com/watch?v=zDZFcDGpL4U
Sir Ken Robinson may be one of the most entertaining and yet insightful and sophisticated contemporary analysts of education. In this animated video, he explains the disconnect between former and current goals for schools. As a summary of how the goals of yesterday's schools have lingered in and derailed today's schools, this succinct explanation is one of the best.
Nikhil Goyal. *Do We Still Need Schools?* (TEDxDanubia 2014). (15 minutes). https://www.youtube.com/watch?v=AMxgSgAgwbk
Goyal argues that the historic purpose of schools, to create compliant workers and citizens, is deadening for children. He sees a problem in having adults make every decision for students and argues for transforming schools into democratic sites where students are in charge. Should the goal of schools be to help students do and be whatever they want to do and be? It's an idea worth at least thinking about.
The School of Life. *What's School For?* (5 minutes) https://www.youtube.com/watch?v=HndV87XpkWg
This video (produced by a group in London, UK) has a simple answer to the question of what schools are for: preparing students for life. Of course, different people will have different ideas about what "life" requires. See what you think of the vision proposed in this video. You might think about which idea/s you like, and why—which you object to, and why. It might be useful as well to consider how the ideas here might connect to ideas presented in this chapter.

Notes

1. San Antonio Indep. Sch. Dist. v. Rodriguez, 411 U. S. 1 (1973).
2. See, for example, Leachman, M., Albares, N., Masterson, K. and Wallace, M. Most states have cut school funding, and some continue cutting. (2016, January

25). Center on Budget and Policy Priorities. Retrieved from http://www.cbpp.org/research/state-budget-and-tax/most-states-have-cut-school-funding-and-some-continue-cutting

3. Southern Education Foundation. (2009). No time to lose: Why America needs an education amendment to the Constitution. Retrieved from http://www.southerneducation.org/getattachment/43e3f5bb-714f-47c3-85ad-ece27529f99f/No-Time-Lose-Why-America-Needs-an-Education-Amendm.aspx

4. For a discussion of the issue, see this article from *The Atlantic*—https://www.theatlantic.com/education/archive/2013/10/why-doesnt-the-constitution-guarantee-the-right-to-education/280583/. The Constitute Project is a searchable database of constitution documents from around the world. It was developed at the University of Texas at Austin and can be found at www.constituteproject .org. Also interesting, the World Policy Center has a searchable map generator. Find an interactive global map that illustrates the question, "Does the constitution guarantee citizens the right to education or a specific constitutional right to primary education?" See: https://www.worldpolicycenter.org/policies/does-the-constitution-guarantee-citizens-the-right-to-education-or-a-specific-constitutional-right-to-primary-education

5. A 2016 report from the U. S. Department of Education found that in the 2011–2012 school year, 82% of teachers were White, while only 51% of students were White. See https://www2.ed.gov/rschstat/eval/highered/racial-diversity/state-racial-diversity-workforce.pdf

6. Harris, K. (1999). Aims! Whose aims? In Marples, R. (Ed.), *The aims of education*, 1–13. New York: Routledge.

7. https://www.thomasmore.org

8. https://www.aclu.org

9. For a snapshot of this movement, see http://www.fairtest.org/testing-resistance

10. Tyack, D. (1974). *The one best system: A history of American urban education.* Cambridge, MA: Harvard University Press.

11. Linder, D.O. (n.d.) Scopes "Monkey" Trial (1925). *Famous Trials* website. Retrieved from http://www.famous-trials.com/scopesmonkey

12. Wilson, R. (2017, January 27). New wave of anti-evolution bills hit states. *The Hill.* Retrieved from http://thehill.com/homenews/state-watch/316487-new-wave-of-anti-evolution-bills-hit-states

13. An enjoyable way to learn the details of this ongoing debate would be to watch the PBS documentary from the NOVA series, *Judgment Day: Intelligent Design on Trial.* See http://www.pbs.org/wgbh/nova/evolution/intelligent-design-trial.html

14. Editors. (2009). Why everyone should learn the theory of evolution. *Scientific American.* Retrieved from https://www.scientificamerican.com/article/why-everyone-should-learn-evolution/

15. Clark, C. (2017, April 12). Where corporal punishment is still used in schools, its roots run deep. *National Public Radio*. Retrieved from http://www.npr.org/sections/ed/2017/04/12/521944429/where-corporal-punishment-is-still-used-its-roots-go-deep

16. Dewey, J. (1915). *The school and society*. Chicago: University of Chicago Press.

17. For a more complete look at Utopian aspirations, see John Dewey's "Dewey Outlines Utopian Schools," first published in the *New York Times* on April 23, 1933, and delivered initially as an address at Teachers College, Columbia University.

18. *Mr. Smith Goes to Washington* is a classic 1939 film many people consider among the best films of all time. Its plot involves the efforts of an honest U. S. senator, the film's hero, who is caught up in the machinations of corrupt colleagues.

19. The terms "equal" and "equitable" are often conflated, despite having significantly different implications. Simply, "equal" implies "the same," whereas "equitable" implies "what is fair." The Education Trust explains the difference, which we will get to later: https://edtrust.org/the-equity-line/equity-and-equality-are-not-equal/

20. Mann, B. (2014). Equity and equality are not the same. *The Education Trust*. Retrieved from https://edtrust.org/the-equity-line/equity-and-equality-are-not-equal/

21. Jencks, C. (1988). Whom must we treat equally for educational opportunity to be equal? *Ethics*, *98*(3), pp. 518–533. Available from the JSTOR database.

22. If in case you think there are no homeless students, be aware that in 2013–14, some 1.3 million students were homeless—double the number of the previous decade, according to a report by the National Center for Homeless Education. See http://www.npr.org/sections/ed/2016/06/13/481279226/as-the-number-of-homeless-students-soars-how-schools-can-serve-them-better

23. Counts, G. (1932). *Dare the school build a new social order?* New York: John Day Company.

24. If you are unfamiliar with this phenomenon, see the following for an example: https://qz.com/866771/drug-wholesalers-shipped-9-million-opioid-painkillers-over-two-years-to-a-single-west-virginia-pharmacy/

25. Bell, B., Gaventa, J. and Peters, J. (Eds). (1990) *We make the road by walking: Conversations on education and social change*: p. 180. Philadelphia, PA: Temple University Press.

26. Freire, P. (2004). *Pedagogy of indignation*. Boulder, CO: Paradigm Publishers.

27. For a good understanding of the demands of minimum wage work, see Ehrenreich, B. (2011). *Nickel and dimed*. New York: Macmillan.

28. Jacobsen, R. and Rothstein, R. (2006). The goals of education. *Phi Delta Kappan 88*(4). Retrieved from the Economic Policy Institute website, http://www.epi.org/publication/webfeatures_viewpoints_education_goals/

29. Littky, D. and Grabelle, S. (2004). Chapter 1: The real goals of education. *Big picture*. Alexandria, VA: ASCD. Retrieved from http://www.ascd.org/publications/books/104438/chapters/The-Real-Goals-of-Education.aspx

30. Labaree, D. F. (1997). Public goods, private goods: The American struggle over educational goals. *American Educational Research Journal 34*(1), 70.

THREE

∾ Whither and Whence Curriculum?

A merely well-informed man is the most useless bore on God's earth.
—*Alfred North Whitehead,* The Aims of Education

CURRICULUM MAY BE ONE OF the most popular vocabulary words in education, but the fact that everyone has heard it doesn't ensure that everyone thinks it means the same thing. It's easy to jump to the quick conclusion that curriculum is what is explicitly taught in schools, or the subject-area content. Right? Well, yes, obviously. But curriculum *also* happens outside the classroom. Much like just about everything else in education, curriculum is a complicated topic. Competing ideas exist about what a school's curriculum should (and should not) include, whether curricula should (or should not) differ for different student populations, and who should (or should not) have the power to make such decisions. A look at common assumptions will help build an inclusive definition, and a look at various goals that various curricula pursue will help demonstrate how curricula shape student experiences, knowledge, skills, and character.

Assumptions about Curriculum

Curriculum is the subject area content.

It would be silly of us to argue that the school curriculum *doesn't* include subject area content; of course it does. In fact, a quick Google search on "what is curriculum?" will lead readers to all sorts of materials that specifically define "curriculum" in terms like *the content of a course of study*. Curriculum defined in this way can be a ready-to-use packaged product, including some products that include an explicit script for the teacher to simply read to classes. Conversely, it can be wholly teacher generated. Or, it can exist in many other iterations. From this perspective, curriculum is essentially a body of information delivered to students. Thinking about it like this, we imagine the curriculum as something deliberate, well planned, concrete, and easily identifiable. So far, so good. But when we think of curriculum *only* as explicit information intentionally delivered, we're missing a large and important part of a bigger picture. Textbook or teacher-taught lessons in subject matter are far from the only lessons students learn during their school experiences. Thinking about curriculum as *what students learn* expands the territory considerably.

For example, when students attend classes in a building where rainwater drips steadily into hallways and classrooms, they learn something about how the larger society values them and their community. Or, when teachers use sarcasm to put students down, the students learn something about how a more powerful person can treat a less powerful person. In short, students learn many nonacademic lessons in schools. And, what is explicitly *not* taught is also a form of curriculum. As obvious examples, when a child of color sees only books with White families, or when a child with two mommies or two daddies sees only families with one of each, she learns that her family is not represented in the world of textbooks, suggesting that her family is somehow "not normal," no matter how happy and normal it feels to her.[1] Many scholars and novelists have done much to explain the varied sources of lessons in schools beyond those found in textbooks.[2] Generally, the following basic categorizations are widely accepted and helpful in conceptualizing the various types of curricula that students experience.[3]

Explicit, or intended, curriculum: Simply, the explicit curriculum is the publicly acknowledged curriculum described previously.[4,5] Depending on which version of school reform was in vogue when a teacher entered the classroom, the teacher might assume the right and responsibility to develop her own content, or the responsibility to align his curricula with specific standards or assessments, or the need to "deliver" a ready-made, standards-aligned curriculum (complete with assessments) designed by a commercial vendor. Whatever the source, the explicit curriculum represents the content that someone, or some organization, has said the students should learn.

School reform policy (which we will explore more deeply in the Chapter 6) at both the state and national level highly influences the intended curriculum in any given school or system. In particular, the No Child Left Behind Act (NCLB)[6] passed by Congress and the Common Core State Standards (CCSS)[7] that many states have adopted voluntarily have significantly influenced the academics now taught in schools. While neither of those mandates a specific curriculum (we'll get to that next, in a discussion of Common Core), they nevertheless greatly influence classroom activity. For example, in an analysis of the impact of NCLB, researchers found that the act significantly influenced school curricula. Data indicated that in the first ten years NCLB had been in force, the curriculum had narrowed in order to emphasize tested areas, consequently shrinking or eliminating attention to such areas as social studies, art, music—and even recess. Researchers also found a tendency for schools and systems to narrow exactly what teachers taught within specific subject areas as well the methods they used.[8]

Researchers surveying teachers found a similar, if not stronger, relationship between Common Core implementation, curriculum, and teaching methodology.[9] For example, more than 70% of English teachers and more than 80% of math teachers surveyed indicated that CCSS implementation required changing more than half of their instructional materials, while more than 20% of English teachers and nearly one-third of math teachers reported changing nearly all of their instructional materials. Similarly, more than three-quarters of all teachers surveyed indicated that they changed at least half of their teaching methods, with nearly 20% indicating that they changed all of them. Clearly, policy can have a dramatic impact on the intended curriculum of a school, both in terms of content and teaching strategies.

Implicit, or hidden, curriculum.[10] As the name suggests, implicit curricula include those things the schools may teach without acknowledging them—perhaps without even realizing they *are* teaching them. While few schools would say "We teach discrimination," many school policies do just that. Refusing to let two girls or two guys have a prom date teaches that only heterosexuality is an acceptable sexual orientation. The same lesson is taught when adults in a school tolerate bullying of gay students, saying that a student who acts "too gay" invites abuse. The lesson is reinforced when adults allow adolescent males to "playfully" insult each other with terms like "fag" or "fairy." In addition, as we point out in Chapter 5, when educators enforce dress codes on girls so that they don't wear anything that might "distract" boys, they cast girls in the role of sex objects and boys as both potential predators and as the half of the student body whose education is more important (since no one seems to worry about girls being distracted by what boys might wear). Who can and should be discriminated against is only one of the many areas included in the implicit curriculum. The physical characteristics of teachers also often teach lessons beyond subject matter. If only males teach math and science, then students learn that math and science is a guy thing. If all teachers are White, then students learn that teaching is a White thing. What students see, hear, and experience all provide potentially educative experiences touching on a wide range of areas.

School and classroom routines are other common sources of implicit lessons.[11] Bells teach students to expect that others will control their person (as is the case in factories and in some corporations as well). Forcing students to sit in rows without talking to their neighbors teaches students they are on their own and should not seek help when in difficulty (because it's cheating, or because only the teacher has answers). In contrast, allowing students to sit at tables teaches them they are community members, while seating them in a circle for a conversation teaches them their voices are legitimate—and expected in the work of the classroom. Having uniformed police routinely prowl hallways and conduct searches of bags and lockers teaches students that adults perceive them all as potential criminals unworthy of adult trust (and how might that make them feel?). All of these examples, and more, are powerful communicators of social and cultural norms, values, and beliefs.

We'll have more to say about the hidden curriculum in Chapter 5, but we trust that this discussion has given readers a basic understanding of the implicit curriculum. Before moving on, though, we do want to note that implicit lessons can be positive as well as negative. Adults who can say "I don't know" teach students that no one knows everything, so it's not bad to admit not knowing something. Adults who publicly act against unfairness, even if it's an unpopular stance, teach children that sometimes courage is necessary to do the right thing. Teachers who return graded papers promptly teach students that deadlines are as important for adults as for students. And so on. We have provided fewer of these examples because we think that most often, teachers actually are conscious of "practicing what they preach" and try to act as role models for the values they promote and the behavior they would like to instill in students, understanding the power of the modeling they do to reinforce their explicit lessons.

Null curriculum. The null curriculum consists of things—topic or skills, for example—that are consciously excluded from school experience.[12] The example of the student with two mommies or daddies offers a good example, because books with gay parents are frequently banned in or removed from classrooms.[13] Many schools avoid any mention of homosexuality at all, refusing to acknowledge its existence as a part of reality. Other areas frequently subject to what is essentially censorship increasingly include science topics perceived to challenge religious beliefs (evolution, for example) and/or corporate profit (global warming, for example). In addition to content, certain kinds of thinking can be excluded as well. In many schools, for example, students are discouraged from asking questions that in any way seem to challenge existing authority in the school or that question other authorities— clergy, police, political leaders and so on. Failing to teach students to question narrows the likelihood that tomorrow's citizens will feel free to question and challenge public authorities, something many people consider a major requirement of citizenship.

Some would argue that what students don't learn may be as important as what they do, including a noted curriculum scholar who said:

> [I]gnorance is not simply a neutral void; it has important effects on the kinds of options one is able to consider, the alternatives that one can examine, and the perspectives from which one can view a situation or problems.[14]

In short, the null curriculum is a concern because not learning anything about contentious topics will likely leave tomorrow's citizens ill-equipped to take part in public policy discussions on any number of crucial issues.

There is a single body of core knowledge that all students need to know.

As we discussed in Chapter 2, there is healthy controversy around what is or should be *the* goal of education for the masses. Such controversy is unavoidable around curriculum as well, because curriculum is essentially the path educators use to reach their goals. To create literate citizens, for example, reading and writing must be part of the curriculum.

E. D. Hirsch is likely the best known proponent of the "every American *must* know this" school of thought. In 1987, he published the seminal work *Cultural Literacy: What Every American Needs to Know,*[15] followed in the next year by his *Dictionary of Cultural Literacy.*[16] Essentially, these texts are big books containing a treasure trove of information that the author believed every person must know, the information he and other scholars he consulted considered the shared cultural heritage of Americans. He argued, and in fact still argues, that such knowledge is necessary for, among other things, the ability to make sense of newspapers that contain frequent references to such things as Armageddon and the Cold War. Hirsch subsequently founded the Core Knowledge Foundation,[17] which makes the Core Knowledge Curriculum available for multiple content areas, including science, history and geography, and language arts; other specific topics include such cultural icons as George Washington and Abraham Lincoln. In addition, Hirsch has founded Core Knowledge Schools,[18] based on his curriculum.

Hirsch's work is important because it is likely the strongest current implementation of the idea that there can be a one-size-fits-all curriculum. This approach assumes that a single body of common cultural knowledge and vocabulary is necessary to function within society and that having such knowledge leads to economic prosperity.[19] People who don't have it, usually the poor or otherwise marginalized, occupy lower places in the social hierarchy than those in the "educated" classes,[20] who often attend expensive private schools that stress such information.

On the face of it, this theory makes sense: give the poor the same information the rich have, and they will prosper. But not everyone agrees, and whether the economic future of students in the Core Knowledge schools will be substantially improved by their schooling remains to be seen. It would seem that if the poor could become wealthy just by learning a standard set of facts, then any country with a national curriculum should have largely eliminated poverty—but France, for example, still has about nine million people living below its poverty line despite its insistence that every French citizen must share a common body of knowledge.[21]

When one-size-fits-all curricula like Hirsch's is criticized, it's typically because the content is shaped by a narrow perspective, one that is White, male, and Western. Critics point out that people like W. E. B. Du Bois and Sojourner Truth had major historical roles but rarely make an appearance in what we might call *traditional* curricula. In fact, just about any time anyone announces a single curriculum in any area for every student, there are objections about the many people and things necessarily excluded. The problem raised here returns to the null curricula: whose culture is important, and whose is disposable? Who is most worth knowing about, who isn't, and what does that mean for everyone excluded? Or more pointedly, which students see themselves reflected in the curriculum, which do not, and what do the exclusions teach them?

It's hard to argue against the idea that members of a society should share a pool of cultural knowledge or that students currently need a certain type of language to enter the world of the powerful. But as yet, no one has developed a single curriculum that has escaped criticism for excluding some topics while overemphasizing and thus privileging other topics.

Students are best served by being tracked into career paths.

Just as Hirsch's argument that everyone needs to know the same things makes some sense (however hard it may be to identify those things), so too does the argument on the other side of that curricular fence, the one in favor of providing different students with different kinds of educational experiences. Proponents of differentiated curricula, which most often takes the form of tracking, perceive a standard curriculum as the equivalent of giving every student a road map to Miami—even if many of them hate hot weather, and even if they are actually interested in going to Chicago or San Diego. Every experienced educator has heard students wail "But why do I need to learn *this*? I am never going to need to know *this* for the rest of my life." When the California student who has never seen snow or woods asks this question about the classic Frost poem "Stopping By Woods on a Snowy Evening," it's a pretty tough question to answer if you're not a Hirsch disciple. Adapting curricula to specific locales and students makes a lot of sense. But as we keep seeing, what sounds like terrific common sense can have problematic outcomes, as is the case here.

The first problem is that while schools *claim* that curricula serve the needs of different students differently, too often that is not the reality of student experience. That is, educators tell students they can be anything they want even as the hidden, and sometimes not-so-hidden, curriculum pushes them toward college as the surest route to economic success. One psychologist summarizes this reality in the article titled "All Kids Should Go to College: A Great American Myth," noting that

> The cultural critic, Camille Paglia, was quoted in the *Wall Street Journal* as saying that what's driving the push toward universal college graduation is "social snobbery on the part of a lot of upper-middle-class families who want the sticker in their car window. . . ." That's being a little harsh on parents who just want the best for their kids, but it is time to take a fresh look at these core prejudices. [22]

The prejudice isn't hard to spot. While in school, college bound students usually enjoy being taught by the very best teachers, who are typically assigned to college preparatory courses, and they are typically the group whose members staff student government or edit the school newspaper; as a result, they "[walk] around campus with an air of promise."[23] Meanwhile,

> [H]istorically the vocational curriculum itself has not adequately honored the rich intellectual content of work . . . vocational education [has] "emphasized job-specific skills to the almost complete exclusion of theoretical content." And the general education courses—English, history, mathematics—that vocational students [take are] typically dumbed down and unimaginative. Reforms over the past few decades have gone some way toward changing this state of affairs, but the overall results have been uneven.[24]

Such signals from multiple directions that college is the best, perhaps only, route to success have enormous and often disastrous consequences. Students who would not choose college if left to their own devices experience one set of consequences, while students who might have thrived there experience another. Both suffer, and the end result is a great deal of squandered human potential.

We'll consider first students pushed into college prep tracks whether they want to be there or not. Recently, a student at one prestigious, affluent high school posted a Change.org petition asking the administration to address the high stakes and high academic pressure climate at the school—launched within a few days of a *second* "unexpected death of a student" during this academic year:

> At [our school] there is one path to success. This path is made clear from the day high school anticipation begins, and is reiterated until graduation. From the age of 13 every prospective . . . student understands that this path makes no exceptions, and those who wander off or fall behind are left for failure. Everyone here understands that there is no worse fate than failure.[25]

The petition ends with a plea to the administration,

> And you, the . . . administration, must work with us. Stop teaching us . . . there is only one way to be a student. Stop treating community colleges, trade schools, and apprenticeships like failing destinations. Stop paving the one true path to success . . . [a]nd start treating us like people, not GPAs or test scores. Start letting us choose how we wish to be defined. Start helping us find our dreams, and give us the tools we need to achieve them. Start understanding our priorities instead of implementing yours. Start defining success as any path that leads to a happy and healthy life. Start teaching us to make our own paths, and start guiding us along the way.

At the time we were drafting this text, the petition had over 2000 signatures, and a number of comments as to why people signed it. Although many of the comments came from students and alumni, many more represent students at other schools, as well as parents, teachers, and community members both inside and outside the school attendance boundaries.

Such unreasonable pressure is far from the only consequence of the "college or bust" mentality, however. Students who are not intrinsically interested in academics but who are nevertheless nudged into college classrooms also frequently acquire crushing loan debt and uncertain job prospects post-graduation—*if* they manage to graduate at all.

> Just 56% of students who embark on a bachelor's degree program finish within six years. . . . Just 29% of those who seek an associate's degree obtain it within three years . . . [and] just 46% of Americans complete college once they start. . . . The system is incredibly wasteful.[26]

It seems, then, that the first problem with the idea of different educational paths for different students is that too often it appears in rhetoric while not being realized in practice. Too often, tracks pay lip service to alternatives while in practice promoting and supporting only one.

But of course, some schools *do* actually provide strong vocational programs, and things can go better in such cases. For example, in areas with a strong agricultural base, schools may provide strong and well-respected agricultural programs and provide a home for thriving chapters of Future Farmers of America. This makes sense, because members of farming communities are likely to value an educational program that reflects its interests and values. The same is true of schools that are situated in locales with high concentrations of other industries, like technology. Such alignment with the character of a community is precisely why much control of schools is delegated to local school boards: to allow local people to shape schools that reflect the nature and needs of their particular communities.

However, it's important not to confuse what might be good for the community with what might be good for students themselves. Things go wrong here when specific segments of the student population are channeled into particular tracks based not on their interests, but on the assumptions that post-graduation, students will remain in the same geographic and socioeconomic places they occupied before high school. But students in farming communities may not be best suited for farming. Students in communities where most folks work for WalMart may not be best suited for WalMart jobs.

Pam once worked at a large comprehensive high school on the southwest side of Chicago, for example, that had a thriving career and technical education program, including partnerships and apprenticeships with local businesses and further technical education opportunities. To argue that these programs were not good for the students and the community would be ridiculous—they were, and many students thrived in them. Still, there's an important question to ask about them: did the school have a strong career and technical education program because of the philosophy that providing both strong academic and vocational tracks allows all kids to find a good path? Or was it because the school was in a diverse working class neighborhood, so that it was assumed that technical, trade, or service level jobs were most appropriate for students from a working class background? While we can't know the answer to that question with any certainty, we know enough about tracking to know that students from certain socioeconomic groups are routinely tracked by social class rather than by talent or interest. For example, we know that low-income students of color in urban schools are often tracked into vocational and service-oriented courses that lead to low-paying jobs, rather than into college prep or Advanced Placement opportunities—if such courses even exist in their schools.[27]

There is little question that the existence of tracks in schools creates hierarchies that rarely serve students well. Pam's experience offers another example. Once when she served as a school improvement researcher at another large and thoroughly diverse high school, she was part of a team working through the push by one group of parents to recast career and technical education courses as less vocationally oriented and more aligned with arts and culture. She recalls in particular a powerful discussion about reframing the basic welding course as "metal sculpture." First, this group of parents perceived greater symbolic value in presenting the course as an art, a pursuit with cultural and social cachet, rather than as a technical skill. And second, they believed that "metal sculpture" would benefit students both because it would "look better on college applications" than welding and because it would constitute an additional art elective for students. Such a proposal suggests how creatively even vocational education itself can be twisted to directly serve the interests of a college bound student population: art and culture? Yes, important. Welding? No. Better that students in the academic track should take "metal sculpture" than that vocational students should take "welding." (By the way: these parents got what they wanted. Parents of the vocational students didn't have the time or political skill to mount successful opposition, and the school yielded to the loudest parental voices instead of protecting the integrity and strength of the vocational track.)

Different educational paths for different students make a lot of sense. And yet, they also have caused a great deal of harm, and not only to students who suffer being shoved into intense college preparation. Tracking systems also often close off college to those who might have done well there, and they do much to return students to the social class they were born into.[28] It's easier to promise good alternatives for everyone than it is to create them.

The Common Core State Standards are a curriculum.

Simply, no—but we know that many people have that mistaken idea. Common Core State Standards (CCSS) are *not* a curriculum, a curriculum guide, or anything that can be construed as *curriculum* itself. The CCSS are a set of academic *standards* that were developed by the National Governors Association Center for Best Practices and Council of Chief State School Officers.[29] Essentially, a *standard* is a goal set for students; curriculum is what schools choose to have students study and do in order to reach a goal. For example, a standard might say that students should be able to identify a main character in a work of fiction. To meet that goal, students might discuss the main character in Melville's *Moby Dick*—or in one of Rowling's *Harry Potter* novels.

A key goal of CCSS is to provide a set of "high quality" standards states can adopt, essentially creating national agreement about what American schools should ensure children know and be able to do, no matter where they attend school. Many people believe that if schools all pursued common standards, then teachers as well as students could be assessed more easily through standardized tests, with schools and especially individual teachers being held "accountable" for what students do and don't learn. Adoption of the standards is voluntary, but as this book was being published, forty-two states and the District of Columbia were using the Standards to guide curriculum and instruction.

In a nutshell, then: the *standards* tell schools what is expected of students at particular grade levels, while the *curriculum* includes the course materials and strategies used to teach the students what they need to learn.

Controversy has surrounded the CCSS since they appeared in 2010. Proponents argue that high standards for all children in all schools isn't a bad thing. And really, it isn't: who among us would argue that having high expectations for the academic outcomes of all of the nation's children is a bad thing? But critics (including parents, teachers, politicians, and others) from all points on the political spectrum have taken issue with the standards.[30] For example, challenges include questions about standards development (who developed them, using what process?) and about whether the content is appropriate for all children (especially the demands on very young children); the lack of research to document effectiveness of a standards-based approach; the implications for teacher evaluation (using student standardized test scores to evaluate teachers is problematic);[31] and a perceived override of local authority (too much federal intervention in community decisions). Some critics, including former presidential hopeful Rick Santorum, have gone so far as to suggest that the CCSS represents an attempt to "nationalize the curriculum"[32]—despite the fact that standards and curriculum are not the same thing, as we've explained. That said, research does indicate that implementation of the Common Core has very real implications for curriculum development and teaching practice.

Curriculum should be neutral and free of controversy.

In Chapter 2, we pointed out that nothing that happens in schools is value-free (if you have read that chapter, you will remember our discussion of the evolution controversy). The idea that curriculum should be neutral warrants a much closer look than we provided in that chapter. The fact is that no matter which curriculum we are talking about, you can be sure values are deeply embedded.

Many people imagine schools to be fact focused, much like Mr. Gradgrind in Dickens' *Hard Times*:

> Now, what I want is Facts. Teach these boys and girls nothing but Facts. Facts alone are wanted in life. Plant nothing else, and root out everything else. You can only form the minds of reasoning animals upon Facts; nothing else will ever be of any service to them.[33]

While this sounds like a pretty straightforward plan, the reality is much more complicated. *Which* "facts" are to be included, and who decides? For example, American history books often talk about Manifest Destiny, the idea that White people were destined to "civilize" the United States from coast to coast. Who decided these are *the* "facts"? What about those "facts" over there—the ones noting that Native American tribes had their own civilizations before Europeans arrived, thank you very much, and that what Manifest Destiny meant to Native Americans was the theft of their land and the genocide of their people? The questions of "which facts" and "who decided" and "what about *those* facts" are crucial. Too often we assume that what we teach and learn in school is "the Truth,"[34] and we don't take the next step to think about where that "Truth" might come from, or what interests that "Truth" might serve, or whose version of a story that "Truth" might tell. As Chinua Achebe has said (referencing a proverb), "Until the lions have their own historians, the history of the hunt will always glorify the hunter."[35]

That the lessons taught and learned in school might be only partial truths, only one side of multifaceted stories, can be a difficult concept to swallow, especially if we have devoted our professional lives to educating young people. To think that as teachers we could be teaching students things that aren't exactly true feels antithetical to our professional responsibilities. But the hard reality is that we can't teach everything—every side of every story, every possible interpretation of every fact. And when we select this fact or story but not that fact or story, we unavoidably bias the curriculum.

Of course, "we" school personnel are often not the ones making these decisions. They are frequently made far outside local schools and classrooms by noneducators—like, for example, legislators who mandate that this-or-that must (or must not) be included in a curriculum. Local control is also eroded by the fact that many schools serving disadvantaged communities are under-resourced and, lacking essential staff and supplies, school personnel feel obliged to accept free curricular materials that many sources are only too happy to provide.

For example, corporations and industry lobbies increasingly strive to shape the curriculum in significant and controversial ways. According to a 2011 *Washington Post* article,

> Industries such as information technology and aerospace have crafted lesson plans aimed at training future employees. Some have purchased advertising space on school websites and buses. In the Washington area, defense contractors have made donations to several school systems and sponsored school engineering clubs ... But critics say the energy industry often goes much further than the typical school donations. Groups with a stake in oil, gas or coal frequently train teachers and shape lesson plans on controversial subjects.[36]

A well-known instance appeared in 2009, when the American Coal Foundation partnered with the major education publisher Scholastic, Inc. to develop fourth grade curriculum materials called the *United States of Energy*. This particular curriculum caused both a media frenzy and back-tracking by Scholastic. The materials did give a nod to other forms of energy production by featuring wind turbines, solar panels, oil wells and nuclear plants alongside illustrations of what the organization Rethinking Schools refers to as "shimmering piles of coal." The Rethinking Schools critique of the curriculum, however, points to what is not included—the null curriculum of these particular materials: "the lessons in the curriculum fail to alert children that there might be any problems with the mining, washing, transport, and burning of coal."

Interestingly, in the grid showing how the lessons align with national standards, the very first standard states that children should learn "that different types of energy (e.g., solar, fossil fuels) have different advantages and disadvantages." Sure enough, the lessons are full of "advantages," but there is not the slightest hint—none—that coal might have any problems.

> Nothing about the mountains being scraped away throughout Appalachia, or the resulting flooding that has destroyed people's homes, or how communities' water supplies have been poisoned. Nothing about the busting of unions or the exploitation of nonunion miners. Nothing about the billions of gallons of toxic waste created by washing coal and, of course, by burning it. Nothing about the poisonous coal dust that blows off trains and barges as the coal travels from mine to coal-fired plant. Nothing about the toxins released when coal is burned—like sulfur dioxide, mercury, and arsenic—which kill many thousands of people a year, according to the American Lung Association.[37]

The author notes that a full explanation of the realities of coal fuel might be overwhelming for fourth graders, but his point is this—leaving the challenges out entirely fundamentally misrepresents the usefulness and the dangers of coal. Of course, to the American Coal Foundation that funded this curriculum's development, that's not a problem at all.

Rethinking Schools partnered with the Campaign for a Commercial-Free Childhood and Friends of the Earth to get Scholastic to stop distributing the materials. And they succeeded. After what Rethinking Schools characterized as a "two-day publicity nightmare,"[38] the Campaign for a Commercial-Free Childhood (CCFF) reported that

> In response to pressure from tens of thousands of parents, educators and grassroots advocates, Scholastic Inc. has agreed to drastically limit its practice of partnering with corporations to produce sponsored teaching materials. Scholastic's announcement is the culmination of a three-month campaign led by the Campaign for a Commercial-Free Childhood.[39]

But that wasn't all.

Buoyed by this victory, CCFC expanded the Scholastic campaign to ask for reforms to Scholastic's InSchool Marketing Division, a component of the company that produces a variety of corporate, government, and nonprofit funded curriculum materials. The CCFC explains the InSchool Marketing objectives here:

> Scholastic's InSchool Marketing program has been used to market everything from ice cream to Hollywood movies in children's classrooms. Clients have included McDonald's, Cartoon Network, Shell, SunnyD, Nestle, and Disney. According to Scholastic, the program was designed "to promote client objectives" and "make a difference by influencing attitudes and behaviors."[40]

An article from the *New York Times* detailed other corporate-sponsorships turned-curriculum,

> In addition to the coal curriculum, Scholastic distributed a program stressing the environmental wrongs of plastic water bottles, sponsored by Brita, which sells water filters. It also had a $3 million Microsoft campaign in which schools could earn points toward prizes for each Microsoft search, as well as a program featuring Playmobil's small plastic figures.[41]

Scholastic responded by not only discontinuing production of the *United States of Energy* curriculum, but more significantly, by agreeing to limit its production of corporate sponsored teaching materials.[42] Additionally, Scholastic cut its InSchool Marketing program by nearly half, even more significantly decreasing corporate sponsored materials. In addition, it instituted a "partner review board," comprised of a curriculum editor, a teacher, a school administrator, a child psychologist and a parenting expert.[43]

It's not just the lobbying arm of big business that can impact the curriculum. We see the impact of personal and institutional values at work in other places, too. Populous states like Texas and California use a huge number of textbooks, and as a result, they have an extraordinary amount of influence on the content of textbooks used nationwide. The number of K-12 school textbooks purchased in Texas is so significant that many publishers pander to the often extreme and politically driven agendas of powerful and monied Texans, affecting state level curriculum policy and the decisions of the Texas Board of Education. Put another way, this means that anyone with enough money, power, and influence can play a decisive role in what becomes part of the explicit and null curricula, not just in Texas, but by default, across the nation. For example,

> In 2009, the nation watched in awe as the state board worked on approving a new science curriculum under the leadership of a chair who believed that "evolution is hooey." In 2010, the subject was social studies and the teachers tasked with drawing up course guidelines were supposed to work in consultation with "experts" added on by the board, one of whom believed that the income tax was contrary to the word of God in the scriptures. [44]

According to the *Washington Post*, this 2010 revisioning of the social studies curriculum was intended to "[restore] balance" after "years of liberal bias in history education."[45] But that's not all. Five years later the *Washington Post* reported,

> Five million public school students in Texas will begin using new social studies textbooks this fall based on state academic standards that barely address racial segregation. The state's guidelines for teaching American history also do not mention the Ku Klux Klan or Jim Crow laws.

And when it comes to the Civil War, children are supposed to learn that the conflict was caused by "sectionalism, states' rights and slavery" — written deliberately in that order to telegraph slavery's secondary role in driving the conflict, according to some members of the state board of education.

Slavery was a "side issue to the Civil War," said Pat Hardy, a Republican board member, when the board adopted the standards in 2010. "There would be those who would say the reason for the Civil War was over slavery. No. It was over states' rights."[46]

To say that the State of Texas is unilaterally responsible for the content that appears in major publisher textbooks would be inaccurate, but as one author stated, "its size, its purchasing heft, and the pickiness of the school board's endless demands—not to mention the board's overall craziness—certainly made it the trend leader."[47]

Texas isn't the only state in which the legislature has opened the door for special or individual interests to impact school curriculum. Tweeted by Scientific American[48] and reported in *Nature*, eleven bills have been introduced across the United States in 2017 that are aimed at specifically altering science education standards.[49] Many of these measures employ language like "academic freedom" and "teach the controversy," phrases that are generally attributed to liberally-oriented interests. But this brand of curriculum-busting is far from progressive. According to *Frontline*,

In Idaho, lawmakers removed references to climate change from the state's science standards. In Alabama and Indiana, they passed resolutions urging support for educators who teach "diverse" views on climate change, evolution and human cloning. And in Florida, the legislature on Friday adopted one bill that would give educators and students more freedom to express religious beliefs in school, and a second that would give residents new power to oppose classroom materials they dislike— including science textbooks.

Across the country, proposals that would influence how topics like climate change and evolution are taught in public schools have gained traction. Eleven such measures have been introduced in nine Republican-dominated states since January.[50]

And in May of 2017, the Florida legislature approved a measure that

> enables any tax-paying resident of a given county to file complaints
> about the curriculum of the schools in their district. A complaint would
> trigger a public hearing to determine if the material in question is
> "accurate, balanced, noninflammatory, current, free of pornography . . .
> and suited to students' needs," according to the legislation.[51]

Given the long arm of corporations and the whims of politicians, letting
tax-paying residents protest specific topics *might* seem like a good idea. And
its apparent common sense is exactly why of all the measures introduced
this year, this one may have such critics as the National Coalition Against
Censorship, the Florida School Boards Association, and the National Science
Teachers Association especially worried. The authors of these "academic freedom" bills use the word "controversy" in ways that make it difficult to coun-
ter.[52] As *Frontline*[53] explains the Florida bill,

> school districts must issue lists of all materials in classrooms, school
> libraries and reading lists. Districts would provide an outside "unbiased
> and qualified hearing officer" to consider objections and make
> recommendations to school boards, which would have the final say.

The Florida Citizens Alliance, the group behind the bill, have compiled an
extensive document that targets, among other subjects and material, science
education, the Common Core, critiques of Reaganomics, and the idea that
Thanksgiving is complicated for Native Americans.

Bills such as these are not new. The National Center for Science Education
has been keeping track of these kinds of proposals for over a decade. What is
alarming is that since 2004, more than fifty of these kinds of "academic freedom" proposals have seen the light of day in twenty states. They are becoming
more frequent and are getting farther in the legislature,[54] threatening to turn
control of curriculum over to groups essentially dedicated to seeing that only
one side of many issues ever makes it into schools, walling out much that is
widely accepted as valuable information in formal academic circles.

Clearly, turning a blind eye to the power of stakeholder groups that privilege political, ideological, or financial gain merely serves to open the door for

even more partisan, corporate, or ideologically driven content to make it into the classroom. Whoever controls what people believe to be true about the world, about themselves, or about others, controls the people as well.

Frameworks for Curriculum

To say that there are many ways to envision curriculum would be a gross understatement. We cannot say that in selecting curriculum, school or district personnel choose among options A, B or C—or even among options A to Z. Possibilities are endless and not mutually exclusive. For example, an academic curriculum can be, and often is, accompanied by some character building curriculum; because each of those two components can vary widely, possibilities for exactly what a combination of those two areas might look like in a single school seem nearly endless. In addition, and by their very nature, hidden and null curricula aren't publicly acknowledged, even though their effects are significant. Adding those into the mix means still more possibilities for combinations in practice. When we define curriculum as "what students do and do not learn, intentionally or unintentionally," the task of thinking clearly about it can feel overwhelming—as it felt even to the authors trying to streamline and organize the topic for this introductory chapter.

The bottom line here is that curriculum is a topic that exceeds by far what we can explain in a single chapter and that appears in so many versions it's likely impossible to catalogue them all. Still: it's essential to try and think as clearly as possible about curriculum because there is perhaps nothing more important than what students learn in schools. In the following section, we offer two routes we hope will help you clarify your own thinking about what content, skills, values and so on you might endorse as a professional: classroom approaches to curriculum, and typical goals for curriculum. We hope these overviews prove useful in thinking about the thorny question of what it is exactly you think schools should teach.

Classroom Approaches to Curriculum

Banking versus Problem-Posing Curriculum. Although any number of curricular approaches have come and gone, a dichotomy that many people find useful is a well-known one offered by the renowned Brazilian philosopher and educator Paulo Freire: the "banking v. problem-posing" model. The dichotomy he presents (in his seminal text *Pedagogy of the Oppressed*) is used in studies of curriculum to illustrate the divide that separates what many understand as traditional versus modern modes of teaching, learning, and curriculum development. Essentially, Freire believed that teachers frequently see themselves as holding all knowledge in a classroom and dispensing it to students.[55] In this model, the students aren't much more than passive receptacles for information. The teacher "deposits" information into them, and the teacher "withdraws" it from students in oral drills, on worksheets, or on exams. The teacher has absolute authority, and students have no space in which to challenge or question what they are told.

In contrast to this authoritarian model, Freire's vision of problem-posing education serves personal freedom; it is something that enables people to think for themselves rather than to expect and accept that others have the right to tell them how and what to think. Students are "critical coinvestigators" who work toward understanding with their teachers, perhaps generating new understanding for teachers as well as students. The work of the classroom is to explore real world problems that students identify in their own experience and to devise strategies to alleviate them. In this model, teachers empower students to think for themselves, and all members of the classroom community help generate learning.

In practical terms, the difference might easily be seen in two different curricula on the coal issue previously discussed. The industry-provided materials might be used in either approach. In the banking approach, students would likely be told both by the curricular materials and by the teacher that coal is a wonderful fuel and an essential complement to other forms of energy. Teacher questions would likely focus on the technical process of mining and on coal's usefulness in generating energy, with students asking no questions of their own (except perhaps to clarify understanding of the materials). In contrast, in a problem-posing model, a teacher might explain to students the importance of determining whether information they receive is trustworthy and assign the "problem" of determining the trustworthiness of the coal curriculum. In this case, students might explore who developed the materials, what their goals might be, whether information provided was factually correct, and what information had been left out. In the process, students would research the many aspects of coal mining in coal mining communities, including not only how it might contribute to the financial health of families but also its costs in terms of human health and the environment. After their explorations, each student could take an individual stance on whether or not potential benefits outweigh potential harms—perhaps agreeing with others, perhaps not. Or, if the class generally found the curricular materials not to be trustworthy, students might devise some action to help get them removed from classrooms or to see that supplemental information is provided in the future.

Notice that in these approaches, the implicit curriculum varies as well. In the banking model, students learn to trust whatever they are told by an authority. In the problem-posing model, however, students learn they can question what they are told and determine its trustworthiness for themselves.

Standards-based Curriculum. As we've said, standards do not themselves constitute curriculum. Many states have their own standards (and have for many years), but many states have adopted Common Core. That has created a large market for "standards-based textbooks" that publishers have rushed to fill. States too have been developing specific curricula to help schools meet Common Core standards; New York is just one example.[56] But individual educators often are free to develop specific classroom plans of their own—as long as students are prepared to take the standardized tests intended to hold schools and teachers accountable. The fact that major flaws have been found in standardized tests based on Common Core assessments[57] and on other standardized assessments as yet has not freed students and teachers from the need to prepare for them.

Still, the standards themselves often leave open which specific materials teachers might use—although teachers might often feel shoved toward the kind of traditional curriculum favored by people like E.D. Hirsch. For example, here is a standard for ninth and tenth grade literature instruction:

Integration of Knowledge and Ideas:
CCSS.ELA-LITERACY.RL.9-10.7
Analyze the representation of a subject or a key scene in two different artistic mediums, including what is emphasized or absent in each treatment (e.g., Auden's "Musée des Beaux Arts" and Breughel's *Landscape with the Fall of Icarus*).[58]

Based on the language of the standard itself, a teacher might choose to compare a scene from one of the Harry Potter books with the same scene in the movie based on the book, or might compare treatment of the topic of drug addiction in the classic James Baldwin story "Sonny's Blues" with its treatment in the James Taylor song "Oh Brother."[59] Such alternatives might at least help introduce students to the concept under study, providing an entrée to discussion of more culturally elite works, if such works appear on the specific test students have to take. Standards in and of themselves are not bad things, in that they generally denote skills that teachers frequently target in any event—like how the medium can affect a message. The goals identified in standards may have less influence over student experience than the classroom approach teachers use to meet those goals.

Scripted curriculum. Scripted curriculum is exactly what it sounds like: teachers are given scripts that tell them exactly what to say and do. Exactly. At one time, the scripted approach was found primarily in under-resourced communities[60] or "no excuses" charter networks. Now, however, it is becoming more commonplace, thanks in part to increased school privatization and its need to reduce teacher salaries in order to increase profits. Widespread adoption of and confusion about Common Core has also expanded the adoption of scripted materials, because they may promise to help educators find their way through Common Core standards and related assessments.

Advocates of scripting claim that scripted lessons serve to "teacher-proof" the curriculum, ensuring that even teachers unfamiliar with the content will be able to successfully "deliver" lessons. That said, others argue that scripted lessons undermine, even subvert, teacher autonomy, professionalism, and ability to be genuinely responsive to student needs. While scripted lessons are being used in a wide variety of educational contexts, there appears to be insufficient attention to the quality of popular materials. Consider this example, in an article about a phonics lesson in which the teacher, Karen, was forced to work from scripted materials:

Karen turns toward the marker board and writes *superman*. Two children call out "Superman!" right away. They are precocious readers and volunteer many of the words Karen writes. The transition has been wordless as the children watch their teacher shift from reading the scripted story to writing a word on the board. They are used to the routine; it's almost October, and they've been at this for weeks.

Karen erases the *n* in superman and puts a *d* at the end to make the nonword *supermad*. Some of the students in Karen's class believe it is a word, and one child suggests that if you are very mad at someone, you "are supermad at them." Next Karen puts an *n* back in place of the *d* but then places a *d* after the *n* to make *supermand*. The children slowly work to say the nonword. One calls it out, and a few others echo. They look at their teacher; "What is supermand?" asks one.

Karen says, "It is not a word."

Karen erases *supermand* and writes *baboon*, which is read by one of the same two precocious readers. Karen changes it to *baboot*. Some of the children say it; others echo it. Some are silent.

Next Karen writes *alphabet*; the same two children read it. Others echo it. Karen changes it to *alphabed*. Some children chuckle as they say it; others echo and wait for the next word. Some are silent.

When Karen writes *schoolbus*, again some say the word, and others echo it or are silent. Someone suggests, "Like The Magic School Bus [books]"... as Karen turns it into *schoolbun* by erasing the *s* and replacing it with an *n*. One child frowns and calls out, "What is a schoolbun?"

Another responds before Karen can answer, "Like, when you're at school, if they have hot dogs for lunch, they give it to you on a schoolbun." Karen smiles.[61]

Any experienced literacy educator would argue excitedly against a lesson that taught students *not* to expect that what they "read" will make any sense in the real world. In cases like this, materials actually force teachers to mis-educate students.

It's important to remember that the point of corporations is to make money, and that is as true for textbook publishers as for any other type of corporation. Pat has been involved in development of commercially developed curricular materials and assessments, and her experiences have led her to look at commercial products with a highly skeptical eye. We suggest that education personnel who have any role in shaping curriculum acquisition do the same. This is especially true for scripted materials—written far from the

classroom and possibly by someone who has never taught in a classroom—
which take control completely away from classroom professionals.

Co-created curriculum. The notion that students should be involved in
creating curriculum in the classroom isn't a new one, but it's always been
perceived as a bit radical. This may be particularly true in the current climate
of prescriptive, top-down reform initiatives that place little faith in students
or their teachers. But throughout his body of work, John Dewey[62] advocated
for including students in creating curriculum in a number of ways, and more
recently Freire's problem-posing model relies on active participation of both
teacher and learner in the process. More contemporarily, Pedro Noguera[63] argues that students in classrooms possess valuable insight into and knowledge
about effective teaching and learning, and Brian Schultz[64] demonstrates that
"spectacular things" really can happen in classrooms when children are given
the space to imagine, create, exercise agency, and learn *alongside* their teacher.

Rather than a cookie cutter recipe, this model begins with the teacher
listening to and learning from students, asking such questions as "What do
these students know and what do they want to know?" "How do they learn
best?" "What are their priority concerns, and how might these concerns be
addressed within the context of academic work?" "How might these interests and concerns be incorporated into the classroom while simultaneously pursuing the goals/standards imposed by outside authorities?" If young
children are interested only in games, a great deal of math, language, history
and finance can be learned during a project to design a marketable game. If
middle-schoolers have no safe place to gather socially after school, they can
acquire a good bit of academic information and develop any number of skills
by crafting a proposal for a specific place to be revamped for them and sub-
mitting it to funders.

Students know the difference between content that is relevant and applica-
ble and that which is removed or disconnected from their experiences. And,
as we've pointed out repeatedly, many core academic skills, including critical
thinking, can be practiced on a wide variety of content. When youth have a
stake in the creation and manifestation of their learning in terms of content
and experiences, they transition from being mere receptacles of information
to being active participants in knowledge generation and skill development.
And, engaged learners are more successful learners.[65]

Typical Goals for Curriculum

Provide students with a body of knowledge and skills. As we've said, subject area content and basic skill development are at the heart of the intended curriculum in schools. In the most basic sense, it is the goal of the intended curriculum to provide information in such key areas as history and science and to develop such basic skills as literacy and numeracy.

We have already detailed Hirsch's Core Knowledge curriculum, which is one example of a curriculum that functions to provide students with a specific body of knowledge. Commercial publishers can function as default curriculum designers, because often whatever textbook a school or district has adopted becomes the de facto curriculum. At one time this kind of curriculum resource might have been limited to two texts, a teacher edition and student edition of the classroom textbook—maybe three, if a workbook was included. Today, publishers have increased profits by supplementing texts with a variety of print, media, and data tools. For example, promotional materials for one social studies program consists of eight slick pages indicating how with the "right mix of print materials and dynamic online resources" teachers can "explore more, discover more, and do more!"[66] to help students meet standards from the National Council for the Social Studies. The materials include what is available for students (text, multimedia, assessments, and customized interactive opportunities) and the teacher (teacher's edition and online lesson center, lecture guides, prealignment to standards, and access to data, data, and more data).

Everything a teacher needs in order to meet the goal of communicating a body of information to students is in this one-stop curriculum shop, neatly packaged and ready to go. When dominant publishers create such materials, they keep an eye on potential selling points like "aligned with *xyz* standards" and "including assessments" that mirror popular standardized assessments— hence their widespread appeal (and, often, the notable size of the null curriculum, since any topics likely to spark controversy are typically assiduously avoided).

Cultivate attitudes favorable to particular brands or industries. We've already discussed the *United States of Energy* curriculum and explained that many organizations, notably including corporations, attempt to influence curriculum in order to influence opinions on potentially controversial topics and to develop brand loyalty. In addition to advertising on school buses and athletic fields and to providing full curricula on specific topics, for example, corporations have managed to have pictures of Nikes and Oreos appear in textbook math lessons.[67] While specific strategies vary, the goal remains to bias students in favor of a particular product or point of view.

Because there are environmental and health risks involved with such things as pipelines and the fracking process (used in extracting natural gas),[68] they are highly controversial. As a result, energy is an area where there have been great efforts to influence curricula by providing free materials to schools. For example, the Education Outreach program of The Offshore Energy Center[69] has developed several curricula as well as teacher professional development products. Teachers can choose among: the *Knowledge Box*, which showcases the oil and gas industry through interactive technology, hands-on activities, posters and multimedia presentations; *Playing with Petroleum*, which provides multidisciplinary hydrocarbon-based energy education; the *Mobile Oilfield Learning Unit*, which offers six self-contained learning centers with curriculum-based, hands-on activities about energy and the technologies and sciences involved with the oil and gas industry—delivered in a trailer truck; and *Earth's Energy: The Science of Offshore Drilling*, which informs students about rock and carbon cycles, petroleum and natural gas, offshore drilling, environmental issues and careers in the offshore energy industry. It's a pretty good bet that exploration of those environmental issues provides reassurance to students by minimizing, or negating, environmental concerns. In fact, one element in particular of the Education Outreach Program mission statement makes clear exactly the direction it plans to sway student perception and opinion: the program seeks, in its own words, to have students "develop an understanding of offshore energy's contribution to the environment and our quality of life."[70]

Cultivate good character in students. As we've noted, most people assume that schools will help students develop "good character," although different people define that term very, very differently. Character education has in the past been taught subtly, often through the content of academic texts. For example, Pat has a copy of a grammar book from the mid-1900s in which students had to find grammar errors in a funny story—with the story being about an obviously stupid Russian guard. Since the book was used during the Cold War, it's no surprise now to see efforts to cultivate an anti-Soviet attitude in textbooks from that period. In the last several decades, however, character education has increasingly taken the form of explicit criteria.

It's actually harder to use explicit texts because they make clear which definition of "good character" is being taught. While the values of honesty and integrity would likely be acceptable to most people, others are not. For example, while some parents tell their children to "turn the other cheek" in the face of violence, others preach "an eye for an eye." Even "cooperation" has been challenged by parents who worry that the world outside school is competitive, and cooperation is poor practice (and even, sometimes, considered a characteristic of communism rather than capitalism).

Still: explicit curricula have been developed and do exist. The *Character Development and Leadership* curriculum is one example.[71] This commercially available curriculum uses a role model approach in lesson modules promoting eighteen character traits.[72] The developer provides lesson plans as well as suggestions for how to integrate the curriculum into a school program. It is designed for middle through high school grades, and is aligned with the Common Core State Standards for English/Language Arts. For each character trait taught, a role model is offered. For example, Pat Tillman (killed in Afghanistan—perhaps by friendly fire) is the role model for sacrifice (though pacifists and parents might not approve). Booker T. Washington (who advocated that Black people be patient and advance through education and entrepreneurship rather than political activism against Jim Crow laws) is the role model for perseverance (though we know W. E. B. Du Bois did not approve).

Help students take responsibility for their own learning and for the world around them. Unlike other models, this goal produces a curriculum based not in a standard set of materials but instead in a fluid and flexible process. Here, the teacher is key in crafting the curriculum out of the interests and concerns of the students.

Project Citizen, an interdisciplinary curriculum developed by the Center for Civic Education, is one example.[73] The Center is a nonpartisan group that promotes learners' responsible and competent participation in local and state government. The *Project Citizen* curriculum is intended to help participants develop a better understanding of the public policy process as well as learn ways to have an impact on public policy themselves. Related objectives of the curriculum include helping participants develop an appreciation for democratic values and principles, tolerance, and feelings of political efficacy. Key elements of the curriculum include having students and teacher:

1. Work cooperatively to identify and research a local public policy issue or problem,
2. Discover and evaluate alternative solutions,
3. Develop a public policy solution and action plan, including ways to involve local or state authorities in the adoption of the proposed solution,
4. Present findings and materials at a community public hearing and contact public officials.

The *Project Citizen* curriculum provides teachers with the framework necessary to guide a local project that helps students develop the skills necessary to envision and accept responsibility for attaining a better state of affairs in their own communities.[74]

Choices for Educators

Curriculum is a case of bad news/good news for educators. The bad news—which in-service teachers know all too well—is that recent years have brought increasing efforts from people far outside schools to limit and control the efforts of educators within schools. Scripted curriculum is, of course, the most extreme example, but the accountability movement has also placed limits on what must be and what can't be taught in the time and space allowed. Teachers have not been quiet about their resentment.[75] Yes, there are limits.

There is also, however, good news. Teachers are not powerless, as we tried to indicate when we pointed out that teachers can choose how to use materials they must use in the classroom—as in our example of teaching a unit on coal. They may substitute one set of materials for another in pursuit of the same goal—as in our example of substituting Harry Potter for icons of Western culture alien to student interest and experience. Nor are teachers and administrators necessarily powerless outside the classroom. They can volunteer for curriculum committees. They can identify sympathetic stakeholders, including parents, and begin to lobby for and against curricula and curricular influences as they think best, at local, state and even national levels. *The* key choice here is whether to accept powerlessness and teach whatever curriculum is handed over by the state, or by the school board, or even by last year's teacher or to accept responsibility for helping to ensure curricula seems best suited to serving the interests of the students populating the school and district.

Of course, first it's necessary to think through what seems desirable and undesirable. Perhaps thinking about the following questions and exploring the suggested additional resources will help.

Things to Think About

1. Curricula are intended to be useful to students in their lives after school. Think back over your K-12 years. Of everything that teachers tried to teach you, what did you take away with you when you left high school? Can you say why it was important and how you learned it? What does that—and the fact that there's almost surely much more you didn't take with you than you did—suggest about the curricula you experienced?

2. Think of three examples of hidden curriculum you believe were present in your K-12 experience or are present in your higher education experience. (Remember that hidden curriculum may teach desirable as well as undesirable lessons.)

3. This is a long and detailed chapter. Find three paragraphs or sentences you felt strongly about—either because you found them wholly accurate or totally unbelievable or for some other reason—and explain why they struck you that way. Discuss your reactions with others who have read the chapter.

4. Do you believe students can be good partners with teachers in shaping school experience? Why or why not?

Things to Explore

Readings

Babits, C. (2015, May 27). Another perspective on the Texas textbook controversy. (Blog post). NOT EVEN **PAST.** Available from http://notevenpast
.org/another-perspective-on-the-texas-textbook-controversy/
  While the contemporary Texas textbook controversy has gotten a lot of

press, Babits takes a historian's look back and traces the long-standing culture war at the heart of many struggles over curriculum. This highly informative piece is an easy read, leaving the reader with much history painlessly learned.

Klass, P. (2017, January 16). The banned books your child should read. *New York Times.* Available from https://www.nytimes.com/2017/01/16/well/family/the-banned-books-your-child-should-read.html?_r=0
This brief article offers a look at some frequently banned books for kids, explaining why people object and why kids should be given access anyway. The piece offers good insight into how sensitive what information is given to students is and it also provides links to some other pretty interesting places.

Liu, E. (2015, July 3). What every American should know: Defining common cultural literacy for an increasingly diverse nation. *The Atlantic.* Available at https://www.theatlantic.com/politics/archive/2015/07/what-every-american-should-know/397334/
We introduced you to E. D. Hirsch, his Dictionary of Cultural Literacy, *and the Core Knowledge curriculum. This article contains a history of the cultural literacy movement as well as a contemporary critique of what is essentially the traditional curriculum.*

Meyer, R. J. (2003). Captives of the script: Killing us softly with phonics. *Rethinking Schools.* Available at http://rethinkingschools.aidcvt.com/special_reports/bushplan/capt174.shtml
Although we quoted heavily from this article on scripted teaching, we believe it's worth the time it takes to read the whole piece. It's hard to believe teachers and students are being subjected to such materials—but they are.

Videos

Public Broadcasting Corporation, *Precious Knowledge.* (75 minutes) http://www.pbs.org/independentlens/films/precious-knowledge/
This is a documentary about the Mexican American Studies program at Tucson High School in Arizona. With its 100% graduation rate and 85% college attendance rate, the program was hailed as a national model for the educational success of Latino/a students, who as a group tend to drop out of school at a rate near 50%. The film follows students and teachers in their fight to save the program from a state-mandated order to dismantle it.

Chimamanda Ngozi Adichie, *The Danger of a Single Story* (TED Talk) (18 minutes) https://www.ted.com/talks/chimamanda_adichie_the_danger_of_a_single_story
This engaging talk from a Nigerian novelist illustrates the distorted perceptions that arise from reading literature from a single culture and from failing to ask how a story might be told differently. The importance of what is left out of curriculum is evident here.

Public Broadcasting Corporation, *Judgment Day: Intelligent Design on Trial*: http://www.pbs.org/wgbh/nova/evolution/intelligent-design-trial.html
This Nova film documents Kitzmiller v. Dover, the first legal test of intelligent design—proposed as an alternative to evolution—as a scientific theory. The case arose out of an attempt by the school board to force teachers to read a statement to students indicating that intelligent design is a valid counter-theory. Teachers refused. And the community was ripped apart.

Heathwood Press, *The Hidden Curricula of Education* (60 minutes) http://www.heathwoodpress.com/the-hidden-curricula-of-education-douglas-kellner/
In this hour-long video lecture, Douglas Kellner, a professor from UCLA, explains many aspects of the hidden curriculum, offering much more detail on how it is that schools often reproduce the social order that is already in place, keeping people in place rather than helping them move upward.

Websites

National Center for Science Education https://ncse.com/

American Library Association: Banned & Challenged Books http://www.ala.org/advocacy/bbooks/about

Campaign for a Commercial Free Childhood http://www.commercialfreechildhood.org/

Notes

1. For a powerful demonstration of how texts representing only a single culture affect students' perceptions, explore Chimamanda Ngozi Adichie's TED Talk, "The Danger of a Single Story," listed in video explorations at the end of the chapter.

2. See, for example, scholar Lisa Delpit's text *Other People's Children*, or novelist Toni Morrison's *The Bluest Eye*.

3. Although there are numerous people who have written extensively about curriculum, the work of Elliot Eisner is straightforward and easy to understand. You can find more about Eisner's framework for curriculum here: Eisner, E. (1985). *The educational imagination: On the design and evaluation of school programs*. (2nd ed.). New York: Macmillian Publishing Company.

4. Schubert, W. H. (2010). Intended curriculum. In Kridel, C. A. (Ed.) *Encyclopedia of curriculum studies*, 488–489. Thousand Oaks: Sage.

5. Although we have explored some of the primary ways that curriculum is thought of in schools, there are many more important conceptualizations that exist that are not within the scope of this chapter or this text. For example, often the "intended" curriculum is differentiated from the "taught" curriculum, the "tested" curriculum, and the "learned curriculum," and much, much more. Here, the differentiation between "intended" and "taught" makes it clear that how a teacher interprets and delivers the curriculum might be different from what the institution intends. Similarly, in our current climate of massive standardized testing, the "tested" curriculum can be distinct from the intended and the taught curriculum. For more on these more nuanced types of curricula, we suggest exploring the *Encyclopedia of Curriculum Studies* referenced earlier.

6. No Child Left Behind Act of 2001, P.L. 107-110, 20 U.S.C. § 6319 (2002).

7. National Governors Association Center for Best Practices & Council of Chief State School Officers. (2010). Common Core State Standards. Washington, DC: National Governors Association Center for Best Practices, Council of Chief State School Officers.

8. Dee, T. S., Jacob, B. A., Hoxby, C. M., and Ladd, H. F. (2010). The impact of No Child Left Behind on students, teachers, and schools. *Brookings Papers on Economic Activity*. Washington, DC: Brookings Institution., 149–207.

9. Kane, T. J., Owens, A. M., Marinell, W. H., Thal, D. R. C., and Staiger, D. O. (2016). Teaching higher. Educators' perspectives on Common Core implementation. Cambridge, MA: Harvard University Center for Education Policy Research.

10. Philip Jackson is often credited with coining the term "hidden curriculum." Read more about this idea and life in elementary school classrooms here: Jackson, P. W. (1968/1990). *Life in classrooms*. New York: Teachers College Press.

11. Boostrom, R. (2010). Hidden curriculum. In Kridel, C. A. (Ed.) *Encyclopedia of Curriculum Studies*, 439–440. Thousand Oaks: Sage.

12. Quinn, M. (2010). Null curriculum. In Kridel, C. A. (Ed.) *Encyclopedia of Curriculum Studies*, 613–614. Thousand Oaks: Sage.

13. Human Rights Campaign Staff. (2013, September 26). LGBT Inclusive Books Frequently Censored in Banned Books Week. Human Rights Campaign. Retrieved from http://www.hrc.org/blog/lgbt-inclusive-books-frequently-censored-in-banned-books-week

14. Eisner, E. (1985). *The educational imagination: On the design and evaluation of school programs.* (2nd ed.). New York: Macmillian Publishing Company.

15. Hirsch, E. D. Jr. (1987). *Cultural literacy: What every American needs to know.* Boston: Houghton Mifflin.

16. Hirsch, E. D. Jr., Kett, J. F., and Trefil, J. (1988). *The dictionary of cultural literacy.* Boston: Houghton Mifflin.

17. More about E. D. Hirsch and the Core Knowledge curriculum can be found here: https://www.coreknowledge.org

18. See https://www.coreknowledge.org/our-schools/

19. Hirsch, E. D. Jr. (1987). *Cultural literacy: What every American needs to know.* Boston: Houghton Mifflin.

20. Tozer, S. E., Violas, P. C., and Senese, G. (2002). *School and society: Historical and contemporary perspectives.* (4th ed.) New York: McGraw Hill. If you can find this edition of this text, Chapter 9, "Liberty and Literacy Today," is an absolutely wonderful piece of work. Here, the authors help us understand the important differences between various kinds of literacy (basic, functional, cultural, and critical), as well as the social, political, and economic implications of such on all sorts of populations. This version, which is from an older edition of the text, is particularly powerful. More recent versions of this text do not do these ideas justice.

21. The Local. (2016, November 18). Revealed: The truth about rising poverty in France. Retrieved from https://www.thelocal.fr/20161118/revealed-the-truth-about-poverty-in-france

22. Hicks, M.R. (2014, December 11). All kids should go to college: A great American myth. Retrieved from https://www.psychologytoday.com/blog/digital-pandemic/201412/all-kids-should-go-college-great-american-myth

23. Rose, M. (2012, December 9). Who should go to college? Truthdig. Retrieved from http://www.truthdig.com/report/item/who_should_go_to_college_20121209?mob_no_redirect=true

24. Rose, M. (2012, December 9). Who should go to college? Truthdig. Retrieved from http://www.truthdig.com/report/item/who_should_go_to_college_20121209?mob_no_redirect=true

25. Baker, S. (2017, April 14). Student petition says too much pressure to succeed at Naperville North. Retrieved from http://www.chicagotribune.com/suburbs/naperville-sun/ct-nvs-203-naperville-north-petition-st-0414-20170413-story.html

26. Weissmann, J. (2012, March 29). Why do so many Americans drop out of college? *The Atlantic.* Retrieved from https://www.theatlantic.com/business/archive/2012/03/why-do-so-many-americans-drop-out-of-college/255226/

27. Cool, J. (2005, September 1). Still separate, still unequal: America's educational apartheid. *Harper's Magazine,* 311(1864). Retrieved from https://harpers.org/archive/2005/09/still-separate-still-unequal/

28. Anyon, J. (1980). Social class and the hidden curriculum of work. *Journal of Education*, 62(1), 67–92.

29. You can examine the Common Core State Standards for ELA here: http://www.corestandards.org/ELA-Literacy/ and the Common Core State Standards for Math here: http://www.corestandards.org/Math/

30. Strauss, V. (2016, April 30). A revealing new twist in the Common Core State Standards controversy. *Washington Post*. Retrieved from https://www.washingtonpost.com/news/answer-sheet/wp/2016/04/30/a-revealing-new-twist-in-the-common-core-state-standards-controversy/?utm_term=.812dc456877a

31. See, for example: Fairtest. (2016). Teacher evaluation should not rest on student test scores (Revised). Available at http://www.fairtest.org/teacher-evaluation-fact-sheet

32. Sherman, A. (2012, August 30th). Rick Santorum says Barack Obama wants to "nationalize curriculum." Politifact Florida. Retrieved from http://www.politifact.com/florida/statements/2012/aug/30/rick-santorum/rick-santorum-says-obama-wants-nationalize-curricu/

33. Dickens, C. (1854). *Hard times*. New York: Harper and Brothers, Publishers.

34. It's beyond the scope of this text to explain the difference between "little t truth" and "big T Truth," but conventionally it's understood like this: "big T Truth" is used to refer to ideas that are generally understood as "absolute Truth," or something that is absolutely, positively "true," and "little t truth" is used to refer to that which we as individuals believe to be true, regardless of whether or not it is believed to be true by everyone.

35. Quinn, A. (2013). Chinua Achebe and the bravery of lions. http://www.npr.org/sections/thetwo-way/2013/03/22/175046327/chinua-achebe-and-the-bravery-of-lions

36. Sieff, K. (2011, June 2). Energy industry shapes lessons in public schools. *Washington Post*. Retrieved from https://www.washingtonpost.com/local/education/energy-industry-shapes-lessons-in-public-schools/2011/05/25/AGRaXYHH_story.html?utm_term=.63333340c1c3

37. Bigelow, B. (2011). Scholastic Inc.—Pushing Coal. A 4th-grade curriculum lies through omission. *Rethinking Schools*, 25(4). Retrieved from https://www.rethinkingschools.org/articles/scholastic-inc-pushing-coal--2

38. Bigelow, B. (2011). Scholastic Inc.—Pushing Coal. A 4th-grade curriculum lies through omission. *Rethinking Schools*, 25(4). Retrieved from https://www.rethinkingschools.org/articles/scholastic-inc-pushing-coal--2

39. Campaign for a Commercial-Free Childhood. (2011, August 1). Scholastic Inc. agrees to limit corporate-funded teaching materials, bowing to pressure from parents and teachers. [Press release]. http://www.commercialfreechildhood.org/scholastic-inc-agrees-limit-corporate-funded-teaching-materials-bowing-pressure-parents-and-teachers

40. Campaign for a Commercial-Free Childhood. (2011, August 1). Scholastic Inc. agrees to limit corporate-funded teaching materials, bowing to pressure from parents and teachers. [Press release]. http://www.commercialfreechildhood .org/scholastic-inc-agrees-limit-corporate-funded-teaching-materials-bowing-pressure-parents-and-teachers

41. Lewin, T. Children's publisher backing off its corporate ties. *New York Times.* Retrieved from http://www.nytimes.com/2011/08/01/education/01scholastic.html

42. Bigelow, B. (2011). Scholastic Inc.—Pushing Coal. A 4th-grade curriculum lies through omission. *Rethinking Schools,* 25(4). Retrieved from https://www .rethinkingschools.org/articles/scholastic-inc-pushing-coal--2

43. Lewin, T. (2011, Autust 1). Children's publisher backing off its corporate ties. *New York Times.* Retrieved from http://www.nytimes.com/2011/08/01/education/01scholastic.html

44. Collins, G. (2012, June 21). How Texas inflicts bad textbooks on us. *New York Review of Books.* Retrieved from http://www.nybooks.com/articles/2012/06/21/how-texas-inflicts-bad-textbooks-on-us/

45. Birnbaum, M. (2010, May 22). Texas board approves social studies standards that perceived liberal bias. *Washington Post.* Retrieved from http://www .washingtonpost.com/wp-dyn/content/article/2010/05/21/AR2010052104365 .html?tid=a_inl

46. Brown, E. (2015, July 5). Texas officials: Schools should teach that slavery was a "side issue" to Civil War. *Washington Post.* Retrieved from https://www .washingtonpost.com/local/education/150-years-later-schools-are-still-a-battlefield-for-interpreting-civil-war/2015/07/05/e8fbd57e-2001-11e5-bf41-c23f5d3face1_story.html?utm_term=.9ae8ad2cda0c

47. Collins, G. (2012, June 21). How Texas inflicts bad textbooks on us. *New York Review of Books.* Retrieved from http://www.nybooks.com/articles/2012/06/21/how-texas-inflicts-bad-textbooks-on-us/

48. Scientific American [SCIAM] (2017, May 16). Eleven bills designed to alter science-education standards have been proposed this year across the United States. Retrieved from https://twitter.com/sciam/status/864646706113261570

49. Ross, E. (2017, May 12). Revamped "anti-science" education bills in United States find success. Legislation urges educators to "teach the controversy" and allows citizens to challenge curricula. *Nature.* Retrieved from https://www .nature.com/news/revamped-anti-science-education-bills-in-united-states-find-success-1.21986

50. Worth, K. (2017, May 8). A new wave of bills takes aim at science in the classroom. *FRONTLINE.* Retrieved from http://www.pbs.org/wgbh/frontline/article/a-new-wave-of-bills-takes-aim-at-science-in-the-classroom/

51. Ross, E. (2017, May 12). Revamped "anti-science" education bills in United States find success. Legislation urges educators to "teach the controversy" and

allows citizens to challenge curricula. *Nature.* Retrieved from https://www
.nature.com/news/revamped-anti-science-education-bills-in-united-states-find-
success-1.21986

52. Gilnskis, E. (2017, April 25). Climate denial in schools. A new wave of state
bills could allow public schools to teach lies about climate change. *VICE News.* Retrieved from https://news.vice.com/story/six-states-trying-to-pass-climate-denial-
in-education-legislation

53. Worth, K. (2017, May 8). A new wave of bills takes aim at science in the classroom. *FRONTLINE.* Retrieved from http://www.pbs.org/wgbh/frontline/article/a-
new-wave-of-bills-takes-aim-at-science-in-the-classroom/

54. The National Center for Science Education has provided a Chronology of
"Academic Freedom" Bills here: https://ncse.com/creationism/general/chronology-
academic-freedom-bills

55. Freire, P. (2000). *Pedagogy of the Oppressed* (30th Anniversary Edition). New
York: Continuum.

56. See https://www.engageny.org/common-core-curriculum-assessments

57. See https://fairtest.org/common-core-assessments-factsheet

58. http://www.corestandards.org/ELA-Literacy/RL/9-10/

59. http://www.azlyrics.com/lyrics/jamestaylor/ohbrother.html

60. See, for example, Jonathan Kozol's description in *Shame of the nation.*

61. Meyer, R. J. (2003). Captives of the script: Killing us softly with phonics.
Rethinking Schools. Retrieved from http://rethinkingschools.aidcvt.com/special_
reports/bushplan/capt174.shtml

62. See for example *My pedagogic creed* (1987), *The child and the curriculum*
(1902), *Moral principles in education* (1909), *Democracy and education,* (1916), and
Experience and education (1938).

63. Noguera, P. (2008). *The trouble with black boys . . . and other reflections on race,
equity, and the future of public education.* San Francisco: Jossey-Bass.

64. Schultz, B. (2008). *Spectacular things happen along the way: Lessons from an
urban classroom.* New York: Teachers College Press.

65. Klem, A. M. and Connell, J. P. (2004), Relationships matter: Linking teacher
support to student engagement and achievement. *Journal of School Health,* 74(7),
262–273. doi:10.1111/j.1746-1561.2004.tb08283.x

66. http://ecommerce-prod.mheducation.com.s3.amazonaws.com/unitas/
school/program/networks-2018/networks-program-overview.pdf

67. Hayes, C. L. (1999, March 21). Math textbook salted with brand
names raises new alarm. Retrieved from http://www.nytimes.com/library/
national/032199textbooks-ads.html

68. See, for example: Seville, L. R. (2014, August 25). Danger beneath: "Fracking" gas, oil pipes threaten rural residents. Retrieved from http://www.nbcnews
.com/news/investigations/danger-beneath-fracking-gas-oil-pipes-threaten-rural-
residents-n187021

69. See the Offshore Energy Center here: http://www.oceanstaroec.com/education.htm

70. See the mission statement of the Offshore Energy Center here: http://www.oceanstaroec.com/edu_mission.htm

71. See the Character Development and Leadership website here: https://www.characterandleadership.com

72. See the curriculum overview here: https://www.characterandleadership.com/curriculum-overview/

73. Read more about the Center for Civic Education and Project Citizen here: http://www.civiced.org

74. We list the Project Citizen overview video as a suggested exploration in Chapter 4, but if readers are curious now, it appears at http://www.civiced.org/resources/multimedia/featured-videos

75. Walker, T. (2016, January 11). Teacher autonomy declined over past decade, new data shows. *neaToday.* Retrieved from http://neatoday.org/2016/01/11/teacher-autonomy-in-the-classroom/

FOUR

What Does It Mean to Educate for Citizenship?

Democracy needs to be re-born in each generation and education is its mid-wife.
—*John Dewey,* The Need of an Industrial Education in an Industrial Democracy

A s we said in Chapter 2, it's unlikely anyone would doubt that public schools, funded by taxpayer dollars, have as a key responsibility educating students for citizenship in a democracy. That is why each November, crayoned portraits of Pilgrims appear in the windows of elementary schools nationwide and why the U.S. school day typically begins with students pledging allegiance to the flag. But when we ask the question that serves as title for this chapter—*What does it mean to educate for citizenship?*—we find any number of rarely discussed assumptions, despite those assumptions often being contradictory, sparking decades of fierce fights over curriculum and textbooks. While such spokespeople as Thomas Jefferson have written clearly about the need to educate citizens to serve as guardians of their constitutional rights, such foundational thinking seems a far cry from the many assumptions guiding policy and practice for citizenship education today. Following are a few of the most influential.

Assumptions about Educating for Citizenship

Educating for citizenship means inculcating patriotism.

Well, sure: like every other country in the world, the United States needs patriots. Governments pay for state-sponsored schools not because of concern for the welfare of youth, but because the survival of any government depends upon the goodwill and loyalty of its citizens. This is no less true for the United Stated than it was for Nazi Germany:

> Schools played an important role in spreading Nazi ideas to German youth. While censors removed some books from the classroom, German educators introduced new textbooks that taught students love for Hitler, obedience to state authority, militarism, racism, and antisemitism.[1]

Sadly, their efforts were wildly successful. While most readers will no doubt cringe to have Nazi educational goals and methodology set alongside U.S. methodology, nevertheless the fact is that in schools world-wide, *patriotism* is often defined in the same way and taught toward the same ends: love of country and loyalty to its leaders, with any unflattering material kept out of classrooms. Schools in the United States use many of the same routines that other countries do to ensure citizens' support. The similarities are unmistakable and, to some extent, defensible.

It would be silly to deny that if we want the democracy to survive, our schools should teach patriotism. It would make no sense—indeed, it would be a form of state suicide—for U.S. schools to teach theocracy, monarchy, oligarchy and democracy as equally desirable forms of government. We should expect that many school routines are in place to cultivate loyalty to the government. In fact, obvious evidence that the United States uses public schools as an important tool for that goal lies in Puerto Rican history. Within a very few years after the United States took control of Puerto Rico from Spain, the island's schools had been thoroughly "Americanized" through language, textbooks, and school routines. English was mandated as the official language of schools, U.S. flags flew over schoolyards, children started learning songs like "America the Beautiful," and American textbooks filled classrooms:

> [T]extbooks were almost all in English and even Spanish translations were culturally exotic to Puerto Rican children, e.g., white Christmases; light brown-haired Bill, blond Mary and their dog, Spot; the small-town American suburban house with its white picket fence; and the total absence of Blacks and dark-skinned people.[2]

These policies eventually fell apart largely because English could not be effectively mandated as the language of instruction when most teachers didn't speak it (and many Puerto Ricans refused to abandon their native language). Still, this example illustrates that American schools are a traditional vehicle for promoting the typically assumed definition of *patriotism*: loyalty to a particular government and its leaders.

So yes, let's agree that U.S. public schools do, and should, work to cultivate a patriotic citizenry. It's what governments *do*.

If we think just a bit more deeply, however, we find that not everyone assumes that *patriotism* is necessarily uncritical or that loyalty is necessarily unquestioning. There are, minimally, two perspectives on the issue. We might call one the "America-love-it-or-leave-it" definition and the second the "loyal-opposition" definition. The love-it-or-leave-it patriots consider it dangerous to cultivate a questioning stance toward government. Instead, they believe the best way to cultivate citizens' loyalty is by using schools to teach students the best possible story about American history and accomplishments—about the many things the United States has to be proud of, like its many military victories and its cultural heroes, like George Washington.

In contrast, the loyal opposition camp believes that it is the responsibility of every patriot to keep a critical eye on government functions. From this perspective, loyalty is to democratic principles rather than to leaders. As we noted in Chapter 1, Thomas Jefferson took this stance, arguing that public education was necessary to prepare citizens to recognize their civil liberties and to protect them by monitoring the actions of government leaders. Educated citizen voters, Jefferson believed, were the best way to prevent any strong personality or group from ever gaining so much power that the democracy itself would be in danger of slipping into some form of authoritarianism. From this perspective, patriots have an obligation to speak out if leaders appear to be veering from a democratic path or to be violating a founding democratic principle, such as freedom of speech. In one of the articles cited for further reading at the end of this chapter, theorist Joel Westheimer refers to the two perspectives briefly described here as *authoritarian patriotism* (unquestioning) and *democratic patriotism* ("questioning, critical, deliberative").

It is these two very different perspectives that have produced decades of struggle over curriculum and textbooks, not to mention incredibly bland and boring history and social studies texts. If unquestioning loyalty is wanted, then students must be taught that America's leaders and policies can be trusted, always. This means that textbooks must eliminate, or minimize, government's past shameful acts and policies and instead emphasize triumphs. If students are to have only admiration for their country, then telling them about past missteps would undermine the goal. For this reason, few history textbooks detail, or even mention, historical events like the Trail of Tears, the forced march in which some 4,000 Cherokees died of cold, hunger and disease. It is why the westward takeover of Native American lands that prompted the Trail of Tears is flatteringly described as Manifest Destiny, with scant attention (if any) paid to the peoples whose lands were being taken. It is why a textbook in Texas referred to the slave trade as a movement that brought "millions of workers" to Southern plantations, causing the descendants of slaves to protest the misrepresentation.[3] The substance of most history and social studies textbooks consists primarily of introducing cultural heroes like George Washington, praising U.S. military victories, and celebrating technological advances like the cotton gin that brought much prosperity (at least for some segments of the population).

Proponents of democratic patriotism see things very differently. They argue that events like the Trail of Tears and policies like legal slavery are precisely the kind of topics that must be included in texts. They argue that rather than being hidden, questionable or shameful events of the past need to be honestly confronted so that tomorrow's citizens can learn from them and understand their weighty responsibility to keep a watchful eye on government leaders, laws and policies. Again, German history is illustrative. That country's current school curriculum includes extensive attention to the Holocaust so that nothing like it will ever happen again in that country. In essence, U.S. educators endorsing democratic patriotism have worked to broaden the curriculum, to bring the history of exploited peoples like African Americans and Native Americans into the country's narrative about itself and to raise awareness of the need for citizens to be ultimately responsible for ensuring the country stays on a democratic and just course.

Toward this alternative pedagogical goal, educators endorsing democratic patriotism have worked to craft alternatives to traditional instruction in authoritarian patriotism. For example, James Loewen's award-winning book *Lies My Teacher Told Me: Everything Your American History Textbook Got Wrong* is a national bestseller. The Zinn Education Project provides educators extensive resources for what the site calls "a more accurate, complex, and engaging understanding of United States history than is found in traditional textbooks and curricula" (https://zinnedproject.org), and the organization Rethinking Schools (http://www.rethinkingschools.org/index.shtml) offers a wide variety of related publications, including teaching resources like *Rethinking Columbus* that challenge some of the many myths perpetuated by mainstream history texts.

Here, assumptions set up stark opposing alternatives in terms of teaching for unquestioning versus questioning patriots. It seems unwise to endorse a specific text or curriculum without first having a serious discussion about which vision will govern choices in a specific public school.

Educating for citizenship means having teachers teach facts about government.

Again, as tools of the state, public schools are obviously responsible for teaching about government. How are citizens to vote for legislators and presidents as well as monitor their performance if they don't understand the roles various government leaders play in the American three-branch system of checks and balances? From this perspective, teachers must teach the structure of government.

However, there's also a common fallacy underpinning this assumption: *If a teacher teaches something, we can assume that students have learned it.* Any adult who has forgotten any of the many things taught by high school teachers (or who has failed a high school exam) can bear witness to the absurdity of this assumption. And there's a second complication here. That is, anyone holding a democratic definition of patriotism would argue that knowing about government becomes almost beside the point if students don't learn about their rights and their responsibilities as citizens—and the *actions* that those elements of citizenship imply. Let's take a closer look at those two points: *Does teaching facts about government mean students learn them? And, does having facts about government structure provide adequate preparation for civic life after school?*

It would be a rare American indeed who didn't agree that high school graduates should know the basics of U.S. government. And it would be a rare student indeed who, during twelve years of public school, never heard that the U.S. government has three branches (executive, legislative and judicial).

And yet, everyone (or almost everyone) also agrees that very few Americans can remember that basic information. Countless surveys have demonstrated widespread ignorance in recent years. The following typical description of the problem comes from a 2011 survey report from the Campaign for the Civic Mission of Schools:

- Only one-third of Americans could name all three branches of government; one-third couldn't name any.
- Just over a third thought that it was the intention of the Founding Fathers to have each branch hold a lot of power, but the president has the final say.
- Just under half of Americans (47%) knew that a 5-4 decision by the Supreme Court carries the same legal weight as a 9-0 ruling.
- Almost a third mistakenly believed that a U.S. Supreme Court ruling could be appealed.
- When the Supreme Court divides 5-4, roughly one in four (23%) believed the decision was referred to Congress for resolution; 16% thought it needed to be sent back to the lower courts.[4]

It's difficult to understand how citizens can be expected to either support or monitor a government without understanding, for example, the role of the Supreme Court in aligning laws with the Constitution or the constitutional limits on the power of the president.

Oddly, even though many Americans readily confess they retain little information they were tested on in school, there seems to be a pervasive cultural belief that if students must be tested on something, then they *must* learn it. The failure of the No Child Left Behind act to produce universally proficient students on a deadline seems to have done nothing to undermine this belief. And so, out of concern for widespread ignorance about the structure of American government among the U.S. citizenry, a movement to require high school students to pass the same test that immigrants must pass when applying for citizenship has spread nationally like wildfire. In January of 2015, Arizona became the first state to adopt the citizenship test as a high school graduation requirement[5]; thanks largely to promotion by a project called the Civics Education Initiative, by March of 2017, a total of 15 states had adopted the requirement and another 23 had pending legislation to do so.[6]

The 100-question test requires such knowledge as how many Constitutional amendments exist, which rights are listed in the Declaration of Independence, and how long a U.S. senate term is.

However, many who argue that assuming factual information is central to education for citizenship are missing a much bigger picture. Critics charge that information in and of itself is sterile and the testing movement misguided. Mandating yet another test ignores the reality that information presented in classrooms is often forgotten; in addition, it neglects vital elements of citizenship central to democratic life—like moving people to vote after researching candidates. The assumption underpinning this perspective is that understanding government is not an end in itself, but instead a component of the critical task of educating for *active* citizenship. For example, in an article titled "Why Are We Teaching Civics Like a Game Show?" Joseph Kahne writes:

> Forcing students to study and then regurgitate ... facts will point students and their teachers in the wrong direction. We need young citizens who are committed to helping make their communities better and who can assess policy proposals, not merely youths who know how many voting members of the U.S. House of Representatives there are. . . . Democracy thrives when citizens think critically and deeply about civic and political issues, when they consider the needs and priorities of others, and when they engage in informed action.[7]

Here the focus is on skills, on things citizens must be able to *do*, not simply related information.

Many spokespersons and organizations promote this emphasis on action rather than information. For example, in a 2013 position paper the National Council for the Social Studies (NCSS) characterizes "effective citizens" as having "four common traits": being informed and thoughtful, participating in their communities, acting politically, and exhibiting moral and civic virtue.[8] The Campaign for the Civic Mission of Schools similarly calls for citizenship education to foster "informed and engaged participation in democratic life";[9] it includes "participatory skills" as one of four categories it considers essential for citizenship education.[10] Kei Kawashima-Ginsberg, director of another organization at Tufts University dedicated to reforming civics education,[11] details the kind of actions being targeted:

Ideally, K-12 civic education would fully prepare young people to participate in myriad aspects of civic life: voting, volunteering, deliberating on issues, and advocating for a cause, for starters. Acquiring these skills begins with a solid grasp of foundational knowledge. But it also requires students to experience civic engagement through experiential learning—service learning, community-engaged research, and nonpartisan electoral activities—that facilitate and encourage real-life civic participation.[12]

While acknowledging that information is important, organizations and spokespersons like these offer their own assumption that meaningful education for citizenship must aim beyond retention of basic information and look toward far more engaging curricula and to far more complex assessments than multiple choice exams to assess essential skills and dispositions. Suggested alternative assessments include digital badges, ePortfolios, rubrics, games, and simulations.[13]

Perhaps the strongest support for a more active conception of citizenship appears in the failure of vast numbers of Americans to exercise their right to vote. There is a well-documented problem in that about half of Americans eligible to vote accept the responsibility to do so. In 2016, the Pew Research Center reported that "U.S. turnout trails most developed countries," with 53.6 of the eligible voting population participating in national elections.[14] Even in the hotly contested presidential election of 2016 (Hillary Clinton versus Donald Trump), only some 60% of those eligible to vote actually did so.[15] Citizenship confers rights . . . but it also confers responsibilities. It's clear that whatever schools are doing in terms of citizenship education, they are not effectively nurturing in students a commitment to the most basic of citizens' responsibilities. Perhaps that's not their job—but perhaps it is.

Education for citizenship means teaching students to obey laws.

Like other common assumptions, it seems a self-evident truth that students need to learn to respect authority and obey the law. The United States is, after all, a society in which the rule of law prevails. This assumption aligns nicely with the concept of authoritarian patriotism. Since government leaders, laws and policies are to be supported without question, then students must be taught to obey laws. Period. And again, in alignment with the authoritarian perspective, this assumption has led to keeping morally questionable laws out of textbooks. For example, it is hard to imagine any text detailing the compulsory sterilization laws born of the eugenics movement in the United States that resulted in the sterilization of some 60,000 Americans in the early decades of the twentieth century, including many unfortunates who were disabled, mentally ill, or simply from lower socioeconomic classes.[16]

For the same reason, texts include few, and highly selective, examples of civil disobedience. To portray civil disobedience as an effective mechanism to change unwise or unjust policy, as it was during the Civil Rights and Vietnam War eras, would be to invite challenges to the country's leadership. This is why those endorsing democratic patriotism argue for loyalty not to leaders, but to democratic principles. The principle of equal protection under the law has been repeatedly violated in episodes already discussed—like forced sterilization—as well as in countless other episodes including, to name just one other example, the incarceration of Japanese American citizens during World War II.

The reality is that sometimes laws and policies are unjust and in violation of democratic, and sometimes humanitarian, principles. And an additional reality is that unjust laws and policies have been abandoned in the past because citizens have called the government to task and taken action to oppose and undo them.

Segregation became illegal only after the efforts of Civil Rights leaders came to the attention of the entire nation, when television news showed their nonviolent protests being met with fire hoses and billy clubs. Government leaders moved to end the Vietnam War only after the nation saw young men burning draft cards and massive demonstrations protesting the deaths of tens of thousands of young Americans as well as the massacres of civilian Vietnamese women and children. History shows that there have been times when the actions of a citizenry, outraged by the loss of life and liberty, persuade government leaders to bring national practice into line with democratic principle.

If schools do not teach about the power of civil disobedience, about the need to take action to change unjust law and policy, how are tomorrow's citizens to know how to monitor a democratic government, how to take action to effect a necessary course correction—as those endorsing democratic patriotism insist they must? And yet, since the nation is ultimately governed by "rule of law," who can argue against teaching young people to be law-abiding and to respect authority—as those endorsing authoritarian patriotism do? Who would argue for the individualized, vigilante justice of the Wild West? Society would crumble if no one accepted any authority but his or her own. This is troubling territory.

In addition, the issue of respect versus resistance is further complicated by the fact that citizens cannot be vigilant in protecting their rights if they are unaware of what those rights *are*. Here again, authoritarian versus democratic concepts come into play, largely because schools are typically a bit schizophrenic: teachers may *tell* students they have constitutional rights while school policies simultaneously force them to yield many of those rights. For example, students have a constitutional right to privacy—but not at school, where drug-sniffing dogs have become common in classrooms and where cameras often follow students' every move inside and outside of school buildings, as well as on school buses. Students have a right to free speech—but not in school newspapers, which school authorities may censor, and increasingly not online in texts and web pages, as schools increasingly seek authority over students' out-of-school electronic communications. If students learn to consider such restrictions normal over twelve years of schooling, how are they to remember to guard against intrusions on their rights in life after school? Especially when, in a post-9/11 world, all citizens' privacy has already been sorely compromised?

Of course, many of these restrictions have to do with safety. No one thinks students should be dealing drugs out of their backpacks, and electronic bullying clearly has implications for school students since it is not only epidemic but also known to have a wide range of negative consequences—including student suicide.[17] School authorities have to . . . well . . . have *authority* over students in the interest of maintaining a safe and orderly environment for all students, just as police must have authority to ensure a safe and secure environment for citizens at large. But where is the balance between student liberty, and student safety and security? And how are students to learn to use their voices as school citizens against unjust policies and decisions, against bullying by school personnel—and later by police—if schools are not environments that allow for, and still less promote, student activism in defense of their own and other people's constitutional rights?

Education for citizenship means teaching students to be good neighbors.

Just like other assertions about citizenship, it appears to make perfect sense to say that students should be good neighbors. Typically, that platitude means something like not throwing trash on the streets everyone shares, or respecting private property by not barging into and through it, and so on. But such typical injunctions seem to imply a fairly passive view of neighborly responsibility: don't make messes that other people will have to clean up, and don't trample on other people's stuff. That's fine—as far as it goes. But just how far does one person's responsibility go, how far *should* it go, in the interest of being a *good neighbor*?

If every citizen is responsible only for his or her own behavior, then obviously no one should create problems or messes for others. But what if someone sees someone else robbing a neighbor? Does one community member have a responsibility to intervene in a harmful act someone else is committing? That is, is a good community member someone who doesn't break the law—or someone who also intervenes when a law is being broken? Or, does responsibility extend even beyond the realm of what is legal? For example, as the statement attributed to Jesus goes, the poor will always be with us. So then, what, if anything, can a well-meaning, good citizen/neighbor do about and for community members who might be hungry or homeless? Give the hungry person a fish to ease his hunger? Teach the person to fish so that he can find a way to catch his own fish? Or ask about what is going on in the community or country that has created conditions that leave some citizens hungry and homeless in the interest of identifying a more lasting solution via social change?

Often, school personnel respond to local social issues by encouraging students to contribute to community efforts like food drives, asking them to bring some canned goods to school or nudging them to join a group bagging groceries for a Thanksgiving dinner give away. This, of course, fits in with the notion of giving someone a fish—providing food for the hungry. Increasingly popular are various types of service learning, which are more formal efforts that involve students working for some organization on a more regular basis. The rationale is that in sharing their time and talents, students will come to understand community needs and to value lending a hand to ensure that the basic needs of all community members are met. And of course that may happen, and it's true that sometimes student volunteers do help make an organization and its impact stronger. Moreover, schools also benefit from such efforts when local TV news programs showcase the contributions school groups make to local charitable organizations.

However, given one of the author's experiences in a soup kitchen, she can testify that while some students learn to give of themselves generously and compassionately, many other students force-marched into a volunteer role spend their mandatory hours with hands in their pockets trying as hard as possible not to touch anything or to make eye contact with anyone in the building—especially the diners. For too many students, volunteering is just one more thing to do to check off a school requirement or a requirement on a college application, with no serious investment of either effort or reflection. Generally, as one experienced administrator of a charity noted, volunteers sent into organizations by their schools "can be as much a curse as a blessing, especially to an organization that lacks the administrative structure and money to train and supervise students."[18]

Moreover, people sometimes argue that volunteering for community organizations can be the equivalent of putting a band-aid on a bone-deep wound. It serves more as a distraction from attending to deeply rooted social pathologies. Yet again the issue is more complex than it appears. Surely we don't want people to go hungry, and communities are better off with volunteers in organizations like soup kitchens than without them. But the potential cost here is huge, if we teach young people that as long as we do a little of this or that to alleviate a social problem, then we've done our part to contribute to the health of our communities. We might do well to consider carefully how we might do both: alleviate suffering in the moment but also attend to identifying the root cause of the problem (*Why are so many people in my community hungry?*) and noticing that we have national as well as local social problems. Given that among developed nations only Romania has a higher percentage of children living in poverty than the United States does,[19] there might be more important lessons students can learn than how to beef up a college application with some volunteer hours.

Of course it's a really good thing to be a good neighbor—but defining what *good* means and identifying the actual boundaries of *our community* can be pretty tricky tasks.

Frameworks for Citizenship Education

While standardized testing may have largely squeezed civics education out of schools, fossilized school routines like the pledge to the flag and the celebration of national holidays like Thanksgiving maintain at least superficial attention to national loyalty and pride. In some schools there is little else to suggest that those in charge of school objectives and curriculum have given much thought to cultivating whatever qualities may be considered desirable in citizens. Maybe a school has some sort of student council, but typically it either has no power, or it plans themes for dances rather than having any real input into school policies and decisions. Still, many other schools *do* invest greater effort, on a kind of sliding scale of attention and ambition, from the most minimal and least obtrusive efforts to the most focused efforts, sometimes even targeting ambitious goals of nurturing students to become social change agents.

The numerous individual elements of citizenship education—texts, student activities, disciplinary systems and so on—together combine to characterize schools along the authoritarian/activist continuum described earlier. Precisely because several elements of schooling together constitute "citizenship education," it can be difficult to either identify or plan coherent, schoolwide efforts targeting a clearly articulated conception of a good citizen. Indeed, it's not unusual for some elements of citizenship education to undermine other elements, as when students are taught to rejoice in their right to free speech while simultaneously accepting the right of administrators to censor discussion of topics students care about in student newspapers.

To promote clarity as educators work to think through their citizenship goals and plans, several theorists and researchers have worked to identify clusters of elements that form basic patterns in various ways. The following is a brief overview of some frameworks that have been developed to illuminate typical conceptions of citizenship education. Perhaps this systematic thinking will help readers put the pieces of their own thinking on various assumptions together into a single coherent vision. If and when that is the case, we encourage readers to seek out relevant articles condensed here. Readers should bear in mind that the following descriptions omit some interesting and useful detail found in the original texts; what we can offer here constitutes only a minimal sketch of the complex positions they represent.

Westheimer and Kahne: Conceptions of Citizenship Embedded in School Routines

Joel Westheimer and Joseph Kahne[20] have developed a framework to identify how certain kinds of pedagogical projects in schools align with certain conceptions of a *good citizen*. After studying programs in place in schools, the authors conclude that there are essentially three conceptions of a good citizen underpinning various school pedagogies: *personally responsible, participatory* and *justice-oriented citizens*.

The Personally Responsible Citizen

The *personally responsible citizen* respects authority and lends a helping hand when asked. The authors describe this orientation as "citizenship devoid of politics":

> [Educational efforts promoting this perspective] often promote service but not democracy. They share an orientation toward volunteerism and charity and away from teaching about social movements, social transformation, and systemic change. These programs privilege individual acts of compassion and kindness over social action and the pursuit of social justice.

School efforts aligned with this conception often promote volunteerism in one way or another, and they often talk about building character. They encourage not only charity but also such qualities as integrity and respect for others—typically the fairly passive respect previously described as not harming others or their property.

This perspective is advanced by interest in what is generally called *character education*. The core idea is that social problems can and will be alleviated when the character of youth is shaped appropriately. The authors cite the *Character Counts!* organization[21] as typical of this perspective. Its "Six Pillars of Character" include trustworthiness, respect, responsibility, fairness, caring, and—although it claims to be apolitical—citizenship. Its description of citizenship makes clear the underlying assumption that a good citizen is one that has a good character, as defined by the other endorsed values. Students are admonished to:

Do your share to make your school and community better. Cooperate. Get involved in community affairs. Stay informed; vote. Be a good neighbor. Obey laws and rules. Respect authority. Protect the environment. Volunteer.[22]

Generally, these are the attitudes and behaviors that characterize personally responsible citizen: exhibiting good character, lending a hand, and respecting authority.

The Participatory Citizen

The *participatory citizen* goes beyond simply contributing to a community effort like a food drive by also providing leadership. Understanding that people who come together can focus on and accomplish specific tasks, a participatory citizen may organize events such as food drives. While the participatory citizen is more active than the personally responsible citizen, his or her efforts generally lend support to existing structures, suggesting that the status quo be accepted as a given rather than a changeable situation open to critical questioning:

> Educational programs designed to support the development of participatory citizens focus on teaching students about how government and other institutions (e.g., community-based organizations, churches) work and about the importance of planning and participating in organized efforts to care for those in need, for example, or in efforts to guide school policies.

In line with this more active (if apolitical) conception, schools might encourage students to engage in some kind of project in service to the community—organizing a community recycling program, for example—but not pay any attention to such issues as the role of policy in protecting the environment. Students learn about government, but primarily as a supportive resource, not as an entity to be monitored or possibly challenged. Benefits to the community may at times be substantive, but engagement does not typically extend to political engagement.

The authors discuss one example of an educational program promoting this conception. It included student projects to determine whether citizens in a community were interested in county trash pickup and another project that developed a five-year plan for the fire and rescue department. The authors note that while students learned much doing such projects, there was no effort to cultivate engagement with such larger political issues as causes of poverty or fairness of tax policies. This orientation, like that of the personally responsible citizen, takes what is often perceived to be a neutral political path by avoiding troublesome political and economic terrain.

The Justice-Oriented Citizen

Westheimer and Kahne call the third conception the *justice-oriented citizen.* This is perhaps the least common orientation, and the one often explicitly avoided in mainstream textbooks and curricula. Rather than simply providing relief for community members in distress, or supporting something like a specific war simply because it *is* a government policy at a particular moment, these citizens maintain focus on democratic principles and pursue just and equitable conditions for all segments of the citizenry. Rather than feeling content to feed the hungry, these citizens ask why hunger plagues so much of the U.S. population when the United States is one of the richest countries on earth. In the words of Westheimer and Kahne:

> [T]he justice-oriented citizen . . . calls explicit attention to matters of injustice and to the importance of pursuing social justice goals. Justice-oriented citizens critically assess social, political, and economic structures and consider collective strategies for change that challenge injustice and, when possible, address root causes of problems. [Justice-oriented programs] emphasize preparing students to improve society by critically analyzing and addressing social issues and injustices.

Programs embracing this conception of citizenship "are less likely to emphasize the need for charity and volunteerism as ends in themselves and more likely to teach about social movements and how to affect systemic change." Much of the material banished from the classroom in mainstream texts, such as the history of labor or of voting rights for women, becomes part of the curriculum in order to illustrate to students the power of organized citizen efforts, which are cast as essential responsibilities in the face of inequitable power arrangements, leading to severe disadvantages for certain segments of the population.

This orientation in educational activities that encourage students to work for structural change faults not individuals but instead entrenched social and economic structures that maintain structural inequities. As one student who participated in a social-justice oriented program reported:

> "[W[hen the economy's bad and people start blaming immigrants or whoever else they can blame, they've got to realize that there are big social, economic, and political issues tied together, that it's not the immigrants, no it's bigger than them."

Rather than avoiding political issues related to social problems that plague individual communities as well as the nation as a whole, the justice-oriented perspective encourages student analysis of structural causes of the problems and efforts to provoke change in them. Citizenship in this case involves on-going critical analysis to determine where tenets of democracy seem to have been violated or abandoned and working to get things back on course.

Abowitz and Harnish: Discourses of Citizenship

Kathleen Knight Abowitz and Jason Harnish[23] looked at the language both within and outside of schools to see what particular language habits—or *discourses*—indicate about alternative conceptions of citizenship. Language, as researchers and theorists are acutely aware, is not neutral. As a simple example, consider the terms "government monopoly schools" and "public schools," terms describing the same thing used by two opposing camps, with very different perspectives on school funding. After examining a wide variety of texts, Abowitz and Harnish identified distinctly different conceptions of citizenship embedded in language patterns. They found two discourse patterns that are dominant in schools, another family of related discourses that challenge entrenched conceptions of citizenship, and still one more discourse that is emerging from ever-expanding global interaction.

Civic Republican

The first conception of citizenship that the researchers found widely in evidence in schools they call *civic republican*, an orientation that stresses strong political community. Values include love of country, self-sacrifice, loyalty, and service to the political community, including such activities as voting and participating in political parties. This discourse also stresses what we might call traditional patriotism, the form of patriotism that honors such symbols and icons as the flag and the Founding Fathers and that stresses the accomplishments of American history. Because of the focus on a common identity, such topics as world history, multicultural education, historical missteps are of little or no concern—and even counterproductive to the love for and loyalty to country that this conception promotes. Some proponents feel strongly that such efforts have distracted young people from critical elements of citizenship. The researchers report a sense among those promoting a civic republican perspective that:

> [Y]ounger generations erroneously understand democracy to be an exercise of rights rather than a structure that equally obligates them to certain duties. . . . Our democracy . . . is broken because of growing cynicism, apathy, and a selfish focus on individual rights over collective responsibilities.

From this vantage point, much greater stress on the admirable and the traditional in American history needs to drive citizenship education.

In schools, this orientation means practice in such symbolic rituals as the Pledge of Allegiance and other time-honored practices. This description of post-9/11 school activity remains common in many schools:

> Kids are pledging allegiance in Pennsylvania, singing "God Bless the USA." in Arkansas, wearing red, white and blue to school (for a "Patriotism Day" assembly) in Maryland. And much more. (Chester Finn, 2001, quoted in Abowitz and Harnish)

Other typical parts of the curriculum include a strong emphasis on American history, including such seminal texts as the Constitution, to teach pride in heritage, as well as community service projects to teach duty to others. Together, such activities and curricular efforts are designed to foster pride in America's uniqueness and its many accomplishments. They are also intended to cultivate the kind of willingness to sacrifice that has in the past motivated so many young Americans to volunteer for military service unhesitatingly in time of war. For example, Ohio's social studies standards for grade 5 calls for students to learn how citizens' participation in civic life promotes the common good and how historical events resulted in the rights contemporary American citizens hold dear (Abowitz and Harnish).

This orientation is widely promoted by groups with a politically conservative orientation—the Fordham Foundation, for example, and the Veterans of Foreign Wars, whose website pages on youth and education is listed at the end of this chapter.

Liberal Citizenship

The second widespread conception Abowitz and Harnish call *liberal citizenship*, which privileges individual liberty. The authors identify two primary values: "freedom from the tyranny of authority" and "the deliberative values of discussion, disagreement, and consensus building." Each citizen is free to make personal choices and commitments—although every other citizen has the same right to personal choices. Given the U.S. population's wide range of such characteristics as ethnic background, religion, cultural values and beliefs, political commitments, and so on, and given that each citizen has the same right to self-determination as every other citizen, disagreements on public policies are to be expected. From this perspective, deliberation—defined as a thoughtful process in which multiple perspectives and options are carefully examined[24]—becomes the engine of decision making. Such reasoned rational or considered deliberation is essential to maintaining the democratic political system that enables each individual's liberty.

To be prepared for citizenship that prioritizes deliberation and that accepts responsibility for helping protect liberty for all, students need to learn to listen to other voices, to consider and critique other arguments, to provide support for their own positions, and to hammer out compromise and consensus. Of course, they will need a good understanding of American government and of the opportunities for contributing to important public discussions, but they also need to be open-minded if they are to fairly assess alternative perspectives.

Such open-mindedness in turn is cultivated at least in part through some degree of familiarity with and respect for other cultures—including familiarity with the history of marginalized populations. To understand issues in the present means understanding the past. As just one example, consider the fact that many students don't know that the United States seized much of its current southwestern territory from Mexico by force (giving rise to a saying common in the Southwest, "We didn't cross the border, the border crossed us"). Many Mexican American families never moved to the United States, legally or otherwise; instead, families are living in the same place their ancestors lived in the mid-1800s, having become Americans by conquest, not by choice. How are students who don't understand this history going to understand the Mexican American perspective on immigration, or on the issue of an imposing, extended wall between the current borders of the two countries?

As the authors note, many educators and policymakers do take this perspective and promote teaching for cultural understanding as well as for protection of individual liberty. Ohio's standards for tenth grade, for example, include not only the study of civil disobedience but also such government missteps as the McCarthy era (Abowitz and Harnish).[25] In addition to such curricular efforts, schools assuming this perspective might have an active student government, one that provides students practice in the skills of deliberative decision making and empowers them to make decisions on meaningful issues.

Among the organizations that appear to embrace this conception, the authors name the Center for Civic Education, whose website is listed at the end of this chapter.

Critical Citizenships

The third category Abowitz and Harnish describe includes a family of conceptions linked by a common goal: educating citizens to work toward a better United States by analyzing social injustices and strategizing to correct them. The authors' designation here is *critical citizenships*. The term *critical* describes the central goal of identifying how particular groups are kept from full participation in various elements of American life, identifying where power resides and how it might be challenged for the benefit of those marginalized under current power arrangements. Under this critical umbrella, the researchers include four orientations: feminist, cultural, reconstructionist, and queer discourses.

The *critical feminist* orientation addresses the many ways that females and female perspectives are excluded from or marginalized by an entrenched male power structure.[26] While there are various subgroups of feminists that fall within this category, they all share "the centrality of the nation-state and homogenous identity being questioned." Humans are privileged over country, and a one-size-fits-all notion of American identity, or citizenship, is undesirable. Women and men—and those with other differences, like race or culture—should not be forced into preconceived conceptions of their abilities or of the value of their various contributions to communal life. Women should be educated and empowered to pursue greater equity in all realms.

Two of the other groups under this umbrella pursue similar goals, but with a focus on the marginalization of different groups. The perspective of *cultural citizenship* holds that there are ethnic and other cultural differences among vast groups of American citizens, and these should be viewed as assets rather than as threats to be countered by assimilationist education of the republican citizenship model, which stresses commonality and uniformity. Instead:

> Cultural citizenship is an attempt to name citizenship and political membership as an activity that is fraught with struggles over culture; conflicts over representation, naming, language, minority rights, and full inclusion; and a myriad of other issues.

And, the *queer citizenship* orientation similarly aims at education for equality as well as public recognition and affirmation of citizens with a variety of sexual orientations:

> "Queering citizenship" is a civic project that has a powerful normative direction: engaging in dialogue, contestation, and performance to challenge normative structures and discourses that keep certain "undesirable" identities at the margins.

While the issue of sexuality is often contentious in schools and communities, the dangers of bullying and legislative debate around which students may use which bathrooms in schools suggests to many that it is past time to broaden popular ideas about gender identity.

Rather than insisting there is a single ideal American, these orientations would force open various doors that impose separation between *us*—a homogeneous U.S. citizenry (real or imagined)— and those historically marginalized as *them*—the "others" who differ in any number of ways from the traditional, patriarchic model of White American citizenry. Insisting on the value of diversity, this approach calls for all individuals from a wide range of backgrounds (including culture, race, language, gender, and sexual orientation) to be considered equal as Americans.

The final orientation in this critical family is the *social reconstructionist* orientation. The researchers summarize its essence in this way:

> If state-run schooling is about order and loyalty, as is exemplified in some civic republican texts, reconstructionist citizenship is antithetical to state-run schooling in some of its more critical forms.

From this perspective, in light of growing global enterprise and the increasing influence of consumerism and of special interests and big money in politics, tomorrow's citizens need to learn to think critically and learn to question whether various elements of government are functioning on behalf of the citizenry at large or are systematically working to disenfranchise and/or disadvantage citizens as a whole or various subgroups within the citizenry. Whereas other perspectives deem the history and heritage tales of White America as essential, this orientation would have students examine the reality behind many of the traditionalists' most beloved myths—that Columbus discovered America, for example, or that Manifest Destiny involved the great triumph of "civilization" over "savagery" rather than the broken treaties and bloody extermination of peoples and their cultures.

Perhaps obviously, critical perspectives are largely absent from the dominant perspectives governing the vast majority of American schools, where many school personnel assiduously work to avoid open disagreement. There are, however, many theorists and scholars working to inject a critical

perspective into discussions about what citizenship education should accomplish, including nurturing true equality for populations historically marginalized in multiple ways. An important organizational voice in this area is
Rethinking Schools, an advocate and publisher working to influence education reform by, among other things, producing alternative texts for schools.
Its website is listed at the end of this chapter.

Transnational

The fourth orientation Abowitz and Harnish identify is *transnational*, recognizing that all citizens are citizens not only of the United States but also of
the world.

> Transnational citizenship focuses on the local, national, and international
> communities. A citizen in this discourse is one who identifies not
> primarily or solely with her own nation but also with communities of
> people and nations beyond the nation-state boundaries. [It] articulates
> an agenda for citizenship that simultaneously educates students for
> membership in local, national, and international organizations and
> civic organizations. . . . A citizen therefore weighs political and social
> decisions considering both the local and global possible effects.

Under this label, however, are some different views of why it is important
to nurture students' identities as national and world citizens.

For example, there is currently a widespread idea that a priority of schools
should be educating for work, and since many corporate employers are mul-
tinational, tomorrow's workers need to understand the importance of cultural differences and to value cultural and linguistic diversity. In this case,
the mind-set endorsing transnational citizenship privileges neoliberal goals,
especially those that support ever-increasing consumerism. In contrast,
however, when the mind-set guiding choices is concerned with humanity
rather than "human capital" (as workers are so often called in a neoliberal
environment), then universal human rights rather than economic concerns
dominate discussions. For example, rather than accepting cheap goods as an
unquestioned benefit of transnational corporations, this orientation encourages considering whether the human conditions required to produce those

cheap goods—say, child labor or unsafe workplaces—are ethically acceptable. If not, students might be taught to ask what their options are as American citizens to oppose such unethical corporate practices. Thus, transnationalism can address the goals of more than one of the other orientations.

Like the critical approaches, the transnational orientation has had little impact in schools. When it is at all in evidence, it typically appears in geography classes, where students simply learn which countries are where—a far cry from learning about other cultures or about why the school might be teaching from a transnational perspective.

Subedi: Approaches to Global Citizenship

Although, as Abowitz and Harnish note, transnational conceptions of citizenship are not yet widely incorporated, such contemporary conditions as the current ease of global electronic communication and the influence of transnational corporations have promoted sufficient interest in the conception of global citizenship for scholars to have begun debating what exactly global citizenship might mean and what it might look like in schools. Just as conceptions of what it might mean to be a good American citizen differ widely, conceptions of global citizenship have become diverse. Binaya Subedi has contributed a framework to clarify the key theoretical differences among the approaches,[27] which share some similarities with the approaches described earlier. He identifies three: *deficit, accommodation,* and *critical.*

Deficit

Subedi characterizes the *deficit* approach as emerging from the common cultural stereotyping of other countries and cultures—especially those in the Third World—as intellectually inferior, culturally inferior, and even dangerous in the perceived threats of immigration, terrorism, unemployment, and diseases. Ethnocentrism—a perspective that one's own culture has figured out the natural and "right" way to do things—leads to the assumption that all others are "strange" and/or "unnatural."

This attitude leads to a curriculum that devalues other countries and cultures, casting them in terms of world problems that need to be solved, when they are mentioned at all:

The deficit curriculum places emphasis on "problems" in the world and often relies on dichotomous narratives to explain how certain societies are culturally superior while some other societies are inferior. Problem stories often paint a picture of bleak or hopeless conditions in Third World societies, while describing Western industrialized societies as (always) being progressive and democratic and having a geography that is largely free of social problems.

Such an idealized version of the United States as an advanced country that contrasts sharply with other countries given no legitimate space in the curriculum reinforces the *republican* approach to citizenship described previously. Just as the "World Series" of baseball in the United States invites no teams from the rest of the world, "world history" is frequently taught as the (glorious) history of the West, which has surpassed and triumphed over lesser parts of the globe.

Accommodationist

In contrast to the deficit orientation, the *accommodation* orientation does advocate study of other countries and cultures.

The accommodation rationale for the global curriculum is a well-intentioned approach to including global knowledge in classrooms. . . . it seeks to include perspectives that have historically been marginalized. . . . To advocate an inclusive curriculum, the accommodation approach may cite the misconceptions and stereotypes that have developed because of the absence of global perspectives. It may similarly ask that educators go beyond the nation-state approach to conceptualizing ideas such as history and culture, and that they include multiple readings or perspectives on global events and issues in teaching world history and world geography.

As Subedi notes, the approach is well-intentioned, and it is much more inclusive than the deficit approach.

What tends to be left out of the approach, however, seems to be political considerations, so that important questions about how existing power arrangements came to be, or how they are maintained, aren't part of the curriculum. As one example, an accommodationist curriculum might include attention to women's rights worldwide and talk of a "global sisterhood"—but without taking into consideration such contributing factors as race or social class, that produce diversity and complexity within populations. The result can be to promote overgeneralized and superficial understanding of a population.

Decolonization

The *decolonization* approach is aligned with the *critical* approach in Abowitz and Harnish's framework, one that acknowledges diversity between and within cultures and that directly addresses ethical issues related to power and equity. Subedi suggests that this approach has three traits in opposition to the deficit perspective: "antiessentialism, contrapuntal readings, and ethical solidarity." Antiessentialism involves avoiding the tendency to oversimplify other cultures, to assume that each can be reduced to a single set of characteristics. Theorists with this perspective argue that it is essential to acknowledge and discuss differences within cultures—avoiding discussing something like "the role of women" in a culture as if all women of all races, social classes, religions and so on in that culture responded to the same expectations or had the same experiences.

Including "contrapuntal readings" in a global curriculum means bringing not only voices of the dominant groups into a discussion but also the voices of others who have been marginalized, denied equal power and voice. For example, a global perspective on economic issues would include readings not only on prosperity in the West but also on the ways in which that prosperity has been largely enabled by exploitation of poor workers in Third World nations. Or, as another example, a global perspective would avoid either/or depictions of Muslim women "as either being victims of their religion or culture, or as being pawns of Western ideology." In reality, and as a global curriculum would indicate, "Muslim women" are hardly a monolithic group but instead a population with diverse experiences, perspectives and voices. This orientation insists that a wide variety of voices must be heard.

The emphasis on *ethical solidarity* means avoiding simplistic ethical positions that continue to privilege dominant power structures. Key to understanding this characteristic is understanding that when one privileged group sets out to "save" or "deliver" a marginalized group, that construction of the situation assumes that the privileged group has a more enlightened or empowered perspective, thus suggesting that those to be saved are less intelligent or insightful. It also characterizes the group to be "saved" as being without power of its own. In these ways, entrenched power remains entrenched for the privileged while those saved remain characterized as less-than in important ways. This perspective holds that a decolonized curriculum would urge working *with* others to attain a more ethical and just world. Denying the marginalized equal voice, complexity and agency reproduces the original problem of marginalization.

Choices for Educators

It's a pretty safe bet that if asked, representatives of all public schools would immediately say "Yes, my school does teach students citizenship." And yet, it's also a pretty safe bet that it's a rare school where the definition of citizenship has been articulated rather than assumed. And, when the school is operating on unarticulated assumptions, it's also pretty much a sure thing that curriculum has not been consciously aligned with clear goals.

Typically, for anyone to take conscious notice of how citizenship is being taught, people in a community with some specific religious and/or political affiliations don't like what they see children learning. In response, they launch some kind of opposing effort—usually to weed out or force into the school some specific text or practices. For example, a group of state Republican senators initiated a bill to ban a specific high school course in Mexican-American history because they disapproved.[28] While the legislators argued that the course taught students to hate others and promoted rebellion, the teacher in charge argued that he was teaching a more inclusive version of history that included events relative to the U.S. Mexican American population. This is just one recent example of whether government and its policies should be presented in school exclusively as benevolent and righteous or whether the harm it has done, either intended or not, should be acknowledged along with lingering consequences.

The questions are many—and critical. Even a very few point the way to serious, extended deliberation:

- Should schools teach only American citizenship, or also global citizenship?
- Which general orientation to American citizenship should schools embrace? Why?
- How shall we define "civic responsibility"? "Loyalty"? "Patriotism?" Are patriots leaders or followers, unquestioning supporters or responsible critics?
- What is the proper role of symbol and ritual in citizenship education? For example, can/should students wear the American flag? Should they be allowed to burn it?

Decisions on such issues are not made best in times of public strife. And, contemporary America has become a hotbed of public strife born largely of growing income disparity and fractured political alliances. In a time of political unrest and activism, it is especially important for school leaders and faculty to come together and have thoughtful and nuanced discussions of what type of citizen the school would like to nurture and how best to align both formal and informal curriculum and policy with intended goals.

Such questions matter.

Tomorrow's United States will be shaped by its citizens, and different types of citizens will shape different kinds of countries. Is the country to defend against new populations as threats to national identity—or welcome them as a source of new ideas and innovations? Will government be able to depend on the blind trust and loyalty of the citizenry—or will the citizenry enact the responsibility to monitor government activity in the interest of ensuring ethical and humane leadership? The answers to such questions will produce very different results.

For readers willing to wrestle with the difficult questions articulated in this chapter, here are some questions for discussion, some suggestions for further reading, and some websites of potential interest.

Things to Think About

1. Now that you've thought about it: what is your own conception of how schools should define a *good citizen*? Which of the frameworks discussed best matches your own thinking?

2. Do you believe education for global citizenship is important? Why or why not? And if so, which version?

3. What are the various components in your current school (or the school you attended) that shape its citizenship education, either in intended or unintended ways? (For example: What does the social studies or civics curriculum include/exclude? How authoritarian or democratic are school policies? If there is a student government, is it empowered or *pro forma*? Are there efforts to promote volunteerism? Social activism? Political activism? Does anyone ever teach students what the Pledge of Allegiance *means*? Are students ever encouraged to critique government policies? To challenge them?)

4. Now that you've thought about what your school is currently providing in terms of citizenship education, how would you characterize its *implied* conception—or perhaps contradictory conceptions—of citizenship?

5. If you think your school's efforts toward citizenship might be improved—or even reformed—what do you think needs to happen? What can *you* do to trigger efforts toward improvement?

Things to Explore

Readings

Brunner, T. (2013). Censorship in history textbooks: How knowledge of the past is being constructed in schools. *Ursidae: The Undergraduate Research Journal at the University of Northern Colorado 3*(2). Available from http://digscholarship.unco.edu/cgi/viewcontent.cgi?article=1072&context=urj
This student research paper traces the sources of pressure on textbook publishers to keep certain topics out of history books. Included in the discussion are what motivates such attempts at censorship and the negative effects that have resulted. (A bonus of this article is that it's a good example of how good undergraduate research can be.)

McFarland, D. A. and Starmanns, C. (2009). Inside student government: The variable quality of high school student councils. *Teachers College Record, 111*(1), 27–54.

These authors identify variables in student government organizations and consider how differences support or undermine the goal of promoting an engaged citizenry. Interestingly, the authors find critical differences among schools serving various populations.

National Council for the Social Studies (NCSS). (2010). *National Curriculum Standards for Social Studies: A Framework for Teaching, Learning, and Assessment.* Silver Spring, MD: NCSS.

Professional social studies educators have a great deal of experience and research to support their take on what citizenship education should include. These standards, from their professional association, make clear how they believe citizenship education should be defined.

Westheimer, J. (2006, April). Politics and patriotism in education. *Phi Delta Kappan,* 1-8. Available from http://www.democraticdialogue.com/DDpdfs/PoliticsAndPatriotisminEducation.pdf

This piece details two contrasting definitions of patriotism along with their implications for curriculum and pedagogy. The author explains the ways these oppositional understandings create problems in and for schools.

Westheimer, J. and Kahne, J. (2004, April). Educating the "Good" Citizen: Political Choices and Pedagogical Goals. *PS Online, 37* (2). Doi: https://doi.org/10.1017/S1049096504004160

This is the article discussed in this chapter, which offers full detail on the authors' framework. The fact that the authors offer examples of actual school programs to illustrate various approaches is especially helpful in understanding what they say. As we said in the chapter, we really think it's worth the time it might take to read this piece.

Videos

The Center on Congress at Indiana University. *Citizenship Video.* (11 minutes) *This award-winning, animated video embeds many elements that commonly appear in frameworks for citizenship education. It might be useful to try to link ideas (like voting) to framework ideals (like participatory citizenship). It also might also be interesting to consider how effective this video might or might not be with students—and why.*

Center for Civic Education, *Project Citizen Project Overview.* (13

minutes). Available from http://www.civiced.org/resources/multimedia/
featured-videos

In Chapter 3, we discussed a curricular effort called Project Citizen, *one
that teachers use with students to explore local concerns—an effort to have
students experience active and engaged citizenship. This video offers an
overview of this organization's efforts to shape citizenship education nationwide. It's worth asking here, too, about links to the frameworks discussion in the chapter.*

Hugh Evans, *What Does It Mean to Be a Citizen of the World? (TED
Talk).* (17 minutes). Available from https://www.ted.com/talks/hugh_
evans_what_does_it_mean_to_be_a_citizen_of_the_world
*This compelling video not only explains what global citizenship is, but it
offers strong visual and narrative support for the need for global citizenship
education. In addition, it offers some of the strongest evidence we've seen
for just how much change a determined individual can make in the interest
of creating a better world.*

Websites

American Bar Association, Division for Public Education https://www
.americanbar.org/groups/public_education/about_us.html
Campaign for the Civic Mission of Schools (CIRCLE) www.civicmissionof
schools.org/
Center for Civic Education http://civiced.org
Civics Education Initiative http://civicseducationinitiative.org
National Council for the Social Studies http://www.socialstudies.org
National Issues Forum https://www.nifi.org/
Veterans of Foreign Wars: Youth & Education https://www.vfw.org/community/
youth-and-education

Notes

1. United States Holocaust Museum. (n.d.). Indoctrinating youth. Available from
https://www.ushmm.org/wlc/en/article.php?ModuleId=10007820

2. StateUniversity.com. (2017). Puerto Rico—History & background. Retrieved
from http://education.stateuniversity.com/pages/1231/Puerto-Rico-HISTORY-
BACKGROUND.html

3. Fernandez, M. and Hauser, C. (2015, October 5). Texas mother teaches textbook company a lesson on accuracy. *New York Times*. Retrieved from https://www.nytimes.com/2015/10/06/us/publisher-promises-revisions-after-textbook-refers-to-african-slaves-as-workers.html

4. Campaign for the Civic Mission of Schools. (2011). Guardian of democracy: The civic mission of schools. Available from http://civicmission.s3.amazonaws.com/118/f0/5/171/1/Guardian-of-Democracy-report.pdf

5. Wilson, R. (2016, January 16). Arizona will require high school students to pass citizenship test to graduate. Can you pass? *Washington Post*. Retrieved from https://www.washingtonpost.com/blogs/govbeat/wp/2015/01/16/arizona-will-require-high-school-students-to-pass-citizenship-test-to-graduate-can-you-pass/?utm_term=.086522bdcdb0

6. Civics Education Initiative. Retrieved March 19, 2017 from http://civicseducationinitiative.org

7. Kahne, J. (2015). Why are we teaching civics like a game show? *Education Week*, 34(28), 23.

8. National Council for the Social Studies. (2013). *Revitalizing civic learning in our schools*. Retrieved from http://www.socialstudies.org/positions/revitalizing_civic_learning

9. http://www.civicmissionofschools.org

10. Ironically, this group reports that many social studies teachers favor testing civics. They hope that mandated tests might serve as a tool to pry open the door to a more comprehensive civics curriculum, which is often squeezed out of instruction by mandated tests in other areas.

11. Center for Information and Research on Civic Learning and Engagement (CIRCLE), Jonathan M. Tisch College of Civic Life, Tufts University. http://civicyouth.org

12. Kawashima-Ginsberg, K. (2016, September). The future of civic education. National Association of School Boards of Education (NASBE). Retrieved from http://www.nasbe.org/wp-content/uploads/Future-of-Civic-Education_September-2016-Standard.pdf

13. Sullivan, F. M. (2013). *New and alternative assessments, digital badges, and civics: An overview of emerging themes and promising directions*. CIRCLE Working Paper no. 77. Retrieved from http://civicyouth.org/wp-content/uploads/2013/03/WP_77_Sullivan_Final.pdf

14. Desilver, D. (2016, August 2). U.S. trails most developed countries in voter turnout. Available from http://www.pewresearch.org/fact-tank/2016/08/02/u-s-voter-turnout-trails-most-developed-countries/

15. http://www.electproject.org/2016g

16. Kaelber, L. (2012). Eugenics: Compulsory sterilization in 50 American states. Presentation at the Social Science History Association, Vancouver. Retrieved from https://www.uvm.edu/~lkaelber/eugenics/

17. See, for example, NOBullying.com. (2016, October 19). The top six un-forgettable cyberbullying cases ever. Retrieved from https://nobullying.com/six-unforgettable-cyber-bullying-cases/

18. Strom, S. (2009, December 29). Does service learning really help? *New York Times.* Retrieved from http://www.nytimes.com/2010/01/03/education/edlife/03service-t.html

19. Buchheit, P. (2015, April 13). The numbers are staggering: U.S. is "world leader" in child poverty. Retrieved from http://portside.org/2015-04-23/numbers-are-staggering-us-world-leader-child-poverty-developed-countries

20. Westheimer, J. and Kahne, J. (2004, April). Educating the "good" citizen: Political choices and pedagogical goals. *PS Online, 37*(2). Retrieved from https://doi.org/10.1017/S1049096504004160

21. https://charactercounts.org

22. https://charactercounts.org/program-overview/six-pillars/

23. Abowitz, K. K., and Harnish, J. (2006). Contemporary discourses of citizenship. *Review of Educational Research, 76*(4), 653–690.

24. For more on what is meant by "deliberation," see https://www.nifi.org/en/deliberation

25. Note that Ohio's standards for the earlier grades seem to reflect the civic republican conception—indicating that consistency characterizing theoretical frameworks is not necessarily to be expected in practice.

26. Readers who doubt there is an entrenched power structure might consider the relative scarcity of women in political office—including Congress, where in 2017 Senate Majority Leader Mitch McConnell created a media storm by refusing to allow Senator Elizabeth Warren to read a letter written by Coretta Scott King on the Senate floor. A male Senator was later allowed to read the letter, and a new trend in feminist slogans and tattoos was launched. On the original fracas, see, for example, https://www.washingtonpost.com/news/the-fix/wp/2017/02/08/never-theless-she-persisted-becomes-new-battle-cry-after-mcconnell-silences-elizabeth-warren/?utm_term=.b52dabb0d55f

On the tattoo trend, see http://www.cnn.com/2017/02/23/politics/tattoo-parlor-women-slogan-trnd/

27. Subedi, B. (2013). Decolonizing the curriculum for global perspectives. *Educational Theory, 63*(6), 621–638. Doi:10.1111/edth.12045

28. Phippen, J. W. (2015, July 19). How one law banning ethnic studies led to its rise. *The Atlantic.* Retrieved from https://www.theatlantic.com/education/archive/2015/07/how-one-law-banning-ethnic-studies-led-to-rise/398885/

FIVE

❧ How Much Control Does a (Student) Body Need?

At issue are the values of a nation that writes off many of its poorest children in deficient urban schools starved of all the riches found in good suburban schools nearby, criminalizes those it has short-changed and cheated, and then willingly expends ten times as much to punish them as it ever spent to teach them when they were still innocent and clean.

—*Jonathan Kozol,* Shame of the Nation

THERE ARE MANY WAYS IN which the notion of "control" has already come up in this text, so an entire chapter on the topic may seem an odd emphasis. But control is a tricky topic. It would be silly to argue that order isn't preferable to chaos, or that some sort of control, whether of the curriculum, or the behavior of students and teachers, or the climate of the classroom, has no place in schools. Of course there needs to be some sort of oversight of the curriculum. Of course schools are safer and more productive institutions when there are clear expectations for the behavior of individuals within them. And of course there should be consequences for those who egregiously violate those expectations. And to argue that well managed classrooms are unnecessary and always oppressive would be just plain crazy. But somewhere along the way, this idea of control has gotten, well, a bit out of control. We sometimes find ourselves in schools where control has become oppression, places where students and families and even teachers find themselves powerless and without voice. Schools where students seem to leave their personal and civil rights at the door, or where teachers have become automatons, or where environments and cultures look and feel more like prisons than sites of growth and learning. Somewhere along the way toward making schools intellectually stimulating, individually and socially affirming, and physically and mentally safe, too many people in too many educational institutions have veered significantly off the path toward a healthful school culture.

Assumptions about Control in Schools

Perhaps because it is self-evident that control of some kind is essential in schools, many personnel in schools pretty much just go along with assumptions about how much and what kind of control is necessary and desirable. In short, they support existing policies while rarely questioning them. Next are some widespread taken-for-granted ideas that bear a closer look.

Schools have a right to set reasonable boundaries on students' expression of youth culture and identity.

School control over the student body is not limited to keeping students seated in silent rows as teachers lecture. Schools exert control over the appearance of students' bodies as well. Youth culture, as it always has done and will continue to do, pushes boundaries of taste and social convention through individual expression. As a result, schools are compelled to respond in ways that (we hope) are intended to ensure that students are safe and secure, and that the school environment is conducive to learning. Imagine, for example, the distraction of hormonal teen boys if braless girls wore see-through blouses, or of hormonal teen girls if boys suddenly took to wearing bulging, skin-tight shorts. It's an understatement to say that students (especially teenagers) and adults (especially school personnel) don't always see eye to eye on what is school appropriate in terms of clothing, body modification, and other modes of expression. This is apparent through the generations, and will likely continue to vex even the most tolerant of adults into the future. Clashes in schools seem sure to continue, given the fact that both students and school staff have legal rights relevant to student appearance.

In 1969, the landmark Supreme Court case *Tinker v. Des Moines Independent Community School District*[1] established that students in schools do not "shed their constitutional rights to freedom of speech or expression at the schoolhouse gate." At issue in the Tinker case was the right of students to wear black armbands as a form of support for a truce in the Vietnam War. But how far that freedom of expression extends and in what contexts that freedom can be exercised today is often complicated. Although long hair on young men and pants on young women aren't quite the scandal they were in decades past, what constitutes "freedom of expression" in terms of how students choose to dress, modify their bodies (such as with piercings, tattoos, and ear plugs), wear their hair, and express their identities is contentious territory. To what extent should schools be able to control these types of student expression, or at least be able to put parameters on what is and is not acceptable? Relevant policies ultimately impact which students will and which will not be allowed to participate in school.

To help make boundaries clear, dress codes for students and teachers in public schools have long been a part of school life, and in the last two decades, required uniforms in public schools have become more common. According to the National Center for Education Statistics,

> From 1999–2000 to 2013–14, the percentage of public schools reporting that they required that students wear uniforms increased from 12 to 20%. During the 2013–14 school year, a higher percentage of primary schools required students to wear uniforms (23%) than high/combined schools (15%).
>
> In the 2013–14 school year, a higher percentage of public schools located in cities than those in suburban areas, towns, and rural areas reported that they required students to wear uniforms. Also, a higher percentage of schools where 76% or more of students were eligible for free or reduced-price lunch required school uniforms than did schools where lower percentages of students were eligible for free or reduced-price lunch.[2,3]
>
> In the same year, 60% of schools enforced a strict dress code.[4]

These numbers suggest trends toward greater and greater control of dress, and especially so for urban schools with students from low socioeconomic status.

Public school uniform policies and formal dress code policies have met with mixed support and dissention in schools across the nation. According to the 2013 *Lands' End School Uniform and National Association of Elementary School Principals State of School Uniforms* survey, many school officials claim that uniform policies and formal dress code policies have a positive impact on a variety of issues such as student achievement, discipline, bullying and peer pressure, and overall student safety.[5,6] It shouldn't come as a surprise that research partially sponsored by a corporation that has an entire division devoted to producing and selling school uniforms reported favorable results. Just as school uniform and dress code policies have financial implications for families, they also have implications for both local and not-so-local businesses. Research into the impact of uniforms and dress-code policies is uneven; it is as easy to find studies that tout the positive impact of uniform and dress code policies on student achievement, attendance, and discipline as it is to find studies that indicate uniforms have no significant impact on student outcomes or school climate.

The big issue here, however, is not about reasonable parameters on what students can and cannot wear to school, or reasonable punishments for violating dress code policies. In general, dress code policies forbid clothing, accessories, or hair/body styles that are "disruptive" (although that is a loaded term that can interpreted in a number of ways in a number of contexts) and/ or that are gang-affiliated, lewd, or promote drug or alcohol use. For example, reasonable people would agree that a t-shirt with "Hitler was right" is unacceptable, or that a student wearing a hot dog costume on a day other than Halloween is a distraction to students and teachers alike.

However, there are instances where a school's ban seems much more capricious than reasonable. And even more troubling than the capriciousness is the manner in which some uniform and dress code violations and punishments are meted out: policies that target primarily students of color, young women, and youth who are transgender or gender nonconforming are common.[7] School dress codes that disproportionally impact some members of the student population, particularly when simultaneously inconsistently enforced for other members of the student population, are discriminatory and exclusionary. From *Teaching Tolerance* (2017),

An elementary student is sent home from her Texas school for wearing her hair in Afro puffs. A Louisiana senior is forbidden to wear her tux to prom. Three students in Pennsylvania are told they can't use the bathrooms that match their gender identities. An Illinois school releases a dress code flier that features two young women, one labeled "distracting" and "revealing," the other "ladylike."

These are not isolated incidents. Similar stories have been reported in K–12 schools across the United States, and more unfold every day. Nor are they unrelated. Each situation was the result of a policy that treats students differently based on their identities.[8]

School dress code policies that cast certain members of the school population in negative ways or that situates students outside the boundaries of "normal" frame the ways in which these students are perceived by others, perpetuating social assumptions that some cultures or genders or people have more worth than others.

Cultural bias in dress codes is not a new phenomenon. From bars to schools, restrictions against sagging pants and baseball caps have been challenged as racially and culturally discriminatory.[9] Racial, ethnic, and cultural bias in school dress codes has, in some cases, gone a step farther in terms of policies that impact how students can wear their hair for school. Here, we're not talking about students who get suspended for dying their hair pink or shaving their heads to support cancer awareness (although a quick Google search will provide a plethora of links to stories like this one about a third grader who shaved her head to support a friend,[10] and this one about a student who sported a pink Mohawk in support of his mom[11]), or punk rock kids with Mohawks (which some would argue is also as much an expression of culture as it is teenage rebellion). Rather, we are talking about school policies that characterize natural Black hair as unkempt and punish Black students for wearing their hair naturally, or that place restrictions on particular hair styles, such as box braids, cornrows, or dreadlocks. Policies such as these send the message that Black hair is somehow *un*natural or that typically Black hairstyles are somehow inappropriate for school.

Another key criticism of school dress code policies is that they often focus primarily on girls' clothing and have relatively few restrictions for boys. In this way, girls are put in a position of responsibility for the quality and integrity of the education received by boys, and often at the expense of their own. As the founder of The Everyday Sexism Project[12] has observed,

Some of our most powerful and lasting ideas about the world around us are learned at school. Hard work pays off. Success comes from working together. Girls' bodies are dangerous and harassment is inevitable.

This might sound inflammatory, but it is not an exaggeration. It is the overriding message being sent to thousands of students around the world by sexist school dress codes and the way in which they are enforced. [13]

School policy that frames young girls as sexual objects, and similarly, frames all boys as potential sexual predators given enough temptation, sexualizes children in ways that they may not have imagined. Such policies contribute to a culture that normalizes sexual violence by casting it as an expected behavior; in addition, it puts the responsibility for preventing assault on the (assumed to be female) victim rather than on the (assumed to be male) perpetrator. Girls already deal with a bevy of sexual stereotypes in the media, which teaches them to feel shameful about their bodies. School should be a place that counters these narratives, not reinforces them. These issues are further exacerbated when schools inconsistently enforce dress code policy for some students and not others, as in this example from The Everyday Sexism Project:

> I got dress coded at my school for wearing shorts. After I left the principal's office with a detention I walked past another student wearing a shirt depicting two stick figures: the male holding down the females [sic] head in his crotch and saying "good girls swallow." Teachers walked right past him and didn't say a thing. [14]

Perhaps the Hitler shirt (or the hot dog costume) wouldn't be a problem in that school, either, where concern seemed to focus only on clothing some adult thinks makes a girl look too sexy for school.

In fact, sexuality and gender identity are at the root of multiple control issues in schools. As the number of students who openly identify as lesbian, gay, bisexual, queer, and (especially) transgender or gender nonconforming increases, the policy quandaries for school officials increase as well. From enforcing dress code restrictions to enacting policy on which bathroom or locker room students may use (or in some cases, be compelled to use), the control of LGBTQ student bodies is often murky, conflicted, and inconsistent. The National School Climate Survey[15] is GLSEN's biennial report on the experiences of LGBTQ youth in schools. According to the 2015 report, 66.2% of the survey participants indicated that they experienced discriminatory school policies and practices, a number of which are directly related to identity expression. For example,

- 22.2% of students had been prevented from wearing clothes considered inappropriate based on their legal sex.
- 15.6% of students were prevented from attending a dance or function with someone of the same gender.
- 71.2% of LGBTQ students reported that their schools engaged in some form of gendered practice in school activities (for example, graduation attire, homecoming courts, school photographs).
- 50.9% of transgender students had been prevented from using their preferred name or pronoun (19.9% of LGBTQ students overall), and
- 60.0% of transgender students had been required to use a bathroom or locker room of their legal sex (22.6% of students overall).

Fortunately, the GLSEN report does contain some good news. For example, it found an overall decrease in the use of homophobic remarks, a decline in the use anti-LGBTQ language, and lower incidences of verbal assault and physical harassment of LGBTQ students. This is great news. Still, there is more work to be done. Policies and practices that frame students who dress in alignment with their gender identity as "cross-dressers" or imply that these students are in some way deviant do more than just challenge student self-expression: they effectively negate the identity of an individual student. According to the National Center for Transgender Equality,

> Too often, school officials themselves single out these youth by refusing to respect their gender identity and even punishing them for expressing that identity. For example, 59% of trans students have been denied access to restrooms consistent with their gender identity. Rather than focusing on their education, many students struggle for the ability to come to school and be themselves without being punished for wearing clothes or using facilities consistent with who they are. Some are denied opportunities to go on field trips or participate in sports. Together with bullying and victim-blaming, these conflicts can lead to disproportionate discipline, school pushout, and involvement in the juvenile justice system.[16]

Should schools, through dress code policies or other means, be in the practice of dictating how a child can identify, and under what circumstances their identity can be expressed? When school policy privileges the right to learn of one group over another, it is a problem. When school policy serves to slut-shame, force cultural assimilation, and negates a student's identity, it is a problem. What of educators' good intentions to help *every* student thrive?

Students are more successful when their behavior is regulated through schedules, routines, and permission-seeking.

Ask new teachers what they are most concerned about as they anticipate the first day of their first job, and very likely the answer will be something related to classroom management—and for many teachers, novice and experienced, this concern never fully goes away. How will I maintain order in my classroom? How will I make sure kids are learning? How will I ensure that they respect my authority? What will I do if they don't? Popular education writer Alfie Kohn aptly portrays how the purpose of classroom management is often viewed:[17]

> Everyone knows why classroom management skills are considered a critical part of teacher training. The reason we need to minimize "misbehavior" and get students to show up, sit down, and pay attention is so we can teach them stuff. That proposition is so obvious that it's rarely defended or even spelled out, except maybe on the first day of Classroom Management 101. While we may disagree about strategies— for example, the relative merits of discipline versus *self*-discipline (getting kids to regulate and manage themselves)—we take it for granted that the whole point is to create an environment conducive to learning.

Well, of course that's the purpose of classroom management: to create an environment in which teachers can teach and students can learn. However, a vision of what constitutes "an environment conducive to learning" can look very different from a variety of perspectives, and it is highly dependent on one's social, political, and economic position. How any one person or community understands the purpose of education and the role of school in the lives of students will have a significant impact on how that vision is imagined and enacted.

John Dewey, a seminal educational philosopher, questioned traditional classroom structures and practices throughout his body of work, but this piece from *Experience and Education*[18] particularly resonates here:

> The limitation that was put upon outward action by the fixed arrangements of the typical traditional schoolroom, with its fixed rows of desks and its military regimen of pupils who were permitted to move only at certain fixed signals, put a great restriction upon intellectual and moral freedom. Strait-jacket and chain-gang procedures had to be done away with if there was to be a chance for growth of individuals in the intellectual springs of freedom without which there is no assurance of genuine and continued normal growth.

Some of the ideas about "good" classrooms that Pam struggled with as a student and as a teacher (both in her high school classroom and her university classrooms) are previously noted. These include the concept that a good classroom is always an orderly classroom, that a quiet classroom is evidence that learning is happening and outcomes will be reached, and that the ability of students to move around or leave the classroom should be highly regulated and a matter of permission granting. And although she found ways to deal with such an environment as a K-12 student (because "smart kids" tend to have many more privileges than other kids, and early on she learned how to leverage "smart kid capital" for physical freedom in school) and as a high school teacher (close the door, cover the window, and don't send kids to the dean's office for infractions that can be dealt with in the classroom), classroom control became a more immediate challenge as a university professor when she was assigned to teach *Strategies of Classroom Management for Secondary Educators* to undergraduate teacher candidates. That was a problem.

You see, Pam's idea of a well-oiled classroom machine didn't align well (or at all, really) with the classroom management textbook she was being compelled to require for class—and presumably, teach from. The text itself was not so different from any number of commercially available classroom management textbooks which all provide a similar array of strategies for arranging seating, establishing classroom rules, monitoring class participation, and designing discipline strategies. This is not to say that such information wasn't very helpful for a group of students one semester away from student teaching; it very much was. Instead, the biggest challenge Pam experienced with teaching this text was not so much what it included, but rather what it left out. Such textbook visions of good classroom management, of how to run a good classroom, really constituted what Kohn described: successfully "minimiz[ing] misbehavior" and "get[ting] students to show up, sit down, and pay attention is so [teachers] can teach them stuff."

Now, we doubt that anyone who has ever had charge of a classroom would argue *against* teaching a classroom full of students who showed up every day and didn't fundamentally distract everyone from the task at hand. But here's a catch. In Pam's experience, a productive classroom environment wasn't necessarily quiet, wasn't necessarily orderly, and didn't force students to sit still in neat rows for the fifty-five minutes they were there. Instead, it consisted of students being occupied in some way on something they valued (maybe, but not necessarily, occupied in the same way on exactly the same thing), open class dialogue around lessons (instead of hand-raising for permission to speak after hearing a lecture—though training students *out* of these compliant behaviors seemed ironic), and students possessing the freedom to move about or even *out* of the classroom if need be (there was a ridiculously obvious bathroom pass hanging on the door for students to use as *needed*, not as permission was granted). This is not to say that her classroom was an unacademic space, or a space in which learning was haphazard or incidental, or for that matter, that it was always productive. It was high school, these were teenagers, and admittedly, Pam was going on gut instinct regarding what would both motivate and de-motivate students to engage in the work of being a student in her classroom. By coming to teaching with an alternative certificate for a high-need school, she came to this from an untrained perspective; she had not yet had the opportunity to be indoctrinated by a teacher preparation program that taught her that silence is golden, the teacher always knows best, and the less movement the better.

To Pam and to her students, it just made sense that the classroom was a place in which teacher and students co-created community norms, dealt with infractions in context, and worked on building a safe, interesting, and productive space together. And . . . good things happened when all members of the community bought into and respected the community norms. In Pam's view, the proper goal was to create a classroom where each kid was engaged in some way with something they valued, either independently or by collaborating with others. Was everyone working on the same thing at the same time? Of course not, and yes, it was messy. Sometimes very messy, both physically and conceptually. But that's also what made it beautiful and exciting and frustrating. The classroom community worked because the kids and their teacher took on all of the various roles that were needed to make it work. And sometimes it broke down, because everyone in that space was human. Kids misbehaved, and some tried to take advantage of the relative freedoms this environment begat. And sometimes Pam yelled, and on occasion even cried. Again . . . they were teenagers, and she barely wasn't. But almost twenty years later, her former students *still* talk about that experience as transformative in a variety of ways.

Pam's story about her classroom is in many ways not unique (if it is an approach light years removed from one that would include handcuffing five year olds).[19] There are legions of teachers who continue to close the door, cover the window, let kids go to the bathroom when they need to, and teach in ways that they find move their students (and themselves) to better places socially, academically, and as human beings.[20] There also exists abundant support in the scholarly literature that challenges the idea that strategies stressing control produce better outcomes than those encouraging student autonomy. A review of the literature[21] on teacher motivating style illustrates a "paradox" in education, that "although students educationally and developmentally benefit when teachers support their autonomy, teachers are often controlling." The author notes that all teachers at times find themselves in contexts where they are

> pushed and pulled toward a controlling style by a multitude of factors, including social roles; burdens of responsibility and accountability; cultural values and expectations; a misconception that controlling means structured, temporarily unmotivated, or unengaged students; personal beliefs about motivation; and their own personal dispositions.

Still, he says, the literature is clear that "that both students and teachers function better in school when teachers support students' autonomy."

As we pointed out previously in this chapter, the issue of control isn't confined to the classroom; it is part of the environment and culture of a school as a whole. And although characterizing schools as resembling prisons might seem extreme, it's not if we think carefully about the messages that institutions send to the people within them through what might seem to be relatively benign, "normal" structures and routines. As Jean Anyon illustrated in her classic text *Social Class and the Hidden Curriculum of Work*,[22] as early as fifth grade, children are already being socialized into their place in the social order through the routines and mechanisms of the school. Similar to Willis's (1977) argument that "working class kids get working class jobs,"[23] Anyon illustrated how the vastly different types of school and classroom environments that different social classes of children experience serve to reinforce existing social class contexts and subsequent professional hierarchies.

In her work, Anyon identified four types of schools: "working class," "middle class," "affluent professional," and "executive elite." In each environment, the content of the curriculum, the manner in which it was delivered, the structure and governance of the school day, the level of student autonomy, and the emphasis on the building of various skills mirrored in many ways the nature of work that was common in that particular social context. For example, she found that while children in the working class schools experienced lessons aimed at learning to follow procedures, children in the executive elite environments were prompted to think critically and employ reason in their studies. The children in working class schools were expected to respond to orders and directives, and the children in the executive elite contexts were participants in the democratic life of the classroom. While instruction for children in the working class environments often involved a lecture that reiterated what was in the textbook or workbook, children in executive elite classrooms were provided with opportunities to engage with the teacher and encouraged to challenge the text. And so on.

Importantly, Anyon wasn't out to prove that teachers were engaging in an overt type of social engineering in a mindful or purposeful way, and she did not suggest that teachers were going into working-class schools to consciously train working-class kids for life as compliant factory workers. As we discussed in Chapter 3, that's not how the hidden curriculum works. Rather, Anyon's concern was for what was being communicated on a deeper, social level. In short, she noted the power of these tacit messages to reinforce unequal social and economic hierarchies and power relations. If the routines of school truly trained children for their intended place in society, then there was a good chance that the rich would remain more autonomous and get richer and more powerful while the poor would remain complacent and stay poorer and relatively powerless. It is important to take note of these messages that institutional structures and routines communicate to those who have no choice but to abide by them. In this way, schools control not only the behavior and actions of those within them, but also the potential life trajectories of students on the other side of schooling.

Zero tolerance policies create a healthful school environment by keeping bad kids out of schools while keeping good kids safe inside.

"Zero tolerance" is a form of school disciplinary policy that typically involves excluding students from school (and often involves law enforcement) for initial offenses, no matter how minor. Zero tolerance policies began to proliferate in schools in the mid-1990s, after the 1994 Gun Free Schools Act[24] (an amendment to the 1965 Elementary and Secondary Education Act) stipulated that in order to be eligible to receive federal education funding, states were to require local schools to adopt a mandatory one year expulsion policy for any student who brought a weapon to school.

Implementation of zero tolerance policies is based on a set of key assumptions. A researcher from the National Equity Project has neatly outlined them:[25]

1. School violence is at a serious level and increasing, thus necessitating forceful, no-nonsense strategies for violence prevention.
2. Zero tolerance increases the consistency of school discipline and thereby sends an important message to students.
3. The no-nonsense approach of zero tolerance leads to improved school climate.
4. Zero tolerance has made a difference in school safety and improved student behavior.
5. Students learn important lessons from the application of zero tolerance, and ultimately feel safer.

On the face of it, the assumptions listed earlier don't seem unreasonable; a commitment to keeping schools and the people within them safe by drawing a clear line between what is acceptable and what is not seems like a good idea. But . . . many initiatives seem reasonable until tested in practice.

For example, although zero tolerance policies were initially thought to be the best solution for removing dangerous students from school for weapons and drug offenses, over time they have been used as consequences for a wide variety of lesser offenses, such as fighting, smoking, and swearing.[26] As we explored earlier in this chapter, the Internet provides us with an abundance of examples of zero tolerance policies being enforced for the ways students dress and wear their hair as well as which toys they bring to school.[27] And in the twenty plus years since inception, the use of zero tolerance policies for a variety of school infractions, both major and minor, have increased dramatically—despite an overall national *decline* in the juvenile crime rate.[28] Importantly, this type of disciplinary action "does not distinguish between serious and nonserious offenses, [or] adequately separate intentional troublemakers from those with behavioral disorders.[29] Meaning . . . a gun is a gun is a gun, whether it shoots bubbles, is made of Legos, or is simulated in fingerplay, and the possession of a gun in school results in expulsion.

Zero tolerance policies leave school administrators and disciplinarians with little discretionary wiggle room to apply an alternative consequence (or in some cases, reason) to instances in which students may (or may not) deserve to be punished for whatever it was they did to land in the administrator's office in the first place. One researcher has provided a list of examples of infractions and consequences, many of which involve elementary aged children, culled from the Advancement Project, the Justice Policy Institute, and the *New York Times*.[30] These include:

- A nine-year-old on the way to school found a manicure kit with a ten-inch knife. The student was suspended for one day.
- A Pennsylvania kindergartener told her pals she was going to shoot them with a Hello Kitty toy that makes soap bubbles. The kindergartener was initially suspended for two days, and the incident was reclassified as "intent to harm others."
- In Massachusetts, a five-year-old boy attending an after-school program made a gun out of Legos and pointed it at other students while "simulating the sound of gunfire," as one school official put it. He was expelled.

- A five-year-old boy in Queens, New York, was arrested, handcuffed, and taken to a psychiatric hospital for having a tantrum and knocking papers off the principal's desk.
- In St. Petersburg, Florida, a five-year-old girl was handcuffed, arrested, and taken into custody for having a tantrum and disrupting classrooms.
- An eleven-year-old girl in Orlando, Florida, was Tasered by a police officer, arrested, and faces charges of battery on a security resource officer, disrupting a school function, and resisting with violence. She had pushed another student.
- An honors student in Houston, Texas was forced to spend a night in jail when she missed class to go to work to support her family.

Surely such horrifying outcomes were never originally anticipated when such policies were adopted.

Employing zero tolerance policies might have seemed like a good idea to policymakers and school administrators when fears of escalating school violence dominated the media (a 2001 RAND report[31] on school violence indicated that "more than 50% of parents with children in grades K-12[32] and 75% of secondary school students[33] now think that a school shooting could occur in their community"). However, more than two decades of research by both educators and other organizations have shown otherwise. In 2005 for example, the American Psychological Association convened a Zero Tolerance Task Force to examine existing research on the multiple ways such policies impact students.[34] Research included such significant topics as how zero tolerance affected students of color and students with disabilities; how it affected child development, students in general, their families, and their communities; and how it was shaping the relationship between schools and the juvenile justice system. The task force report is extensive, and it concludes with recommendations for both improving zero tolerance policies and implementing alternatives. In summary, researchers found that not only are zero tolerance policies not particularly effective in creating safer schools, but such policies can actually have the opposite effect.

For example, the report shows that the use of disciplinary measures that effectively exclude students from school can contribute to increased behavior issues, higher drop-out rates, and a more direct pathway from the schoolhouse to the jailhouse. Further, the report indicates that students of color are disproportionately overrepresented in out-of-school disciplinary measures. A 2010 report prepared for the Southern Poverty Law Center[35] found that middle school Black boys are three times more likely to be suspended than their White counterparts, and middle school Black girls are four times as likely to be suspended as White girls. And, students of color aren't the only marginalized populations to be disproportionately impacted by zero tolerance measures: in addition, "the poor, students with disabilities, LGBT students, and youth of color [are] suspended, expelled, and arrested at the highest rates, despite comparable rates of infraction" (p. 23).[36] A review of the impact of zero-tolerance policies indicates that these policies "do not make schools safer, they produce perverse consequences for academics, school/community relations, and the development of citizens, they dramatically and disproportionately target youth of color; and they inhibit educational opportunities."[37] It is unclear what the 2017 Department of Education decision to "scale back investigations into civil rights violations" in the public PreK-12 system will have in this area, if any.[38]

The good news is that schools and systems seem to be moving away from highly punitive zero tolerance models and toward more positive, preventative, and justice-oriented models (well, good news for some people since alternative models to zero tolerance policies have also sparked a healthy amount of debate and dissent). For example, the Chicago Public Schools stopped using exclusionary discipline practices and began using "research-based preventative approaches." This means employing restorative practices—practices that focus on accountability, conflict resolution, and relationship re-building rather than punishment—and emphasizing social and emotional learning instead of immediately moving to exclude students from school. According to a September 2016 press release from the district,[39] the out-of-school suspension rate decreased by 67% and the expulsion rate decreased by 74% since the district switched disciplinary gears in 2012. As well, in-school suspensions and police notifications also declined, 7% and 39% respectively. In New York City, Mayor Bill de Blasio and the New York Department of Education have similarly questioned the efficacy of zero tolerance approaches, and they have updated the Discipline Code and moved in the direction of implementing restorative methods in classrooms and schools. Significantly, the administration has banned suspensions for children in K-2 classrooms.[40] As mentioned earlier, these practices are not without criticism; for example, a Hoover Institution Media Fellow took to the *New York Post* with a scathing critique of the restorative practices employed in not just New York, but Chicago, Los Angeles, and Philadelphia as well, among other urban centers.[41] He characterizes restorative justice practice as "therapy" rather than punishment, and likens school environments that use restorative practices to the degenerate society that evolves in *The Lord of the Flies.*

Schools function to equip students for a productive, independent future.

People familiar only with better, more successful schools in the United States typically assume that all public schools function to prepare students for a work life or career after school. However, many schools function very differently. *How* differently is evident in the phrase many researchers use to describe them: the "school-to-prison pipeline." Numerous definitions for the term exist, but whether a particular definition comes from the ACLU, the Anti-Defamation League, Teaching Tolerance, any number of academic researchers, or Wikipedia, the concept is essentially the same. The school-to-prison pipeline is a metaphor for the many ways schools channel primarily poor, undereducated students of color into the juvenile (or adult) justice system. The pipeline has been constructed on the backs of those with the most to lose, from the raw material provided by zero tolerance and other isolating and exclusionary policies, and maintained by the greed and amorality of adults in positions of power and responsibility to care. For example, two Pennsylvania judges were convicted of orchestrating their own pipeline to a privately owned detention center for youth, earning kickbacks of more than $2.6 million in the process.[42] One judge set up the contracts, and the other funneled over 5,000 juveniles who appeared in his courtroom into the center.

Of course, we said that some schools have started moving away from zero tolerance policies which enable such abuses, perhaps raising the question of whether the pipeline metaphor is still relevant. Unfortunately, it is. Smashing the pipeline is not so simple. Zero tolerance approaches to discipline constitute merely one peak (albeit a big one) on a proverbial iceberg of school discipline and the control of students. The school environment (meaning its culture, climate and physical condition) also has a powerful and important impact on students in a number of ways. And when that environment looks and feels more like the county jail than a laboratory for learning, there is a problem.

Take for example this notion: if schools are meant to be places in which society is reproduced and where students learn how to become functioning, productive members of that society, what are students learning when the routines of the school resemble the routines of the penal system? Or when the facilities of the school aren't merely sub-par, but dangerous and decrepit?[43] From *Education as Enforcement: The Militarization and Corporatization of Schools:*[44]

> The shift to a society now governed through crime, market-driven values, and the politics of disposability has radically transformed the public school as a site for a civic and critical education. One major effect can be seen in the increasingly popular practice of organizing schools through disciplinary practices that closely resemble the culture of the prisons. For instance, many public schools, traditionally viewed as nurturing, youth-friendly spaces dedicated to protecting and educating children, have become one of the most punitive institutions young people now face—on a daily basis. Educating for citizenship, work, and the public good have been replaced with models of schooling in which students, especially poor minority youth, are viewed narrowly either as a threat or as perpetrator of violence. When not viewed as potential criminals, they are positioned as infantilized potential victims of crime (on the Internet, at school, and in other youth spheres) who must endure modes of governing that are demeaning and repressive.

The same author also notes elsewhere that the culture of "fear, crime, and repression that [dominates] American public schooling" has increased the amount of school resources, often scarce to begin with, being funneled into "more police, security staff, and technologies of control and surveillance."[45] Another researcher points to the "national frenzy of security equipment purchases" and the elimination of "open" campuses (meaning, kids are not allowed off campus during the school day) that ensued after the 1999 Columbine shooting. That school violence has gone down every year since then doesn't seem to have affected popular thinking on the need for police, security cameras, surprise canine searches, or metal detectors. The point here is that schools increasingly monitor the actions and behavior of students and exert what some would characterize as excessive force over children in schools every day. A quick Google search yields literally pages of (legitimate) news articles, news clips, and YouTube videos chronicling four, five, and six year olds being handcuffed by police for minor infractions.[46, 47]

What might a school like this look and feel like? The text *Police in the Hallways: Discipline in an Urban High School*[48] refers to a "culture of control" that often permeates schools in low-income, urban communities.[49] Such control culture is characterized by the presence of law-enforcement officials in the hallways, the use of discipline strategies such as "body searches, handcuffing, and interrogating," and continual threats to students of a court summons or an arrest.[50] In *Being Bad: My Baby Brother and the School-to-Prison-Pipeline*,[51] a Chicago born and raised researcher illustrates the story of her own younger brother's path from the Chicago Public Schools into the criminal justice system. In a text that is equal parts storytelling and academic research, this author illustrates the multiple social, community, and school contexts that converged like a perfect storm around one young man, and challenges readers to be thoughtful about what it means for young people in systemically marginalized contexts, and in particular, young Black men, to "come of age" in these institutional arrangements.

While the *Police in the Hallways* author notes that despite the wealth of literature available illustrating the pervasiveness and power of the school-to-prison pipeline, that text doesn't represent the story of all Black boys in urban systems, or all youth in poverty, or all youth in urban schools. It's simply unreasonable to believe that all students in these environments will end up in prison. But that being said, the impact on children in these schools is still tangible and powerful:

> To gain sufficient understanding of the everyday life experience of students at the school, it is useful to highlight a more mundane but pervasive phenomenon: how the lives of impoverished urban students are managed by a complex interpenetration of systems. The school, where they are by law required to spend most of their day, becomes an auxiliary to the criminal justice system. These findings show that urban youth get subjected to levels of surveillance and repression that are not the same as long-term incarceration, but nonetheless, as the

school merges with an ideology of street policing, the courts, and even the prison, a particular culture of penal control becomes an aspect of everyday life at school and beyond.[52]

In short, the life that many students experience at school is oppressive, constricting, and for these youth, the only thing they have ever known, so however oppressive it may be, it becomes "normal." And as the renowned theorist Paulo Freire[53] has said, social structures like this result not only in those who are disadvantaged believing that they are responsible for their own disadvantage, but also in their acting to similarly disadvantage others if they should happen to secure some modicum of power. The cycle continues.

In enacting discipline policies, school personnel would never willfully endanger students.

Unfortunately, this assumption is simply incorrect. As we noted in Chapter 1, excessive force and tortuous confinement in "seclusion rooms" (also known as "scream rooms") are sufficiently widespread for Congress to have investigated the use of handcuffs, bungee cords, duct tape and even, shockingly, Taser guns and other devices to control students' bodies. A 2014 report[54] found that in the 2012 school year, students were subjected to such extreme constraints over 267,000 times nationwide—and 75% of the students restrained were known to have physical, emotional or intellectual disabilities. More recent research indicates that in addition to children with special needs, students who are male, Black, American Indian, and LGBTQ also receive a disproportionate share of such punishments—with the odds increasing in large schools for the upper grades that are also in low socioeconomic areas with high crime rates.[55] Injuries, and even deaths, are not uncommon:

- Children have gotten head injuries, bloody noses, broken bones and worse while being restrained or tied down—in one Iowa case, to a lunch table. A thirteen-year-old Georgia boy hanged himself after school officials gave him a rope to keep up his pants before shutting him alone in a room.

• At least twenty children nationwide have reportedly died while being restrained or isolated over the course of two decades, the Government Accountability Office found in 2009.

This cannot be an acceptable outcome of school policy. While the American Association of School Administrators argues that restraint and seclusion are necessary tools to keep order in schools,[56] student deaths and other permanent emotional and physical damage to students cannot be justified in the name of "order."

We reiterate what we said earlier: we do not blame school personnel who are forced to enact disciplinary policies determined by others, especially when they have received no training in alternative methods. But torturing children is surely not something professional educators had in mind when they entered their professional education programs. There are many alternatives, including those listed next. However much control an individual professional or cadre of professionals may believe is necessary, in designing policy or taking a personal stance, professionalism requires setting a clear boundary for what constitutes *going too far* for the sake of control.

Frameworks for Disciplinary Policies

In the wake of abundant research indicating that exclusionary zero tolerance and other extreme disciplinary practices do more to harm children and young people than to help them, and that they disproportionately affect students from various marginalized groups, educators and other policymakers have increasingly designed and employed alternative methods of discipline and conflict resolution in schools. The premise is that students will benefit from staying in school rather than being pushed out for (often minor) offenses. Here we present a few of the contemporary alternatives that school systems large and small are currently employing. A detailed set of principles and action guidelines promoted by the U.S. Department of Education is also available in the department's *Restraint and Seclusion Resource Document*, listed at the end of this chapter as a suggestion for further reading.

Assertive Discipline

Perhaps the approach that keeps most control in adults' hands, assertive discipline is an approach developed by Lee Canter in the 1970s. In this approach, the teacher is firmly in charge, but is not to treat students as "enemies" or to assume hostile or sarcastic attitudes.[57] Rather, the teacher functions more as an unemotional enforcer of clearly stated expectations for student behavior. The essence of the approach lies in some core principles:

1. I will not tolerate any student stopping me from teaching.
2. I will not tolerate any student preventing another student from learning.
3. I will not tolerate any student engaging in any behavior that is not in the student's best interest, and the best interest of fellow students.
4. Whenever a student chooses to behave appropriately, I will immediately recognize and reinforce that behavior.
5. I am an assertive teacher and I am the boss in my classroom.[58]

It is important to note that the approach also encourages clearly identifying and rewarding good behavior, and that fairness—equal application to all students—is also stressed. What is central, however, is the role of the teacher as "boss." The teacher sets a few very clear rules—and enforces them without exception, with negative consequences dispensed for each and every infraction of those rules. The model appeals most to those who believe teachers and schools are properly and responsibly authoritarian.

Schoolwide Positive Behavioral Interventions and Supports

We perceive this approach to move beyond the assertive discipline approach in that it is less authoritarian. In some iterations, it also assigns responsibility for promoting good behavior to the entire school community rather than to individual teachers. Positive Behavioral Interventions and Supports (PBIS or SWPBIS—the schoolwide version) has been widely used as a school behavior and discipline strategy since the 1997 reauthorization of the Individuals with Disabilities Education Act (IDEA). An abundance of research exists regarding the nature, implementation, and outcomes of PBIS strategies in schools. For the sake of simplicity, we turned to the OSEP Technical Assistance Center on

Positive Behavioral Interventions and Supports for a concise explanation of what PBIS is and can do. According to its website,

> PBIS is a framework or approach for assisting school personnel in adopting and organizing evidence-based behavioral interventions into an integrated continuum that enhances academic and social behavior outcomes for all students.
>
> PBIS IS NOT a packaged curriculum, scripted intervention, or manualized strategy.
>
> PBIS IS a prevention-oriented way for school personnel to (a) organize evidence-based practices, (b) improve their implementation of those practices, and (c) maximize academic and social behavior outcomes for students.
>
> PBIS supports the success of ALL students.[59]

In short, PBIS works by putting the emphasis on problem prevention rather than on discipline with punishment and consequences. There are many, many models of PBIS programs, and many modes of implementation. Importantly, PBIS rewards good behavior; for example, students who are "caught being good" are rewarded for exemplifying desirable, pro-social behaviors. These strategies do not replace consequence-based disciplinary methods, but rather focus on providing students with positive behavior strategies and creating a school climate in which positive behaviors are the norm. In theory, the need for consequence-based discipline will decrease in a school culture and climate where students are taught positive behaviors and conflict strategies in an integrated manner.

A key criticism of PBIS models is this: if students are rewarded for positive behavior that is part and parcel of being a decent human in our society, what happens when children are no longer rewarded for being "good"? Do PBIS models assist students in developing positive, pro-social behaviors . . . or do students merely become adept at earning rewards?

Restorative Practices

Restorative approaches to discipline in schools, often called restorative justice, include a nonpunitive set of practices used to resolve conflicts and to

respond to instances in which disciplinary measures, including those that
could exclude students from school, would typically be warranted. As some
researchers note in their recent research review of restorative justice practices
in U. S. schools,[60]

> [Restorative justice] is a broad term that encompasses a growing social
> movement to institutionalize peaceful and nonpunitive approaches
> for addressing harm, responding to violations of legal and human
> rights, and problem solving. RJ has been used extensively both as a
> means to divert people from official justice systems, and as a program
> for convicted offenders already supervised by the adult or juvenile
> justice system. In the school setting, it often serves as an alternative
> to traditional discipline, particularly exclusionary disciplinary actions
> such as suspension or expulsion.

In short, restorative practices aim to "establish a voice for victims, offenders, and community in order to address offender accountability for the harm
caused (rather than the act itself), and to develop a plan to repair and restore
relationships." In contrast to exclusionary practices that punish the perpetrator but often leave the victim without a sense of justice or closure, restorative
practices involve the community and the victim in a process of resolution
with the perpetrator. Restorative strategies in schools include but are not limited to:

> victim-offender mediation conferences, group conferences, and various
> circles that can be classified as peacemaking or restorative. Conferences
> and circles are meetings of the parties that were involved in or impacted
> by the harmful actions. Participants include the victim(s) and the
> offender and a facilitator, but may also include other community
> members (e.g., witnesses, friends, family). The victim(s) could also
> include members of the school community who represent the school
> that was harmed by the perpetrator's actions (e.g., in the case of
> vandalism). Together, the conference participants aim to determine a
> reasonable restorative sanction for the offender. Restorative sanctions
> are sought out during these justice processes rather than employing
> traditional punitive sanctions like suspension. Restorative sanctions

could include such things as community service, restitution, apologies, or specific behavioral change agreements, such as the offender agreeing to comply with certain conditions, sometimes in exchange for incentives. (Stinchcomb, Bazemore, & Riestenberg, 2006, as cited in Fronius, et al.)

In their review, the researchers note that given the relative newness of restorative practices in schools, little research on their effectiveness currently exists. However, there are descriptive accounts that provide important illustrations of what is happening in schools and what kinds of support structures need to be in place. Positive outcomes the authors found throughout the literature include:

an improved school climate (Mirsky, 2007; Mirsky & Watchel, 2007). Other reports indicate that RJ has led to increased student connectedness, greater community and parent engagement, improved student academic achievement, and the offering of support to students from staff (González, 2012). In addition, several descriptive reports highlight decreases in discipline disparities, fighting, bullying, and suspensions as a result of an RJ program (e.g., Baker, 2009; Suvall, 2009; González, 2012; Armour, 2013).

As previously noted, restorative practices are not without critics. Implementation of restorative practices isn't necessarily easy. Programs can be expensive in terms of time, resources, and actual funds. Not all school personnel are adept at facilitating the kinds of dialogue and reconciliatory conversation required of restorative circles. And, these methods don't work well for everyone; there remain students who simply are too much of a danger to others to stay in school. And, implementation can be tricky because there is the possibility that in such situations, restorative methods attempting to change the behavior of the perpetrator can prolong the victim suffering rather than curtail it.

Safe and Responsive Schools (SRS)

Originally developed by researchers at Indiana University and the University of Nebraska—Lincoln in partnership with the U.S. Department of Education,[61] the SRS model is particularly concerned with preventing disciplinary issues at the far end of the misbehavior spectrum: school violence. As the model was conceived, researchers would serve as facilitators to help schools devise plans specific to individual contexts and concerns, using a multistep process. While the project has officially ended, school personnel still might consider employing the model to rethink and reconceptualize existing disciplinary practices. As is true for PBIS, proponents don't consider excluding students from schools an optimal situation. More specifically, the approach has four key goals:

- To ensure the safety of students and teachers.
- To create a climate conducive to learning.
- To teach students skills needed for successful interaction in school and society.
- To reduce rates of future misbehavior.[62]

This approach works to reconcile the real need for safety in schools with a need to help students learn ways to be in the world that don't depend on violent actions.

The process involves a comprehensive team of school personnel, parents and other stakeholders spending a year surveying and analyzing existing conditions and needs. Based on what is essentially a self-study process, the team then surveys best practice options related to concerns and finally lays plans for improved strategies in three areas: creating a positive climate, developing early identification and intervention, and designing effective responses. Following a year of implementation, evaluation of outcomes is used to suggest directions for the future.[63, 64] The clear advantage here is that action is targeted directly to local concerns and constraints.

Alternative Educational Settings

Sometimes, it appears that a school has no choice but to remove a student—or, a student is removed by the juvenile justice system. Over time—at least sixty years[65]—alternative schools have evolved to meet a wide variety of student needs that traditional schools were not meeting. Although alternative schools have been stereotyped as quasi-detention centers for "bad kids," that is often *not* the case. For example, schools like Alliance High School in Milwaukee and Harvey Milk High School in New York[66] provide LGBTQ students an opportunity to learn in an environment free of the typical kinds of bullying and harassment they might experience at a standard public high school. In such cases, the students most at risk of being on the receiving end of violence or of being totally alienated and unsuccessful in a traditional school can find a safe and comfortable haven in alternative schools designed to meet their specific needs.

That said, too often alternative schools *are* conceptualized as schools for "bad kids" and, when they are not carefully regulated, helped to feed the discriminatory school-to-prison pipeline.[67] Like many other well-intentioned strategies, much depends upon how a specific school operates—as a warehouse for students who administrators don't know what else to do with, or as a school dedicated to understanding students and helping them find a way to be successful in and after their school experience. Framing alternative school placements for at-risk learners as opportunities for success rather than as punishment is essential. In our suggestions for further reading, we suggest you take a close look at one successful alternative school (Dominus, 2016); the ways it differs from traditional schools in moving away from punishment and toward restorative practice is evident in great detail.

Choices for Educators

School regulation of student bodies is not limited to the instructional life of the classroom and the relationship between student and teacher. There is an institutional relationship as well. Bells order students to leave one place and go to another, no matter how engaged they may be with a particular problem or task, making them subvert their interests to the mania for order in the school. Rules insist they remain silent and walk in straight lines in hallways—a restriction unheard of in the everyday world outside. Dress codes and uniform policies insist on conformity to standards students usually had no part in formulating. Even which games may be played on the playground, or how loud an "outside voice" may be can be regulated. And in this environment, students are expected to grow into personally responsible human beings capable of living harmoniously in a multicultural world.

And, while many argue that such measures are enacted in the interest of safety and well-being for every member of the school community, not *every* member of every school experiences violation and retribution equally. Some students—sometimes females, sometimes males, and routinely those with special needs, those who don't happen to be White, those whose sexual identity causes others consternation—routinely suffer more, and greater, punishment for who they are and what they do.

Educators who entered professions intending to help *all* students succeed might do well to stop and take the pulse of their classrooms and schools. Potential educators might also consider what kind of future they envision for the many, unpredictable students who will be in their care. Will students emerge as productive citizens—or potential jailbirds? What teachers and schools choose to do in the name of order and discipline will do much to answer that question for countless students.

Things to Think About

1. Can you remember a time when you were outraged by what you thought was unfair punishment by a teacher or administrator? Explain your thinking at the time and speculate about the thinking of the person who was punishing you or someone else. Can you connect any of the mentioned frameworks with either your thinking or the punisher's thinking? What insights, if any, does this give you into your own assumptions about control and discipline?

2. The difficulty of creating disciplinary systems lies largely in the need to balance structures that will ensure safety and a good learning environment while simultaneously allowing for a healthy amount of student autonomy. If you were designing a disciplinary system, how much emphasis would you give to control, and how much to autonomy? Assign a percentage of importance and emphasis to each of these two critical factors. Would you make them even (50% control, 50% autonomy)? Or . . . ?

3. Dress codes are often defended on the grounds that individual eccentricities are distracting. Pat once had a teacher insist a student should not be allowed to have blue hair. The question Pat posed—and remains worth asking—is *who* is distracted by such a personal student choice? Is it distracting to other students—or to teachers, who may be uncomfortable

with a student who has obviously chosen to be different in some way? Is the problem the hair, or others' inability to control their attention?

4. What are three rules for student behavior or appearance that you think a school or classroom absolutely, positively must have? Compare your choices with those classmates or colleagues might, or do, make.

Things to Explore

Readings

Dominus, S. (2016, September 7). An effective but exhausting alternative to high-school suspensions. *New York Times*. Available from https://www.nytimes.com/2016/09/11/magazine/an-effective-ut-exhausting-alternative-to-high-school-suspensions.html?_r=0
This easy to read article illustrates how alternative schools—which are not so easy to implement—can provide a positive alternative to pushing students out of schools. The article details an alternative school in New York City that employs the restorative practices discussed in this chapter.

Gross, A. (2014, October 13). The zero-tolerance trap: How a policy meant to protect a school can ruin students' lives. *Slate*. Available from http://www.slate.com/blogs/xx_factor/2017/06/28/texas_republican_pete_olson_has_an_x_chromosome_but_can_t_get_pregnant.html
Another easy to read article telling the nearly unbelievable story of a zero-tolerance policy gone wrong.

National Association of School Psychologists (NASP). (2002). Fair and effective discipline for all students: Best practice strategies for educators. NASP Center. Available from http://www.naspcenter.org/factsheets/effdiscip_fs.html
This article provides a good summary of research-documented problems with zero tolerance and of positive strategies that serve all students well.

U.S. Department of Education. (2012). *Restraint and seclusion resource document*. Available from https://www2.ed.gov/policy/seclusion/restraints-and-seclusion-resources.pdf
This document both explains what the law requires in terms of honoring students' and parents' civil rights and offers practical guidance for districts and schools that want to devise effective and humane disciplinary policies.

Videos

Kids for Cash Scandal (A 20/20 Episode) (2009) (105 minutes) https://www
.youtube.com/watch?v=2zB8i6ftPU0&t=14s
*An overview of the scandal (in Pat's hometown) in which a highly respect-
ed judge was taking "finder's fees"—known in the justice system as "kickbacks"—for sending kids to juvenile detention systems for minor offenses;
a second judge also profited from the related closing of a public juvenile detention center. (In fairness, let it be said that many citizens still believe the
judges genuinely believed they were doing the right thing and were not motivated by the money. You can decide what you think—reading more about
it if you like. An Internet search will readily turn up much information.)*
School to Prison Pipeline (2014) (45 minutes) https://www.youtube.com/
watch?v=4FCGUaOKRks
*A look at the issue, with various spokespeople—including activists, stu-
dents, researchers—commenting on the conflation of schools and prisons
and noting the profit motive for juvenile detention centers.*
Shame: A Documentary on School Dress Code (2015) (33 minutes) https://
www.youtube.com/watch?v=XDgAZO_5U_U
Written and produced by a high school filmmaker, Shame *documents the
dress code policy at the filmmaker's high school through interviews with
students and school personnel.*
The War on Kids (2009) (95 minutes) Available from many education libraries. Trailer available at: https://www.bing.com/search?q=the+war+on+kids
+trailer&form=IE10TR&src=IE10TR&pc=LNJB
*This powerful video details the many elements of schools that are deaden-
ing students' spirits and providing substantive support for the school-to-
prison pipeline. Especially interesting are (controversial) suggestions that
schools are complicit in the ADHD "epidemic" and that psychiatric drugs
may have played a role in several episodes of school violence.*

Websites

Dignity in Schools http://www.dignityinschools.org/
International Institute for Restorative Practices http://www.iirp.edu/

Notes

1. Tinker v. Des Moines Independent Community School District 393 U.S. 503 (1969).

2. U.S. Department of Education, National Center for Education Statistics. Retrieved from https://nces.ed.gov/fastfacts/display.asp?id=50

3. U.S. Department of Education, National Center for Education Statistics. (2016). *Indicators of school crime and safety: 2015* (NCES 2016-079), Indicator 20.

4. U.S. Department of Education, National Center for Education Statistics. Digest of Education Statistics. Table 233.50. Percentage of public schools with various safety and security measures. Selected years: 1999-2000 through 2013-14. Retrieved from https://nces.ed.gov/programs/digest/d15/tables/dt15_233.50.asp

5. National Association of Elementary School Principals. (2013, July 30). *National survey of school leaders reveals 2013 school uniform trends: Lands' End school uniform and NAESP partner to report the rise of school uniforms* [Press release]. Retrieved from http://www.naesp.org/national-survey-school-leaders-reveals-2013-school-uniform-trends

6. National Association of Elementary School Principals. (2013). The right fit: Principles on school uniforms. *Communicator, 36*(12). Retrieved from http://www.naesp.org/communicator-august-2013/right-fit-principals-school-uniforms

7. Zhou, L. (2015, October 20). The sexism of school dress codes. *The Atlantic.* Retrieved from https://www.theatlantic.com/education/archive/2015/10/school-dress-codes-are-problematic/410962/

8. ———. (2017). Controlling the student body. *Teaching Tolerance.* 55. Retrieved from http://www.tolerance.org/magazine/number-55-spring-2017/feature/controlling-student-body

9. Buford May, R. A. and Chaplain, K. S. (2008). Cracking the code: Race, class, and access to nightclubs in urban America. In Duneier, M., Kasinitz, P., and Murphy, A. (Eds.) 2014. *The urban ethnography reader.* New York: Oxford University Press.

10. Sher, M. (2014, May 26). About the student suspended for shaving her head to support her friend with cancer. *Huffington Post.* Retrieved from http://www.huffingtonpost.com/melissa-sher/about-the-student-suspended-for-shaving-her-head-to-support-her-friend-with-cancer_b_5036728.html

11. Neporent, L. (2014, March 31). Teen banned from track for socially conscious hairdo. *ABC News.* Retrieved from http://abcnews.go.com/Health/teen-banned-track-socially-conscious-hairdo/story?id=23129614

12. The Everyday Sexism Project, created by Laura Bates, is a place to record the stories of women and to chronicle and illustrate the sexism that happens everyday in everyday contexts. While some readers may find content offensive, the site nevertheless details how common and varied sexist events are. Scroll down to see stories at: http://everydaysexism.com/

13. Bates, L. (2015, May 22). How school dress codes shame girls and perpetuate rape culture. *TIME*. Retrieved from http://time.com/3892965/everyday-sexism-school-dress-codes-rape-culture/

14. Bates, L. (2015, May 22). How school dress codes shame girls and perpetuate rape culture. *TIME*. Retrieved from http://time.com/3892965/everyday-sexism-school-dress-codes-rape-culture/

15. Kosciw, J. G., Greytak, E. A., Giga, N. M., Villenas, C., & Danischewski, D. J. (2015). The 2015 national school climate survey. The experiences of lesbian, gay, bisexual, transgender, and queer youth in our nation's schools. GLSEN. Retrieved from https://www.glsen.org/sites/default/files/2015%20National%20GLSEN%202015%20National%20School%20Climate%20Survey%20%28NSCS%29%20%20Full%20Report_0.pdf

16. The "Youth & Students" issues page at the National Center for Transgender Equality can be found at http://www.transequality.org/issues/youth-students

17. Kohn, A. (2915, June 25). What's the real purpose for classroom management? Retrieved from http://www.alfiekohn.org/blogs/purposemanagement/

18. Dewey, J. (1938/2007). *Experience and education.* New York: Touchstone.

19. For more on what has become the movement for an alternative approach to discipline, see the websites at the end of this chapter and also: Curwin, R. W., Mendler, A. & Mendler, B. (2008). *Discipline with dignity: New challenges, new solutions.* Alexandria, VA: Association for Supervision & Curriculum Development.

20. For a truly fabulous story of students taking on responsibility for their own learning, see again Brian Schultz's narrative of a year in his fifth grade classroom in the Chicago Public Schools. Schultz, B. (2008). *Spectacular things happen along the way: Lessons from an urban classroom.* New York: Teachers College Press. For even more examples from more teachers, see his latest work, Schultz, B. (2017). *Teaching in the cracks: Openings and opportunities for student-centered, action-focused curriculum.* New York: Teachers College Press.

21. Reeve, J. (2009). Why teachers adopt a controlling motivating style toward students and how they can become more autonomy supportive. *Educational Psychologist, 44*(3), 159–175.

22. Anyon, J. (1980). Social class and the hidden curriculum of work. *Journal of Education, 62*(1), 67–92.

23. Willis, P. (1977). *Learning to labour: How working class kids get working class jobs.* Farnborough, England: Saxon House.

24. H.R.987—Gun-Free Schools Act of 1993. Retrieved from https://www.congress.gov/bill/103rd-congress/house-bill/987

25. Skiba, R. (2004). Zero tolerance: Assumptions and the facts. *Education Policy Briefs, 2*(1). Retrieved from http://files.eric.ed.gov/fulltext/ED488918.pdf

26. Skiba, R. J. and Keating, K. (2001). Zero tolerance, zero evidence: An analysis of school disciplinary policy. *New Directions in Youth Development*, 92, 17–43.

27. Whitehead, J. W. (2011, May 25). Zero tolerance schools discipline without wiggle room. *Huffington Post*. Retrieved from http://www.huffingtonpost.com/john-w-whitehead/zero-tolerance-policies-schools_b_819594.html

28. Sickmund, M. and Puzzanchera, C. (Eds.). (2014). *Juvenile offenders and victims: 2014 national report*. Pittsburgh, PA: National Center for Juvenile Justice. Retrieved from http://www.ncjj.org/

29. Heitzen, N. (2014). Criminalizing education: Zero tolerance policies, police in the hallways, and the school to prison pipeline. In Nocella II, A. J., Parmar, P. & Stovall, D. (Eds.). *From education to incarceration: Dismantling the school-to-prison pipeline*. New York: Peter Lang.

30. Heitzen, N. (2014). Criminalizing education: Zero tolerance policies, police in the hallways, and the school to prison pipeline. In Nocella II, A. J., Parmar, P. & Stovall, D. (Eds.). *From education to incarceration: Dismantling the school-to-prison pipeline*. New York: Peter Lang.

31. Juvonen, J. (2001). *School violence: Prevalence, fears, and prevention*. Santa Monica, CA: The RAND Corporation. Retrieved from https://www.rand.org/pubs/issue_papers/IP219/index2.html#2

32. Lyons, L. (2002, September 17). Parents concerned about school safety. Retrieved October 5 from http://news.gallup.com/poll/6808/parents-concerned-about-school-safety.aspx

33. Gaughan, E., J. D. Cerio, and R. A. Myers. (2001). *Lethal violence in schools: A national study, final report*. New York: Alfred University.

34. Skiba, R., Reynolds, C. R., Graham, S., Sheras, P., Close Conoley, J., and Garcia-Vazquez, E. (2006). *Are zero tolerance policies effective in the schools? An evidentiary review and recommendations*. A Report by the American Psychological Association Zero Tolerance Task Force. Retrieved from https://www.apa.org/pubs/info/reports/zero-tolerance-report.pdf

35. Losen, D. J. and Skiba, R. (2010). *Suspended education: Urban middle schools in crisis*. Southern Poverty Law Center. Retrieved from https://www.civilrightsproject.ucla.edu/research/k-12-education/school-discipline/suspended-education-urban-middle-schools-in-crisis/Suspended-Education_FINAL-2.pdf

36. Heitzen, N. (2014). Criminalizing education: Zero tolerance policies, police in the hallways, and the school to prison pipeline. In Nocella II, A. J., Parmar, P. & Stovall, D. (Eds.). *From education to incarceration: Dismantling the school-to-prison pipeline*. New York: Peter Lang.

37. Fine, M. and Smith, K. (2001). Zero tolerance: Reflections on a failed policy that won't die. In Ayers, W., Dohrn, B., & Ayers, R. (Eds). *Zero Tolerance: Resisting the drive for punishment in schools*. New York: Free Press.

38. Green, E. (2017, June 16). Education dept. says it will scale back civil rights investigations. *New York Times*. Retrieved from https://www.nytimes .com/2017/06/16/us/politics/education-department-civil-rights-betsy-devos .html?smprod=nytcore-ipad&smid=nytcore-ipad-share&_r=0

39. Chicago Public Schools (2016, September 16). *CPS Suspension and Expulsion Rates Reach Record Low* [Press release]. Retrieved from http://cps.edu/News/Press_ releases/Pages/PR1_09_22_2016.aspx

40. City of New York. (2016, July 21). *De Blasio administration announces new school climate initiatives to make NYC schools safer, fairer and more transparent* [Press release]. Retrieved from http://www1.nyc.gov/office-of-the-mayor/news/628-16/ de-blasio-administration-new-school-climate-initiatives-make-nyc-schools-safer-fairer

41. Sperry, P. (2015, March 24). How liberal discipline policies are making schools less safe. *New York Post*. Retrieved from http://nypost.com/2015/03/14/politicians-are-making-schools-less-safe-and-ruining-education-for-everyone/

42. Urbina, I. and Hamill, S. D. (2009, February 12). Judges plead guilty in scheme to jail youths for profit. *The New York Times*. Retrieved from http://www.nytimes .com/2009/02/13/us/13judge.html

43. If you have not experienced a public school building that is dirty, in significant disrepair, or physically unsafe, see Jonathan Kozol's body of work (in particular, *Savage Inequalities* [1991, Harper] and *Shame of the Nation* [2006, Broadway Books]). For a story of how elementary children in a school building that was dirty, in significant disrepair, and physically unsafe took things into their own hands to change that, see Brian D. Schultz's *Spectacular Things Happen Along the Way* (2008, Teachers College Press).

44. Giroux, H. (2010). Governing through crime and the pedagogy of punishment. In Saltman, K. and Gabbard, D. (2011). *Education as enforcement: The militarization and corporatization of schools*. New York: Routledge.

45. Giroux, H. (2011). *Zombie politics and culture in the age of casino capitalism*. New York: Peter Lang.

46. Campbell, A. (2012, April 17). Police handcuff 6-year-old student in Georgia. *CNN*. Retrieved from http://www.cnn.com/2012/04/17/justice/georgia-student-handcuffed/index.html

47. Dakss, B. (2005, April 25). Handcuffed 5-year-old sparks suit. *CBS News*. Retrieved from http://www.cbsnews.com/news/handcuffed-5-year-old-sparks-suit/

48. Nolan, K. (2011). *Police in the hallways: Discipline in an urban high school*. Minneapolis: University of Minnesota Press.

49. Nolan, K. (2011). *Police in the hallways: Discipline in an urban high school*. Minneapolis: University of Minnesota Press.

50. Nolan, K. (2014). Instituting the culture of control: Disciplinary practices and order maintenance. In Duneier, M., Kasinitz, P., and Murphy, A. (Eds.). *The urban ethnography reader*. New York: Oxford University Press.

51. Laura, C. (2014). *Being bad: My baby brother and the school-to-prison-pipeline.* New York: Teachers College Press.

52. Nolan, K. (2011). *Police in the hallways: Discipline in an urban high school.* Minneapolis: University of Minnesota Press.

53. Freire, P. (2000). *Pedagogy of the oppressed* (30ᵗʰ anniversary edition). New York: Continuum.

54. Vogell, H. (2014, June 19). Violent and legal: The shocking ways school kids are being pinned down, isolated against their will. *ProPublica.* Retrieved from https://www.propublica.org/article/schools-restraints-seclusions

55. Whitford, D. K., Katsiyannis, A., and Counts, J. (2016). Discriminatory discipline: Trends and issues. *NASSP Bulletin, 100*(2). Doi: 10.1177/0192636516677340

56. Vogell, H. (2014, June 19). Violent and legal: The shocking ways school kids are being pinned down, isolated against their will. *ProPublica.* Retrieved from https://www.propublica.org/article/schools-restraints-seclusions

57. Universal Class. (n.d.) Types of classroom management: Assertive discipline. Retrieved from https://www.universalclass.com/articles/self-help/types-of-classroom-management-assertive-discipline.htm

58. Universal Class. (n.d.) Types of classroom management: Assertive discipline. Retrieved from https://www.universalclass.com/articles/self-help/types-of-classroom-management-assertive-discipline.htm

59. OSEP Technical Assistance Center on Positive Behavioral Interventions and Supports (2017). Positive behavioral interventions & supports [Website]. Retrieved from www.pbis.org.

60. Fronius, T., Persson, H., Guckenberg, S., Hurley, N., and Petrosino, A. (2016). *Restorative justice in U. S. schools: A research review.* San Francisco: WestEd Justice & Prevention Research Center.

61. Skiba, R., Ritter, S., Simmons, A. Peterson, R. and Miller, C. (2005). The safe and responsive schools project: A school reform model for implementing best practices in violence prevention. Retrieved from http://www.indiana.edu/~equity/docs/A_School_Reform_Model.pdf

62. Skiba, R. and Karega Rausch, M. (2006). School disciplinary systems: Alternatives to suspension and expulsion. In Bear, G. G. & Minke, K.M. (Eds.). *Children's needs III.* Bethesda, MD: National Association of School Psychologists.

63. See http://www.indiana.edu/~equityiu/previous-projects/

64. Skiba, R. and Karega Rausch, M. (2006). School disciplinary systems: Alternatives to suspension and expulsion. In Bear, G. G. & Minke, K.M. (Eds.). *Children's needs III.* Bethesda, MD: National Association of School Psychologists.

65. For more information about alternative educational placements and dropout prevention in general, see The National Dropout Prevention Center/Network at Clemson University here www.dropoutprevention.org

66. Calefati, J. (2015, June 10). Gay high schools offer a haven from bullies. *U. S. News & World Report*. Retrieved from https://www.usnews.com/education/articles/2008/12/31/gay-high-schools-offer-a-haven-from-bullies

67. Vanderhaar, J. Ed., Petrosko, J. M., & Muñoz, M. A. (2013). Reconsidering the alternatives: The relationship between suspension, subsequent juvenile detention, and the salience of race. The Civil Rights Project. Retrieved from https://civilrightsproject.ucla.edu/resources/projects/center-for-civil-rights-remedies/school-to-prison-folder/state-reports/copy4_of_dignity-disparity-and-desistance-effective-restorative-justice-strategies-to-plug-the-201cschool-to-prison-pipeline

SIX

Ꮼ Reform? By Whom and for What?

It is well-known what strange work there has been in the world under the name and pretense of reformation; how often it has turned out to be, in reality, deformation; or at best, a tinkering sort of business, where while one hole has been mended two have been made.

—*George Horne, attributed*, Day's Collacon

IN 1983, A REPORT COMMISSIONED by then President Ronald Reagan pronounced that failing public schools were threatening the future of the United States as a cultural and economic power. To make clear the extent of the danger, the document used the most alarmist language possible, beginning with its title—*A Nation at Risk*. The first paragraph previews the doom and gloom permeating the full report:

> Our Nation is at risk. Our once unchallenged preeminence in commerce, industry, science, and technological innovation is being overtaken by competitors throughout the world. This report is concerned with only one of the many causes and dimensions of the problem, but it is the one that undergirds American prosperity, security, and civility. We report to the American people that while we can take justifiable pride in what our schools and colleges have historically accomplished and contributed to the United States and the well-being of its people, the educational foundations of our society are presently being eroded by a rising tide of mediocrity that threatens our very future as a Nation and a people.[1]

"A rising tide of mediocrity that threatens our very future"! Oh, dear. Sounds pretty serious. But just to be sure that readers got the point, this: "If an unfriendly foreign power had attempted to impose on America the mediocre educational performance that exists today, we might well have viewed it as an act of war."

"An act of war." Oh, my.

As surely intended, the report's extreme language grabbed national attention as countless news stories headlined such quotes. And, the media continued to produce similar stories pronouncing schools failing on each anniversary of the original report—at five years, ten years, fifteen, twenty, twenty-five and thirty, over and over and over. So, for decades we've had a Greek chorus of reporters, politicians, legislators, business leaders and other commentators constantly trumpeting that American schools are failing and the nation is suffering because of it. This 2013 quote from a Chamber of Commerce blog post (titled "A Nation Still at Risk") marking the thirtieth anniversary of the 1983 report is typical:

> [T]he educational statistics are sobering, to say the least. . . . [T]wo-thirds of fourth and eighth-graders are still unable to read at grade level, 30% of U.S. students fail to graduate high school in four years, and the dropout rate is nearly 50% for African-Americans and Hispanics. Once first in the world, America now ranks 10th in the percentage of young adults with a college degree. Students in other countries like South Korea, Finland, Poland, Singapore, and Australia are continuing to outperform our students on international tests.[2]

Not surprisingly, given such rhetoric, those three decades also saw wave after wave of school reform.

We've had: new state standards and new state testing; the No Child Left Behind mandate to attain 100% student proficiency in math and reading—even for students with little proficiency in English and even for students with learning disabilities; fiscal and other punishments when schools failed to attain high enough proficiency, or to maintain a safe enough school, or to graduate enough students, or even to have a high enough attendance rate; mandated tutoring draining funds from Title I grants, which support low-income children; mass firings of school staff in schools rated as failing; non-profit and for-profit charter schools established specifically to compete with traditional public schools; concerted efforts to impose the equivalence of national standards, known as Common Core; and new accountability measures for teachers, including an insistence that students' standardized test scores serve as the basis for teachers' performance assessment.

All of that (and more) . . . and thirty years later, we appear to be in the same fix, and so: still more must be done.

Or must it? Are schools as bad as they are regularly pronounced to be? Does school reform remain an urgent priority three decades after schools were first pronounced failing? If not, why not? If so, what kind of reform is necessary or desirable? And how might different types of reforms confer different types of benefits on various sectors—say, on students as opposed to entrepreneurs or moguls?

In part because of the endlessly repeating rhetoric of failure, school reform is an area where unexamined assumptions abound. The following are some of the most widespread, which—however ingrained they may have become in public thinking—nevertheless are open to extended questioning. A popular maxim is appropriate here: "If it ain't broke, don't fix it." But if there is a problem to be fixed, the surest way to go astray is to misdiagnose the root cause. So let's look more closely at both assumptions and evidence to see what kinds of choices for educators they may suggest.

Assumptions about Reform

Public schools are failing.

To begin with the most widely accepted assumption: what evidence suggests that public schools are failing? Critics frequently cite statistics, especially student scores on national and international standardized tests. These, from an article on the Pew Research Center site,[3] are typical (as is its title, "U.S. Students' Academic Achievement Still Lags That of Their Peers in Many Other Countries"):

- The 2015 Programme for International Student Assessment (PISA) test, "placed the U.S. an unimpressive 38th out of 71 countries in math and 24th in science."
- "Among the 35 members of the Organization for Economic Cooperation and Development . . . the U.S. ranked 30th in math and 19th in science."

- The 2015 U.S. National Assessment of Educational Progress (NAEP) "rated 40% of fourth-graders, 33% of eighth-graders and 25% of twelfth-graders as 'proficient' or 'advanced' in math."

The researcher who wrote this observed that few people were likely to be surprised by such findings, noting that another 2015 Pew Research Center report found that only 29% of Americans considered K-12 education in science, technology and engineering as above average or the best in the world.

Others find (or project) many other statistics to fault U.S. public schools. In 2013, CNBC reported that only a quarter of high schools students who took the ACT college readiness tests had adequate reading, math, English and science skills necessary for success in either college or a career.[4] And, a report from the organization Education Reform Now contends that "Hundreds of thousands of American families across *all income levels* are spending billions each year in extra college costs because our high schools are graduating too many students unprepared for college" (p. 2).[5] According to the article, one in four high school graduates must pay an extra $3,000 and borrow nearly an extra $1,000 for remedial coursework, which does not count toward degree requirements. Still other reports blame schools for failing quiet students,[6] Black students,[7] Black and Latino males,[8] adolescents,[9] and students with disabilities[10]—and also, incidentally, for failing democracy.[11]

With such a persistent media drumbeat and so many ways for schools to *fail* or be *failing* in headlines, it is no surprise that so much of the American public accepts as a given that American schools are indeed failing—and probably failing most of the students, most of the time (or at least most of other people's children, most of the time).[12,13] If there are people who don't hold this assumption (which may seem hard to believe given the statistics so often cited), then why and how are their assumptions different?

First, many people well-versed in statistics argue that not all statistics are created equal or can be taken at face value. To borrow an illustration used by two noted educational psychologists angered by the way statistics are routinely cited as obviously damning: rather than looking at rank among countries that participate in international testing, we might do well to look at actual scores.[14] As an analogy: a runner who came in fourth in an Olympic race might have been tenths of a second behind the winner's best time. Such placement does not change the fact that the slower time was very near the best in the world and hardly indicates failure—but it could generate a headline like "No medal for U.S. runner—not even third."

In fact, statistics and headlines are so easily manipulated that Pat routinely had first-year college students master such manipulation by using an exercise like following:

> *Assume that there were four students in Group A who took a quiz, and four students in Group B who took the same quiz. The individual grades in Group A were 100, 100, 0 and 0. Those in Group B were 55, 45, 60 and 40. How many different statements (headlines) can you write about these numbers?*

If you think about it (and we hope you actually do), the following statements could each be truthfully, if misleadingly, written about the actual student performances: "Half of Group A earned a perfect score of 100, while no one in Group B earned more than 60." Pretty lousy performance for Group B, right? But wait: "The lowest score in Group B was 40 points higher than the lowest score in Group A." Well, go Group B! But then again: "The scores of both groups averaged only 50." Oh—so maybe the two groups' performance was comparable . . . and not very impressive. But look again at the numbers: clearly the two groups vary in stark ways, and therefore any effective effort to improve the average in both groups would likely have to be very different. A class in which half the class is doing excellent work and half the class failing work is a significantly different context than one in which all the class is hovering around a score of 50. Thoughtful teachers might look at the two groups and try to figure out why scores clustered at two extremes for one group while in the other scores huddled around a central point.

Although this is a simplistic example, the point should be clear (if you've actually been thinking about it). Much as Americans love numbers, statistics by themselves have no inherent meaning but instead must be interpreted by someone. People writing headlines and articles about statistics *assign* meaning to the numbers they choose to focus on. It's risky for a thoughtful person to accept assertions, especially assertions in attention-grabbing headlines based on statistics, without looking more closely at the raw data, whom it was gathered from, how it was gathered, how it was analyzed—and who is doing the interpreting. It's worth noting that good news headlines typically sell fewer newspapers than shocking and damning ones, and that people holding a stake of some kind in school reform can choose among data and headlines in their publications as well.

This point is made repeatedly by those who defend public schools from the kinds of statistical assaults so common in the media. The question of exactly *who* takes a particular test is critical. Without knowing something about test takers, we run the risk of making the proverbial error of comparing apples and oranges. In fact, that is one of the multiple problems with the statistics so often used to damn American schools. Many of the comparison countries have largely stable and homogeneous populations, and many also provide equitable learning conditions for all students. (We'll get to equity next.) In such countries, a random sampling of the student population may well provide a reasonably representative sampling of the population on the whole.

However, the United States tries to educate every student in an incredibly diverse population—those who speak little or no English, who come from a wide variety of socioeconomic backgrounds, who attend generously funded or woefully underfunded schools, who learn from highly experienced or uncertified teachers, and so on. American students taking some widely discussed standardized tests are randomly selected from the ethnically and linguistically diverse U.S. student population. Given the variety of students and schools, it is to be expected that some students will do very well and some not very well—and so the average of their scores may blur both ends of the spectrum, hiding how very good the good schools are and how awful the worst schools are. The situation is much like that of the two groups discussed earlier, where the average of students scoring 100 and 0 was the same as the average for students who all scored around the 50 mark

David Berliner, who has been studying the issue of educational outcomes and media representation for decades, made this point in relation to some 2012 exams:

[O]n the mathematics portion of the 2012 Programme for International Student Assessment (PISA) test, poor students (among those from lowest quartile in family income), who attended schools that served the poorest families (a school in the highest quartile of those receiving free and reduced lunch), attained a mean score of 425. But wealthy students (in the highest quartile of family income), who attended schools that served the wealthiest families (schools in the lowest quartile of students receiving free and reduced lunch), scored a mean of 528. That's a one-hundred point difference![15]

Not looking closely at the populations and scores that produced a ranking is a mistake akin to not checking to see how far behind the winner of an Olympic race one of the "losers" was. And, not considering how close the scores of our best schools may be to scores in countries with higher rankings obscures the fact that our best schools actually do very well.[16] The perception of a "rising tide of mediocrity" in U.S. schools so widely assumed is due at least in part to the misleading use of statistics based on averages in very different schools and among students with very different life and educational experiences.

In addition, the student population is unique in that it reflects this reality: the U.S. has a very large population of its children living in poverty—in fact, the Organization for Economic Cooperation and Development (OECD) reported that based primarily on 2013 statistics, the average percentage of poor children in OECD countries was about 13% while in the United States, it exceeded 20%.[17] Thirty-one countries had the average or a lower percentage, while only four countries[18] had higher rates than the United States. Finland, a country to which the United States is often disparagingly compared, had a child poverty rate of about 5–6%.

This matters, because poverty is known to have serious consequences for children's academic performance, as illustrated earlier in the Berliner quote. In another, much more detailed report on how poverty affects children's health and learning, Berliner includes that poor children often experience low birth weight; inadequate medical, dental and vision care; food insecurity; environmental pollutants like lead; family stress; and dangerous communities with few resources.[19] Several of these affect cognitive development and/or the ability to focus on school lessons. After all, who would be able to concentrate on diagramming sentences when suffering from both an intense toothache and gnawing hunger? The fact that one of every four or five children in the United States is poor has implications for schools that should not be ignored. And yet, despite the challenges of educating every child in a diverse population, American public schools also have much to be proud of—which does not mean they cannot do better.

In truth, there are areas where the numbers are hard to challenge. For example, achievement gaps for some groups (Black and Latino students, for example) are well documented,[20] and too many students earn diplomas without having mastered correct sentence structure and spelling, as well as basic arithmetic. But there are successes, too, and also, importantly, steady improvement:

> Critics are right that achievement scores aren't overwhelmingly impressive and that troubling gaps persist across racial, ethnic, and income groups. Yet scores are up over the past 40 years, and the greatest gains over that period have been made by Black and Hispanic students. They're right that the United States finishes well behind exam-oriented countries like Taiwan and Korea on international tests. But scores are roughly on par with countries like Norway, which was named by the United Nations the best place in the world to live; and students from low-poverty states like Massachusetts outscore most of their global peers. Critics are right that 40% of college students still don't graduate. But almost half of all American high school students now head off to college each year—an all-time high.[21]

So, the nation doesn't seem to actually be at risk from a citizenry of dullards, and there is little evidence to support the wholesale dismantling of public schools, as some interest groups promote. To say that public schools—virtually all public schools—are failing is simply not true. What is true, however, is that there are areas where schools need to do better, so that all students—no matter race, ethnicity, culture, socioeconomic background, first language or special needs—have a truly equitable opportunity to take advantage of a free, public education.

Exactly which strategies might effectively lead to such improvement and should therefore be included in or excluded from the school reform agenda is an incredibly complex question that cannot be adequately explored here. What we *can* manage in the confines of a single chapter in a single text, however, is to examine some of the assumptions around various reforms promoted in recent years.

More money will not improve the outcomes of schooling.

To understand the role of money in education, it's necessary first to understand how public schools are funded. To oversimplify the picture, a public school's budget depends heavily on property taxes in each district, which are supplemented primarily by state funds. The United States is highly socioeconomically segregated (how many millionaires or billionaires live down the block from public housing?), so that there simply is far less tax revenue in poor communities than in wealthy ones. As a result, and as Jonathan Kozol has demonstrated in his classic text *Savage Inequalities* and many books since, per pupil spending in one district is often far lower than in a much wealthier district a town or two over. For example, in 2016, NPR found that the Chicago Ridge School District in Illinois was able to spend $9,794 per student while less than an hour away in the well-to-do suburbs, Rondout District 72 was able to spend $28,639 per student.[22]

Such funding discrepancies produce real world effects. For example, parents in one poor school district in Texas filed a lawsuit over an elementary school, very near to some of the highest funded districts, which had many uncertified teachers, few books . . . and a third floor that had been condemned.[23] It seems simply ludicrous to argue that the things money definitely can buy—varied, current learning materials, certified teachers, buildings that don't pose health hazards, more nutritional food—are irrelevant to improving students' academic achievement. There is little doubt that yes, funding does affect achievement:

A 20% increase in per-pupil spending a year for poor children can lead to an additional year of completed education, 25% higher earnings, and a twenty-percentage point reduction in the incidence of poverty in adulthood, according to a paper from the National Bureau of Economic Research.[24]

In short, money matters. And still, the trend at the state level has been to reduce allocations to public schools.

One 2016 study found that thirty-one states allocated less money to their schools in 2014 than they had in 2008, and at least half of those states had cut support by more than 10%.[25] The report notes as well some of the ways in which funding shortfalls hamper school performance:

Many states and school districts have identified as a priority reforms that would prepare children better for the future, such as improving teacher quality, reducing class sizes, and increasing student learning time. Deep funding cuts hamper their ability to implement many of these reforms. For example, while the number of public K-12 teachers and other school workers has fallen by 297,000 since 2008, the number of students has risen by about 804,000. At a time when producing workers with high-level technical and analytical skills is increasingly important to a country's prosperity, large cuts in funding for basic education could cause lasting harm.

Without adequate funding, it is difficult for schools to attract the most effective teachers, provide the neediest students with adequate individual attention, and maintain even a safe, clean, dry and secure physical plant—much less an attractive and inviting environment.

Acknowledging that funds make a material difference in student experience and achievement and that per pupil spending is often inequitable, a small number of states have begun giving more money to poor schools and less to affluent schools. Unfortunately, as a Rutgers University project to track school funding fairness reported in 2017, many other states continue to fund all schools as if their local resources were the same. And, twenty-one states actually give *less* money to poor schools.[26] Funding per student (adjusted for regional variations) nationwide ranged from $5,838 per student to $18,165, so that some students were funded at more than three times the level of others. (Readers can see findings for their own states by exploring the School Funding Fairness website listed at the end of this chapter.) Complicating the issue is the fact that many states don't fund schools adequately to begin with: nearly every state in the nation has faced a lawsuit intended to force adequate funds from its coffers for schools.[27]

Money is indeed so large an issue that in many schools, shaming students whose parents owe the school lunch money has become a common—and incredibly wasteful—practice. Such policies have resulted from a recent Department of Agriculture requirement that schools have a written policy for children whose parents seem unable to provide lunch money. The Department suggests payment plans as an option, but many schools have implemented shaming instead—a practice the *New York Times* editorial board as well as many others considers "a national disgrace":

> The humiliation inflicted on children whose parents are late paying school lunch bills—or are too poor to pay them at all—is a national disgrace. Cafeteria workers berate the children for being unable to pay, rather than allowing them to eat, or stigmatize them by stamping their arms with messages like "I need lunch money."[28]

The editorial was written in response to an earlier article reporting that when a cashier found that a student had a balance from the prior year, her pizza, cucumber, apple and chocolate milk were thrown in the trash. Another elementary school substituted a sandwich consisting of white bread and a single slice of cheese for the hot lunch being served to other students.[29] And, as we were drafting this text in 2017, there was movement at the federal level to reduce nutritional requirements for school lunches—to help ease school budget issues.[30]

And yet, even with schools operating on tighter and tighter budgets, and with poor schools funded at a level so distant from those in wealthy communities, many argue vehemently against increased funding for public schools—on the grounds that additional funding has already been tried and found to fail. They insist that in fact school funding has increased substantively in recent history and that increases have not yielded improved school outcomes. A prominent and representative spokesperson, Bill Gates, laid out basics of the assumption that increasing heaps of money have actually been spent with no results. In a 2011 editorial for the *Washington Post*, he asserted that:

> For more than 30 years, spending has risen while performance stayed relatively flat. Now we need to raise performance without spending a lot more. . . . Perhaps the most expensive assumption embedded in school budgets—and one of the most unchallenged—is the view that reducing class size is the best way to improve student achievement. This belief has driven school budget increases for more than 50 years. U.S. schools have almost twice as many teachers per student as they did in 1960, yet achievement is roughly the same. . . . Compared with other countries, America has spent more and achieved less.[31]

While the assertion that outcomes haven't improved is commonplace, it is also simply untrue. As explained, the test averages used in international comparisons hide the achievements of our very best schools and do not reflect real gains made in narrowing the achievement gap for many student populations. In addition, the percentage of students attending college has nearly doubled over the last forty years.[32] And, Gates' teacher/pupil ratio figures don't account for the many new federal requirements imposed since 1960 that require an enormous amount of staffing, or for the fact that the student body grew by over 800,000 students between 2008 and 2016 alone.

The claim that the United States spends more than any other country is another that simply does not hold up. Refutation comes from data from the widely respected Organization for Economic Cooperation and Development (OECD):

> Based on 2012 data, the OECD shows that the United States has generous education budgets, spending about 50% more than the average OECD country. But relative to the nation's overall wealth, the United States was at the middle of the pack. Relative to the size of the economy or overall government spending, U.S. levels were within 1% of the OECD average. Additionally, the United States was not the top spender. Luxembourg, Switzerland and Norway each spent more per pupil than the United States. In the case of Luxembourg, about 66% more per secondary school student. And similar UN data puts the United States eighth among all countries, behind several other developed countries and Macau, a semi-autonomous city inside China. . . . In fact, the United States would have to increase per student spending about $8,000 per year just to match Luxembourg at the high school level. To spend quadruple what Luxembourgers do would require a $70,000 per student boost.[33]

So, no, the United States does not spend the most on education. In addition, much of the increase in budgets in recent decades has *not* been spent on instruction, which is the portion of school budgets directly linked to academic achievement.

Making this point—which remains true—over a decade ago, Richard Rothstein argued "[S]pending more hasn't failed. It hasn't been tried."[34]

Rothstein compiled an inventory of where school funding increases had gone in the nearly forty years since 1965. Nearly 30% had helped fund federal mandates for children with special needs based on new regulations. When Rothstein was putting together statistics, he found that school nutrition programs had consumed about 10% of increased costs. In 1965, school nutrition programs primarily sold milk and ice cream and were self-supporting. By 2002, 35% of students were receiving free or reduced-price meals. Indeed, government reports indicate that school meal program costs have risen from $225.8 million in 1960, to $565.5 million in 2002—and to over $6 *billion* in 2012, when it was serving over 50% of all students. By 2016, it had reached $11.6 billion.[35] While better nutrition contributes to more learning, it is misleading at best to suggest that the increased funds allocated to schools have been invested directly into instructional efforts to increase academic achievement.

Rothstein also points out that teacher salaries increased only some 1% over the years and still lagged far behind salaries in other professions, and that transportation costs as more and more students were bused to school also consumed more and more resources. Like many others before and since, Rothstein concluded:

> In sum, special education, smaller classes, school lunches, better teacher pay, more buses, and fewer dropouts account for over 80% of new education money since 1965. That these produced few academic gains is no surprise. It is to the credit of the public schools and the teaching profession that real gains have occurred at all.

Until significant funding increases are dedicated to areas directly related to overall academic achievement, the assumption that money is not the answer has little to prop it up. As Rothstein argues, since little money has not been dedicated directly to enhancing instruction, there is no evidence to support the argument that it can't help.

On the contrary, evidence that more money *will* help improve achievement is emerging. In 2016, a working paper from the National Bureau of Economic Research analyzed achievement in districts that had been forced to finance low-income schools more equitably.[36] In summarizing the outcome of their study, the researchers stated:

[T]he the test score gap has narrowed in states that implemented reforms but has been stable in states that did not. . . . Our estimates imply that additional funding distributed through court-mandated changes in finance formulas is highly productive in low-income school districts.

In fact, additional funding for the poorest scores where achievement gaps are most common may well make good sense.

But unfortunately, rather than actually funding poor schools more adequately and monitoring results, recent reforms have done just the opposite. They have drained money from already underfunded public schools based on another assumption that lacks credible evidence: the most effective route to improving school performance is competition, via school choice.

School choice is an effective route out of failing schools.

With the public largely convinced that public schools are generally failing, and with documentation that some groups of students routinely fare far worse in schools than others, many reform proponents have vigorously promoted school choice as a logical solution to the problem of poor achievement. Their argument is that parents should be allowed to move children out of low-quality schools into more successful ones—a practice not permissible (without cost) under the ubiquitous policy of assigning children to "neighborhood" schools. Assigning schools by street address (often described as "Buy a house, buy a school") has most often kept poor children in poor neighborhoods in chronically underfunded and underperforming schools. Thus, according to this argument, allowing parents to choose schools will enable them to rescue their children from failing schools. A corollary argument holds that if parents have choices and can move children to new schools, then failing schools *must* improve—or else close, if they lose a critical mass of students. Underlying these arguments is the marketplace faith in competition as the key to correcting all failures, including what has increasingly been labeled the failure of a "government monopoly" on education, which has allowed mediocrity and failure to flourish.

Stripped down to essentials, then, the rationale for school choice is based on two key assumptions: choice will allow parents to improve their children's education by moving students from failing schools to successful schools, and competition will force failing public schools to do better. Unfortunately, neither of these assumptions has proven to be reliable. First, experience indicates that choice does not guarantee better outcomes for students, both because it is often illusory and because outcomes are often worse in the newly chosen schools than they were in the original schools. And second, because choice drains funds from already struggling, underfunded public schools, it amounts to asking underperforming schools to do more with less—an improbable approach to school improvement. Each of these points deserves a closer look.

Simply having a school choice system does not guarantee better student outcomes. Prerequisites necessary for the choice strategy to work as promised include parents and students having the information they need to choose wisely and students being able to meet admission standards where they exist; in addition, there must be capacity in high-performing schools to allow for expansion of the student body. Unfortunately, more than one of these enabling factors are often absent in practice.

For example, New York City has a school choice system for its high schools, but students must compete for spaces in the top performing schools. Not only do students in poor neighborhood schools often lack good information on how to select a good school, but they also often have not been academically prepared for admission tests and standards.[37] In a 2017 *New York Times* article detailing the city's system, reporters aptly characterize outcomes as "broken promises." The handicaps they report students experiencing are typical in choice systems:

> Fourteen years into the system, black and Hispanic students are just as isolated in segregated high schools as they are in elementary schools—a situation that school choice was supposed to ease.
>
> Within the system, there is a hierarchy of schools, each with different admissions requirements—a one-day high-stakes test, auditions, open houses. And getting into the best schools, where almost all students graduate and are ready to attend college, often requires top scores on the state's annual math and English tests and a high grade point average.
>
> Those admitted to these most successful schools remain disproportionately middle class and White or Asian, according to an in-depth

analysis of acceptance data and graduation rates conducted for the *New York Times* by Measure of America, an arm of the Social Science Research Council. At the same time, low-income black or Hispanic . . . are routinely shunted into schools with graduation rates twenty or more percentage points lower.

While top middle schools in a handful of districts groom children for competitive high schools that send graduates to the Ivy League, most middle schools, especially in the Bronx, funnel children to high schools that do not prepare them for college. . . .

Ultimately, there just are not enough good schools to go around. And so it is a system in which some children win and others lose because of factors beyond their control—like where they live and how much money their families have.

And even if there were enough good schools, the application process is so complex that even affluent parents need highly paid consultants to navigate it and make good choices. And one more *even if*: even if a child qualifies for a good school that parents manage to identify, a required commute of hours on public transportation places many schools literally beyond reach.

When so many theoretical options remain just that in practice—theoretical—parents and students often really have little or no choice at all. And sadly, even when parents do manage to move their children to a school they think desirable, too often outcomes prove no better than, and sometimes even worse than, those in the schools the children left.

Evidence has been steadily accruing to indicate that not only do better outcomes often fail to materialize, but the school of choice can actually lead to *worse* outcomes. Detailed studies on voucher systems in Ohio, Indiana, and Louisiana all showed that student achievement dropped below levels in the schools students chose to leave.

[In late 2015, researchers] examined an Indiana voucher program that had quickly grown to serve tens of thousands of students. . . . "In mathematics," they found, "voucher students who transfer to private schools experienced significant losses in achievement." They also saw no improvement in reading.

The next results came a few months later . . . when researchers published a major study of Louisiana's voucher program. Students in the program were predominantly black and from low-income families, and they came from public schools that had received poor ratings from the state department of education, based on test scores. . . . [The researchers] found large negative results in both reading and math. Public elementary school students who started at the 50th percentile in math and then used a voucher to transfer to a private school dropped to the 26th percentile in a single year. Results were somewhat better in the second year, but were still well below the starting point.

[A] third voucher study was released by the Thomas B. Fordham Institute, a conservative think tank and proponent of school choice. The study, which was financed by the pro-voucher Walton Family Foundation, focused on a large voucher program in Ohio. "Students who use vouchers to attend private schools have fared worse academically compared to their closely matched peers attending public schools," the researchers found. Once again, results were worse in math.[38]

In addition to these discouraging results from the three states, a report on the federal government's private school voucher program in Washington, DC also reported a statistically significant negative impact on math achievement for some 1,100 students in the capital.[39] Reading scores were also lower, though not at a statistically significant level. For a variety of reasons, and in a variety of locales, it's increasingly evident that simply allowing students to leave one school for another is not the panacea many originally thought.

Perhaps this is not surprising, considering that the theoretical foundation for this reform comes not from educational theory but from market theory—where choice and competition are sacred principles. In addition, at this point it's clear that many choice proponents, including parents already paying tuition for religious and other private schools, were led to support choice not out of concern for equitable opportunity for all students but rather for their own benefit. For example, many parents saw vouchers or voucherlike systems as an opportunity to have taxpayers subsidize the tuition they were already paying to private schools. Others also anticipated financial gain from a choice system, a point we'll consider in the next section. However, if the point of school choice for many people was not truly to improve student outcomes, perhaps it is not surprising that better outcomes have largely failed to materialize.

It is unrealistic to expect failing schools to do better with fewer resources to fund improvements. When students choose to leave a school, the tax dollars allocated to educating them go along too—sometimes to a traditional school in either the same or a different district, sometimes to public charter schools, sometimes to private schools. Obviously, the schools that students leave subsequently have less money to use toward improvements like attracting more certified teachers or providing updated curricular materials and technologies. Choice proponents argue that when the student leaves, the school's cost decreases so that there is no net loss. But, finances are not so simple. Carol Burris, an award winning high school principal, explains:

> Schools have "stranded costs." When a public school loses a percentage of students to charter schools or a voucher program, the school can't reduce costs by an equivalent percent. The school still must pay the same utility, maintenance, transportation, and food services costs. The school must still carry the salary and benefit costs of administrative staff, custodial services, and cafeteria workers. The school may not be able to reduce teaching staff because the attrition will occur randomly across various grade levels, leaving class sizes only marginally reduced.
>
> Students aren't a "one-off" expense. The cost to educate each individual student varies a lot. Students with disabilities or who don't speak English as their first language often cost significantly more to educate. So as a school loses students, it may often find itself left with a larger percentage of its highest-cost students.
>
> When schools lose students, they have to cut services. Because schools can't reduce expenses incrementally, they cut support staff—such as a reading specialist or librarian—and courses—such as art and music— that engage the diverse needs and interests of students.[40]

Hence, the idea that losing students can and will force schools to improve seems . . . well, the kindest adjective we can find is *unrealistic*.

Business can manage schools better.

Early on, when the rationale for school choice was to rescue students from failing schools, states began creating charter schools—new schools created in a district, often by its experienced teachers, intended to allow talented educators to escape from bureaucratic straitjackets and to design and create new, more effective schools. The idea was that innovative and successful charter schools could then provide templates for improvements system-wide. Money followed students, but remained in the district. Many such district charter schools operate successfully today. Over time, however, both the options under the school choice umbrella and the rationale for creating them have morphed, so that it can be difficult to link today's options and arguments with the original charter school design and rationale.

Because the idea of introducing choice into public schools is based on economic rather than educational theory ("competition is the answer"), it's not surprising that the school choice system that has evolved centers largely on economics; today, many charters are run not by districts but by entrepreneurs. The (unfounded) argument that giving schools more money has not improved outcomes has led to the idea that the failures of public schools stem, at least in part, from inefficient management. The vocal critics of public schools have charged teachers and administrators with squandering resources and argued that business, purportedly with much greater management expertise, could and should play an important role in improving public education. Ohio Governor John Kasich, for example, has called for both new and experienced teachers to get some "on-site work experience with a local business or chamber of commerce," since he seems to believe business has critical insights into education that education professionals lack.[41] Faith in the ability of the private sector to do everything better than the public sector—from running golf courses to running schools—has led most states to welcome business into the educational arena either to manage public charter schools or to assume responsibility for their entire operation. As a result, many "public" schools are now in private hands.

What few people realize is that many of the earliest choice proponents, as well as many current proponents (including the Koch and Walton families) are millionaires and billionaires who for decades have been working to privatize public education not out of concern for students in struggling schools, but to reap the profit to be made on the billions of tax dollars supporting public schools.[42] Nearly twenty years ago, one writer noted:

> Education in the United States is undergoing a rapid and dramatic series of changes caused by private enterprise moving into the field.
>
> Education attracts the private sector for three reasons. First, it can be financially rewarding: Education is estimated to be a $600 billion market, more than the budget for the Department of Defense. The biggest single market is kindergarten through twelfth grade (K-12), valued at $310 billion in 1998.[43]

Business has long had its eye on securing a piece of this "market." And, by 2016, over $3 billion of federal tax dollars had streamed into charter schools, supplemented by state tax revenues, much of it with little oversight or regulation.[44] Recent developments include the shifting of education from brick-and-mortar schools to completely online environments, serving children in grades K-12.

Right now, the windfall long anticipated by enterprising entrepreneurs is being realized. In analyzing business strategies common in for-profit charter school operations, two prominent researchers found that:

1. A substantial share of public expenditure intended for the delivery of direct educational services to children is being extracted inadvertently or intentionally for personal or business financial gain, creating substantial inefficiencies;
2. Public assets are being unnecessarily transferred to private hands, at public expense, risking the future provision of "public" education;
3. Charter school operators are growing highly endogenous, self-serving private entities built on funds derived from lucrative management fees and rent extraction, which further compromise the future provision of "public" education; and
4. Current disclosure requirements make it unlikely that any related legal violations, ethical concerns, or merely bad policies and practices [will be] realized until clever investigative reporting, whistleblowers or litigation brings them to light.[45]

It is clear that as education has been increasingly cast as a product rather than as a public good, focus has shifted from student welfare to corporate welfare, spawning rampant, often outrageous, abuse of taxpayer dollars flowing into for-profit "public" schools and school management organizations.[46] For example, the billionaire Turkish owner of Gulen Management, which operates 140 charter schools in 26 states, is under investigation by the FBI "for everything from fraud and malpractice, to misuse of public funds"; in addition, he may be using American taxpayer dollars for education to support his controversial political activities in Turkey.[47]

Pursuing profit appears incompatible with the goal of better educational outcomes. Business management's expertise is, after all, in maximizing profit by streamlining processes and cutting staffing to skeletal levels. In part, the drive for "efficiency" explains why outcomes for students are so often disappointing when students change schools, as even industry representatives have admitted. As one leader of a pro-charter advocacy organization has observed, "You can't make a profit and get good results . . . any dollar converted from being used inefficiently in an inner-city charter school is needed in the school."[48] With profits draining support for instruction, there is little reason to expect improved outcomes.

Perhaps in light of this fact, as business has increasingly infiltrated public schools, the original rationale of choice as a way to improve student outcomes has largely given way to rhetoric promoting choice as a consumer right. For example, in a 2017 speech at the Brookings Institution, Secretary of Education Betsy DeVos suggested that parents have the right to choose a school just as they have a right to choose among a taxi, Uber or Lyft to get somewhere.[49] Outcomes don't seem to enter the picture. This is choice for its own sake, a "consumer right," rather than for the sake of students disadvantaged by being stalled in poor schools.

A complete inventory of issues surrounding the privatization of public education is beyond the scope of this text. But readers should be aware the issues are many, and the Internet can readily provide full detail on all of them. The key point here is simply that when the goal of choice schools is profit rather than performance, improvements for students are unlikely to be forthcoming.

This is decidedly *not* to say that charter schools in general have no promise. In fact, recent research has suggested that the charter school idea may well have merit. However, the specific structure of the charter matters. There is growing evidence that charters do best at improving student performance when they are in public, rather than private, hands. As one *New York Times* reporter summarized after surveying recent research: "[T]he best charters tend to be nonprofit public schools, open to all and accountable to public authorities. The less 'private' that school choice programs are, the better they seem to work."[50]

Evidence to date thus reinforces the reality that there is a difference between a public good and a taxi service. As a result, benefits that a choice system may bring to students are far more likely to be realized when public schools are shielded from the profit motive driving business.

Standardized testing will force improvement.

In Chapter 1, we detailed many of the problems with using standardized tests to assess student achievement, schools and teachers. We won't detail again criticisms we discussed there, which included: narrowed curriculum; developmentally inappropriate tasks for younger and younger children; debilitating test anxiety for kids; unreliable scores; and unreliable teacher assessment. Then, too, there's the problem that the predicted improvements in student achievement have yet to appear. Beyond these issues, however, it may be useful to understand that this is another area where the profit motive may have edged out concern for student welfare.

First, the sheer number of tests students must take creates an enormous market for test producers: students in urban high schools typically take some 112 mandatory standardized tests between preschool and senior year.[51] A 2012 report from the Brookings Institution estimated that state spending on assessment ranges from about $13 to $105 per student; overall, states a few short years ago were spending more than $1.7 billion per year on assessments.[52,53] Defenders of all this standardized assessment point out that this figure represents only one quarter of 1% of education spending. However, when children are shamed by having their lunch thrown in the trash or by having their arms stamped with "I need lunch money" (as noted previously) because schools need every nickel they can get, it seems perverse to ignore the real costs of standardized testing. And, as the report notes, this estimate does not include costs for staff and teacher time associated with administering and sometimes even scoring the tests.[54]

Are the costs—the money, the preparation time, the administrative time, the narrowed curriculum, the unreliable results, the angst—worth it? The question merits some thought and some consideration of the contradictory evidence. Finland, for example, is frequently cited as having a superior educational system. What does it look like, and what role do tests play there?

> There are no mandated standardized tests in Finland, apart from one exam at the end of students' senior year in high school. There are no rankings, no comparisons or competition between students, schools, or regions. . . . The people in the government agencies running them, from national officials to local authorities, are educators, not business people, military leaders or career politicians.[55]

Given that mandatory standardized testing has failed to yield notable improvement in public education since the 2001 NCLB mandate, and given that other nations have realized excellence without it, there's an open question of whether corporate profit may be a major unacknowledged motive here, as it has been in the push for for-profit management of public schools.

Frameworks for Reform

There are countless think tanks and organizations of various kinds promoting their versions of school reform. However, generally they promote one of two distinct visions of what public education should do and be. Rather than providing a wide array of alternatives, the many organizations primarily echo the same arguments for one of those two visions, with the same strategies emerging in support of each. Political labels don't apply: both Republicans and Democrats have provided substantive support for the vision that might be called the corporate reform agenda. The alternative might be best named the progressive—or perhaps democratic—agenda.

At issue is whether education is a public good or a product for private consumption. The answer to that question has implications for school management. If it is a public good, then it likely should be run by professional educators who are public employees; if it is a product for private consumption, then it might logically be managed by educational entrepreneurs. No matter the specific organization setting forth the frameworks, the principles embedded in each side remain much the same. The following are representative organizations, and their assumptions are typical of the competing visions.

Corporate Reform: Education Reform Now

Many organizations supporting reform use language meant to suggest that their interest is genuinely in student welfare, with a profit motive rarely (if ever) being mentioned—outside business publications. No doubt some supporters of some corporate reform organizations *are* genuinely interested in student welfare. On the whole, however, corporate reform organizations often sound like progressives—in the sense that the term "progressive" usually signals a commitment to social justice—but they still lobby for favorite strategies of the corporate community.

This is the case for the advocacy organization Education Reform Now, which actually describes itself as "progressive."[56] In describing its goals, however, it includes "reorient[ing] education policy as a content as opposed to time or place based right for students and teachers" (code for moving instruction online), and "promote new methods of content delivery and tools of influence on teaching and learning" (more direct link to online instruction).[57] Embedded here are two assumptions common to a corporate orientation: technology can and should replace teachers, and education is a matter of "content delivery"—a product. Despite its self-professed progressive goals, the organization's rhetoric makes clear which vision of education it actually pursues. Its key principles are also aligned with principles and strategies that seem better suited to producing profit than to improving student performance:

- "Human capital" (a term directly from economic theory). Generally, the assumption is that traditional teacher education programs do a poor job of preparing teachers and therefore teacher preparation mechanisms and certification requirements should be loosened. This has opened the door to for-profit, non-university-related businesses providing "alternative certification" programs, to placing uncertified teachers in schools (as the Teach for America program does), and to allowing charter schools to run their own "training" programs (as the Aspire schools do, with support from the Bill & Melinda Gates Foundation). Each of these offers opportunity to cut costs for teacher preparation (and salaries for noncertified personnel), as teaching is increasingly presented as delivery of a product rather than a complex, interactive human process.

- "Consumer choice." The intent here is to "focus on systems that re-configure the notion of a traditional school district," including inter-district choice. Among other things, this principle supports the strategy of charter schools moving online and expanding the pool of potential students beyond district, as well as state boundaries.

- "Resource equity." The website is fairly vague on this point, although it cites the discrepancy in per pupil funding between New Jersey (where the cost of living is very high) and Tennessee (where the cost of living is very low), the same general point often cited by reformers on the other side of the theoretical fence. However, putting more money into underfunded schools doesn't appear to be the goal, since the organization notes that "There is a ceiling . . . on what can be achieved through traditional approaches to resource re-allocation." If "traditional" means more money to public schools, then perhaps the plan is for any additional funding to go somewhere else—likely a good bit of it to technological infrastructure for virtual schools.

- "Student motivation." The organization says it will study a variety of ways to engage students' interest in their education, such as "efforts to increase grit; [improve] extracurricular services; [and provide] new and more relevant curricula." No rationale is offered for why this particular organization is better positioned to work on the thorny issue of student motivation than professional educators and education researchers, or how—if instruction remains chained to standardized tests—better curricula are to be provided.

- "Fast track advancement." This is explained as an effort to do away with age-based education: "Tailored instruction to individual student needs can speed attainment, better align education with college and employer demands, and yield substantial savings." Such instruction includes "personalized learning, competency-based education, [and] direct assessment." Such plans are typically put into practice via technology: Prepackaged curricula include online assessments, allowing computers rather than teachers to decide when a student has mastered something and can move on. Moving instruction online eliminates the need to maintain costly physical plants or provide such services as transportation, and it usually leads to far fewer teaching staff as well. Where the accrued savings will go is not indicated.

These are common elements of the corporate reform agenda: de-professionalization of teaching; choice, including for-profit options; moving money out of public schools in local districts into new and sometimes far flung private enterprise; and reliance on technology to reduce the need for human staffing.[58]

We don't mean to suggest that everyone supporting these strategies does so with the intention of increasing profit to the corporate sector—although such profit is likely to accrue despite good intentions, as the funders of such organizations are well aware. As we pointed out in Chapter 2, there are many different conceptions of what schools should do and be. From this perspective, schools are primarily mechanisms to prepare workers who can support themselves by delivering the services business needs—a kind of win-win situation (except for the fact that an abundance of qualified labor generally results in lower wages). And, many people (including many educators and parents) do understand "learning" to involve "delivering" the "product" of knowledge to students. From that theoretical perspective, the corporate agenda makes sense, which helps explain the great inroads it has made into contemporary education reform. But the devil, as they say, is in the details, and the details of reform strategies that have been evolving based on this rationale add up to corporate profit, despite whatever some supporters may intend.

Progressive/democratic: Education Opportunity Network

The core assumptions that characterize the progressive or democratic perspective are in direct opposition to the corporate perspective. Most important, this vision holds that public schools exist to serve the public good.

Corollaries are that education therefore extends far beyond educating a citizenry in preparation for entry into the workforce, and often (if not always) that it is a process rather than a product. This difference is clear in the Education Opportunity Network's "Education Declaration to Rebuild America."[59]

- "All students have a right to learn." The first article of this declaration places students—especially students disadvantaged by socioeconomic status—front and center.
- "Public education is a public good." Specifically, the declaration rejects the "private control, deregulation and profiteering" that permeate efforts to transform education into a product.
- "Investments in education must be equitable and sufficient." This principle attends to necessary elements that money *can* buy—if it's provided: "safe buildings, quality teachers, reasonable class sizes, and early learning opportunities."
- "Learning must be engaging and relevant." The stress here is on "dynamic experience . . . [and] connections to real world problems and to students' own life experiences and cultural backgrounds." Here, education is not a product to be delivered, but an "experience"—one shaped to unique students and contexts, not a prepackaged set of lessons delivered technologically.
- "Teachers are professionals" (rather than human capital). This stance is in direct opposition to the deskilling and de-professionalization of teaching being pursued through alternative teacher education mechanisms and through shifting instruction from teachers to technology.
- "Discipline policies should keep students in schools." The school-to-prison pipeline discussed in Chapter 5 is familiar to many educators in public school classrooms. Again, student welfare is reinforced as a primary concern.
- "National responsibility should complement local control." While local control of education makes sense, students have "the civil right to a quality education." When state and local funding formulas instead instantiate cruel inequities, the federal government should enforce civil rights and ensure that no student is housed in a building where one entire floor stands condemned.

Here, a focus on student welfare is pervasive, and education is understood to be a process involving professionals tailoring experience to specific contexts and students—not a one-size-fits-all prepackaged curriculum.

Choices for Educators

Although we believe the binary visions outlined previously are real, we also are well aware that individuals vary and rarely endorse all of *one* agenda and nothing on the other. Purity is rarely to be found in the real world. Readers might consider sifting through the various assumptions presented here and clarifying what they do individually believe to put together their *own* vision for reform.

Choice is a good example, since how a particular charter school operates makes a great deal of difference. Someone who rejects a for-profit charter might still find that it might make sense for educators within a district to design a charter based on their extensive knowledge of students who aren't thriving in traditional schools. Or, someone who thinks frequent interaction with skilled professional educators is essential to the process of education might nevertheless see some areas where inescapable rote content (the times tables or spelling of homonyms) might indeed be handed off to high quality technological instruction.

When we authors were younger, our parents often cautioned against "throwing out the baby with the bath water"—being careful to dislike one part of something so much that we inadvertently throw out the whole package without thinking carefully about component parts. This is the task we see for readers here: considering which principles for reform they endorse, which they reject, and then identifying strategies in keeping with their commitments.

Things to Think About

1. Do you believe education is a consumer right or a public good? Why?
2. Do you believe education is the delivery of content or a process . . . or some of each? What examples from the classroom illustrate your reasoning? If both, what percentage do you think is product, what percentage is process? What examples from the classroom illustrate your reasoning?

3. What role, if any, do you believe for-profit business properly plays in public education? None? Some outsourced services, like food and bus transportation? Management? Ownership? Explain your thinking.

4. What role, if any, do you believe technology should play in education?

Things to Explore

Readings

Burris, C. (2017, May 3). Three big problems with school "choice" that supporters don't like to talk about. Blog post on *The Answer Sheet*, Valerie Strauss, *Washington Post*. Available from https://www.washingtonpost.com/news/answer-sheet/wp/2017/05/03/three-big-problems-with-school-choice-that-supporters-dont-like-to-talk-about/?utm_term=.3878ff1b3acd
The author has extensive experience as a principal and has been active in promoting democratic school reform. In this piece, she speaks from first-hand experience about that realities of school choice when it moves from the theoretical realm into the daily life of schools.

Kearney, P. J. (2017, April 18). There is no silver bullet for education reform. *Huffington Post*. Available from http://www.huffingtonpost.com/entry/there-is-no-silver-bullet_us_58f52a6be4b048372700daab?utm_hp_ref=education-reform
This teacher talks about being caught between defending public schools from attacks while simultaneously trying to pay attention to real problems that exist. His take on things is that complex problems require complex solutions, not a one-size-fits-all prescription.

Ravitch, D. (2014). Public education: Who are the corporate reformers? Moyers & Company (website). Available from http://billmoyers.com/2014/03/28/public-education-who-are-the-corporate-reformers/
Diane Ravitch is a former Secretary of Education who was once an ardent supporter of school choice. Having watched its evolution, however, she is now one of its strongest opponents. As the title indicates, in this article she presents a "who's who" among the big money backers of choice—especially for-profit choice.

Tierney, J. (2013, April 25). The coming revolution in public education reform. *The Atlantic*. Available from https://www.theatlantic.com/national/archive/2013/04/the-coming-revolution-in-public-education/275163/

Tierney details corporate initiatives and explains why he believes that will be effectively countered by growing resistance. The factors he discusses include the problems with over-emphasis on test scores, with trying to design a one-size-fits-all system, and ineptitude on the part of the companies taking control out of the classroom.

Videos

Democracy Now! *How a $100M Facebook donation for neoliberal school reform sparked a grassroots uprising in Newark.* (2015). (19 minutes) https://www.youtube.com/watch?v=uIy6aO7mTgA
What happened when a philanthropist turned millions of dollars over to politicians who support corporate reforms? This video traces events in Newark, New Jersey, which offer a case study of good intentions gone wrong. It also offers some insight into growing public resistance to this reform agenda.

PBS News Hour. *In the black community, a division over charter schools.* (2016). (8 minutes) https://www.youtube.com/watch?v=PyBUlSrIOh4
While many people are highly critical of charter schools, politicians aren't their only fans. Many parents have had positive experiences and resent efforts to limit their ability to choose schools for their children. This report helps illustrate the complexity of the charter school issue, including the fact that stakeholders from many different groups are at odds on the issue.

Websites

Center for Education Reform https://www.edreform.com
Education Opportunity Network http://educationopportuitynetwork.com
School Funding Fairness http://www.schoolfundingfairness.org

Notes

1. https://www2.ed.gov/pubs/NatAtRisk/risk.html
2. Oldham, C.A. (2013, April 24). A nation still at risk. Blog post. U.S. Chamber of Commerce Foundation. Retrieved from https://www.uschamberfoundation.org/blog/nation-still-risk

3. Desilver, D. (2017, February 15). U.S. students' academic achievement still lags that of their peers in many other countries. Pew Research Center. Retrieved from http://www.pewresearch.org/fact-tank/2017/02/15/u-s-students-internationally-math-science/

4. *CNBC*. (2013, August 21). Three-quarters of high school grads are failing. Retrieved from http://www.cnbc.com/id/100977170

5. Nguyen Barry, M. and Dannenberg, M. (2016). Out of pocket: The high cost of inadequate high schools and high school student achievement on college affordability. Education Reform Now. Retrieved from https://edreformnow.org/wp-content/uploads/2016/04/EdReformNow-O-O-P-Embargoed-Final.pdf

6. Dahl, M. (2016, March 18). How schools are failing their quietest students. *New York Magazine*. Retrieved from http://nymag.com/scienceofus/2016/03/how-schools-are-failing-their-quietest-students.html

7. Misra, T. (2015). New numbers show how America's schools are failing black students. *Fiscal Times*. Retrieved from http://www.thefiscaltimes.com/2015/10/10/New-Numbers-Show-How-Americas-Schools-Are-Failing-Black-Students

8. Mohl, B. (2015, April 7). Boston schools failing black and Latino males. *CommonWealth*. Retrieved from https://commonwealthmagazine.org/education/boston-schools-failing-black-and-latino-males/

9. Strauss, V. (2016, September 26). "Brain-hostile" education: How schools are failing adolescents. *Washington Post*. Retrieved from https://www.washingtonpost.com/news/answer-sheet/wp/2016/09/26/brain-hostile-education-how-schools-are-failing-adolescents/?utm_term=.b3df7873e147

10. Romero, G. (2015, June 9). Schools failing too many special education students. *Orange County Register*. Retrieved from http://www.ocregister.com/2015/06/09/schools-failing-too-many-special-education-students/

11. *Newsweek*. (2016, December 17). How US schools are failing democracy. Raw Story. Retrieved from http://www.rawstory.com/2016/12/how-us-schools-are-failing-democracy/

12. See Delpit, L. (2006). *Other people's children: Cultural conflict in the classroom*. New York: New Press.

13. Despite all the criticism, parents typically like the school their child is in but think all other schools are bad. One report found, for example, "Americans continue to believe their local schools are performing well, but that the nation's schools are performing poorly. More than three-quarters of public school parents (77%) give their child's school an 'A' or 'B,' while 18% of all Americans grade the nation's public schools that well." See: Lopez, S. J. (2010). Americans' views of public schools still far worse than parents'. Gallup. Retrieved from http://www.gallup.com/poll/142658/americans-views-public-schools-far-worse-parents.aspx

14. Berliner, D. C. and Biddle, B. M. (1999). The awful alliance of the media and public-school critics. *Education Digest*. Retrieved from ProQuest Social Sciences Premium Collection.

15. Berliner, D. C. (2017, March 2). The purported failure of America's schools, and ways to make them better. *Equity Alliance Blog.* Retrieved from http://www .niusileadscape.org/bl/the-purported-failure-of-americas-schools-and-ways-to-make-them-better-by-david-c-berliner/

16. "In 2012, Martin Carnoy and Richard Rothstein of the Economic Policy Institute analyzed the 2009 PISA data and compared U.S. results by social class to three top performers—Canada, Finland, and South Korea. They found that the relatively low ranking of U.S. students could be attributed in no small part to a disproportionate number of students from high-poverty schools among the test-takers. After adjusting the U.S. score to take into account social class composition and possible sampling flaws, Carnoy and Rothstein estimated that the United States placed fourth in reading and 10th in math—up from 14th and 25th in the PISA ranking, respectively." See: Walker, T. (2013, December 3). What do the 2012 PISA scores tell us about U.S. Schools? *neaToday.* Retrieved from http://neatoday.org/2013/12/03/ what-do-the-2012-pisa-scores-tell-us-about-u-s-schools-2/

17. Organization for Economic Cooperation and Development. (2016, August). CO2.2: Child poverty. Retrieved from http://www.oecd.org/els/soc/CO_2_2_ Child_Poverty.pdf

18. Chile, Israel, Spain, and Turkey.

19. Berliner, David C. (2009). *Poverty and Potential: Out-of-School Factors and School Success.* Boulder and Tempe: Education and the Public Interest Center & Education Policy Research Unit. Retrieved from http://epicpolicy.org/publication/ poverty-and-potential

20. National Center for Education Statistics. (2015). Achievement gaps. Retrieved from https://nces.ed.gov/nationsreportcard/studies/gaps/

21. Schneider, J. (2016, June 22). America's not-so-broken education system. *The Atlantic.* Retrieved from https://www.theatlantic.com/education/archive/2016/06/ everything-in-american-education-is-broken/488189/

22. Turner, C., Khrais, R., Lloyd, T., Olgin, A., Isensee, L., Vevea, B. & Carsen, D. (2016, April 18). Why America's schools have a money problem. National Public Radio (NPR). Retrieved from http://www.npr.org/2016/04/18/474256366/why-americas-schools-have-a-money-problem

23. Turner, C., Khrais, R., Lloyd, T., Olgin, A., Isensee, L., Vevea, B. & Carsen, D. (2016, April 18). Why America's schools have a money problem. National Public Radio (NPR). Retrieved from http://www.npr.org/2016/04/18/474256366/why-americas-schools-have-a-money-problem

24. Semuels, A. (2016, August 25). Good school, rich school; Bad school, poor school. *The Atlantic.* Retrieved from https://www.theatlantic.com/business/ archive/2016/08/property-taxes-and-unequal-schools/497333/

25. Leachman, M., Albares, N., Masterson, K. and Wallace, M. (2016, January 25). Most states have cut school funding, and some continue cutting. Center on Budget and Policy Priorities. Retrieved from http://www.cbpp.org/research/state-

budget-and-tax/most-states-have-cut-school-funding-and-some-continue-cutting

26. Baker, B., Farrie, D., Johnson, M., Luhm, T. and Sciarra, D.G. (2017). Is school funding fair? A national report card, sixth edition. Retrieved from https://drive .google.com/file/d/0BxtYmwryVI00VDhjRGlDOUh3VE0/view

27. See a map of lawsuits by state at http://schoolfunding.info

28. Editorial Board. (2017, May 5). Shaming children over school lunch bills. *New York Times*. Retrieved from https://www.nytimes.com/2017/05/05/opinion/ shaming-school-lunch-bills.html?smprod=nytcore-ipad&smid=nytcore-ipad-share&_r=0

29. Elias Siegel, B. (2017, April 30). Shaming children so parents will pay the school lunch bill. *New York Times*. Retrieved from https://www.nytimes.com/2017/04/30/ well/family/lunch-shaming-children-parents-school-bills.html

30. Green, E. L. and Hirschfeld Davis, J. (2017, May 1). Trump takes aim at school lunch guidelines and a girls' education program. *New York Times*. Retrieved from https://www.nytimes.com/2017/05/01/us/politics/nutrition-rules-school-lunches-michelle-obama.html

31. Gates, B. (2011, February 28). How teacher development could revolutionize our schools. *Washington Post*. Retrieved from http://www.washingtonpost.com/ wp-dyn/content/article/2011/02/27/AR2011022702876.html

32. NEAToday. (2014). Corporate reformers say money doesn't matter in public schools. The facts say otherwise. Excerpted from: Berliner, D. C. and Glass, Gene V. (2014). *50 Myths and Lies That Threaten America's Public Schools: The Real Crisis in Education*. New York: Teachers College Press. Excerpt retrieved from http:// neatoday.org/2014/05/04/corporate-reformers-say-money-doesnt-matter-in-public-schools-the-facts-say-otherwise/

33. Lathrop, D. (2016). Trump is off on claim that the United States spends the most on education. *Politifact Iowa*. Retrieved from http://www.politifact.com/iowa/ statements/2016/feb/09/donald-trump/trump-claim-united-states-spends-most-education/

34. Rothstein, R. (2002). The myth of public school failure. *American Prospect*. Retrieved from http://prospect.org/article/myth-public-school-failure

35. USDA. (2013). National School Lunch Program. Retrieved from https://www .fns.usda.gov/sites/default/files/NSLPFactSheet.pdf

36. Lafortune, J., Rothstein, J., & Schanzenbach, W. School finance reform and the distribution of student achievement. Working Paper 22011. Cambridge, MA: National Bureau of Economic Research.

37. Harris, E. A. and Fessenden, F. (2017, May 5). The broken promises of choice in New York City schools. Retrieved from https://www.nytimes.com/2017/05/05/ nyregion/school-choice-new-york-city-high-school-admissions.html?_r=0

38. Carey, K. (2017, February 23). Dismal voucher results surprise researchers as DeVos era begins. Blog post, *The Upshot, New York Times*. Retrieved from https://

www.nytimes.com/2017/02/23/upshot/dismal-results-from-vouchers-surprise-researchers-as-devos-era-begins.html

39. Camera, L. (2017, April 7). More bad news for private school choice programs. *U.S. News.* Retrieved from https://www.usnews.com/news/education-news/articles/2017-04-27/more-bad-news-for-private-school-choice-programs

40. Burris, C. (2017, January 23). Do charters and vouchers hurt public schools? The answer is "yes." *Network for Public Education.* Retrieved from https://networkforpubliceducation.org/2017/01/charters-vouchers-hurt-public-schools-answer-yes/

41. Strauss, V. (2017, March 9). Teacher to Ohio Gov. Kasich: "You are in the dark about life in the classroom." *Washington Post.* Retrieved from https://www.washingtonpost.com/news/answer-sheet/wp/2017/03/09/teacher-to-ohio-gov-kasich-you-are-in-the-dark-about-life-in-the-classroom/?utm_term=.419e2d46053d

42. PRWatch Editors. (2016). "National School Choice Week" fueled by major right-wing funders and corporate lobby groups. The Center for Media and Democracy's PR Watch. Retrieved from http://www.prwatch.org/news/2016/01/13024/national-school-choice-week-fueled-major-right-wing-funders-and-corporate-lobby

43. Buchen, I. (1999). Business sees profits in education: Challenging public schools. *The Futurist, 33*(5), 38–44.

44. Graves, L. (2016). Education department releases list of federally funded charter schools, though incomplete. The Center for Media and Democracy's PR Watch. Retrieved from http://www.prwatch.org/news/2016/01/13015/education-department-releases-list-federally-funded-charter-schools-though-incomplete

45. Baker, B. & Miron, G. (2015). The business of charter schooling: Understanding the policies that charter operators use for financial benefit. Boulder, CO: National Education Policy Center. Retrieved from http://nepc.colorado.edu/publication/charter-revenue

46. See, for example, these two articles. 1) Walker, T. (2017, March 31). What the charter school industry can learn from Enron—before it's too late. *neaToday.* Retrieved from http://neatoday.org/2017/03/31/charter-schools-second-coming-of-enron/ 2) Center for Popular Democracy. (2017, May). Charter school vulnerabilities to waste, fraud, and abuse. Retrieved from https://populardemocracy.org/sites/default/files/Charter-School-Fraud_Report_2017_web%20%281%29.pdf

47. Humire, J. M. (2016, March 10). Charter schools vulnerable to controversial Turkish movement. *The Hill.* Retrieved from http://thehill.com/blogs/congress-blog/education/272424-charter-schools-vulnerable-to-controversial-turkish-movement

48. Huseman, J. (2015, December 17). These charter schools tried to turn public education into big business. They failed. *Slate.* Retrieved from http://www.slate

.com/blogs/schooled/2015/12/17/for_profit_charter_schools_are_failing_and_fading_here_s_why.html

49. Weller, C. (2017). Betsy DeVos compared school choice to taking Uber over a taxi—here's why that could be troubling. *Business Insider.* Retrieved from http://www.businessinsider.com/betsy-devos-compares-school-choice- uber-2017-3

50. Carey, K. (2017, February 23). Dismal voucher results surprise researchers as DeVos era begins. Blog post, *The Upshot, New York Times.* Retrieved from https://www.nytimes.com/2017/02/23/upshot/dismal-results-from-vouchers-surprise-researchers-as-devos-era-begins.html

51. Strauss, V. (2015, October 24). Confirmed: Standardized testing has taken over our schools. But who's to blame? *Washington Post.* Available from https://www.washingtonpost.com/news/answer-sheet/wp/2015/10/24/confirmed-standardized-testing-has-taken-over-our-schools-but-whos-to-blame/?utm_term=.f52c9402a694

52. Chingos, M. M. (2012). Strength in numbers: State spending on K-12 assessment systems. Washington, DC: Brown Center on Education Policy at Brookings. Retrieved from https://www.brookings.edu/wp-content/uploads/2016/06/11_assessment_chingos_final_new.pdf

53. Publishers also stand to make a great deal more money by selling texts closely aligned with tests. Pearson, for example, is a major player in test sales—and also in textbooks promoted on the grounds that they prepare students for the tests they create.

54. Nor does it include the cost of various consultants schools may bring in to help raise test scores, or of practice test after practice test as students prepare for the test that counts.

55. Hancock, L. (2011, September). Why are Finland's schools successful? *Smithsonian.* Retrieved from http://www.smithsonianmag.com/innovation/why-are-finlands-schools-successful-49859555/

56. https://edreformnow.org/about-us/what-we-do/

57. https://edreformnow.org/about-us/what-we-do/

58. See, for example, Saul, S. (2011, December 12). Profits and questions at online charter schools. Retrieved from http://www.nytimes.com/2011/12/13/education/online-schools-score-better-on-wall-street-than-in-classrooms.html

59. http://educationopportunitynetwork.org/education_announcement/

SEVEN

∼ The Way Forward

"Unless someone like you
    cares a whole awful lot,
Nothing is going to get better.
    It's not."
—*Dr. Seuss*, The Lorax

WE BEGAN THIS BOOK WITH a story about getting lost on our way, even though we were clear about where we meant to be. Sometimes, that's just the way things go: you strike out in a particular direction that you feel confident is the right one, only to stop and look around at some point and say "This doesn't look right." Or, someone else insists you take a particular path and in the end you find it led you very far away from where you intended to go. In either case, the sense of dislocation, of not being where we had hoped to go, is a signal that it's time to stop and think about the paths we've been on.

Much of what we discussed in the prior pages "doesn't look right" to us. Our experience suggests that at least some of it probably doesn't look right to you, either. Surely we don't want kids to die or suffer emotional trauma when they're in schools. Surely we don't want corporations to find countless ways to make money on children, including marketing ploys to teach them that endless consumption ensures happiness, or corporate reforms that transform children into grist for money-making mills.

In other areas, we may not agree quite as much. There are legitimate arguments to be made for a variety of stances on the best goals for schools and students, on the essential curriculum that will lead to those goals, on what the most important characteristics of citizens are, on how much control is too much, and on what kinds of reforms will lead to better educative experiences for kids, regardless of how we define "better" and "educative." We've posed big questions in those areas, and we think every education professional ought to have thought through and clearly articulated a stance on such critical questions. There's no point in rehashing here the many assumptions and issues that beg for clarity and professional action detailed in the preceding chapters. Instead, we want to return to two specific missteps we laid out in the very first chapter and have left on the sidelines until now: trusting to good intentions and failing to believe we can make a difference.

As should have been evident in issue after issue, actions designed with the very best of intentions can in practice send messages that no educator ever intended: *The sole purpose of schools is to train students for jobs. One test can accurately represent students' talents and potentials. Human interaction is not an essential element of teaching and learning. Non-educators, like politicians and corporate leaders, know better than educators about what makes sense for educating kids.* But when school activity points unwaveringly at college or work readiness, when educators accept that the kids in "this school" or "that class" must receive a dumbed-down curriculum, when instruction is turned over to technology, and when educators passively accept marching orders from legislators and corporate titans, these are exactly the messages that are sent.

As experienced teacher educators, we wonder to what extent such unintended outcomes influence education professionals who walk away from schools. For example, in countries frequently praised for their education systems, like Finland and Singapore, teachers leave the profession at a rate of about 3–4% per year. That is half the rate of attrition for U.S. teachers, which has hovered around 8% for the last decade. And, between 2009 and 2014, enrollments in teacher education programs dropped by 35%, with over 240,000 fewer undergraduates preparing to enter classrooms.[1] Of course, development and retention of the teaching force is a complicated matter, with many factors influencing trends. But our experience tells us that many teachers are unhappy in situations where the outcomes they see are a stark contrast to their own professional goals. Consider, for example, this account from a former teacher of why she left the profession:

Danielle Painton, 34, is a former elementary school teacher from Pennsylvania.

When she landed a full-time teaching job right out of college, Painton counted herself lucky. But after a decade at a public elementary school near Lancaster, she called it quits.

Education has become test-and-data obsessed, she says: "The schools are being run a little bit more like on a business model of constantly collecting data and then (that's) driving all of our decisions."

It's a shift, she says, that eroded emphasis on the craft of teaching and seeing students as individuals.

"I can't see that kid who walks through my door—who didn't have breakfast or whose parents just got divorced—and think that his number on his latest test is the most important thing about that child on that day," she told [reporters].

Painton remembers a fourth-grade girl who, in the middle of a weeklong bout of testing, put her head down on her desk.

"I said, 'Are you okay?' " Painton recalls. "And she said, 'Mrs. Painton, this just isn't fun anymore.'"

That stuck.

"It was haunting me," she says. "I just kept hearing: This isn't fun anymore, this isn't fun anymore. And these are kids."[2]

It is our belief and experience that people enter education, specifically teaching in public schools, because they want to care for, inspire, challenge students—not to hurt or discourage them, not to faithfully execute policies that drive children to put their heads on their desks in despair.

No: good intentions are not enough—not for policy, and not for professional educators who find themselves living in an educational world that "isn't fun anymore," a world that frustrates and depresses them because they see kids suffering, a world in which their role has increasingly been cast simply as faithfully implementing harmful policies they often had no voice in shaping. We wrote this text in large part because we are worried about the possibility that education professionals, who know most about how specific policies are affecting specific children, might choose to walk away or stay away from schools. If that happens, who will have the on-the-ground knowledge—or the heart—necessary to chart a better path? Who will work toward a better educational experience for children who didn't have breakfast, or whose parents are getting divorced? Or who have to work nights to help put food on the table in their homes, or whose friend or relative recently died in a drive-by shooting?

We know, of course, that many of the issues we discussed are not about student suffering but come about due to legitimate disagreements as what kinds of citizens schools should be cultivating or whether every student in every school really must read *Romeo and Juliet*. But if a school community hasn't come together in collegial conversations to discuss those issues, to design and articulate a coherent and meaningful mission statement to serve as a sort of goal-post for their efforts, how are school personnel to measure where policies are going wrong or right? District or school mission statements frequently resemble the boilerplate language of a "mission generator"[3] —like this one: "The mission of [this district] is to work in partnership with students, families and the community to ensure that each student acquires the knowledge, skills and core values necessary to achieve personal success and to enrich the community." More often than not, such statements serve to meet some legislative reporting requirement rather than to guide the policies and actions within the district. Instead, and as we hope this text has helped demonstrate, school personnel need to come together and capture their commitments in meaningful language, they need to come together to specify *which* knowledge, skills and values are necessary. Until they do, there's little hope of students receiving unified messages or growing into the kind of adults that school personnel hope to nurture. Colleagues in a school need to have frank conversations, many of them, to ensure that they are all pulling in the same direction as much as possible.

And to the individual who says "But you don't understand. I'm just one person. I have no power," we say—nonsense. Everyone has agency.

- Anyone can think long and hard about the most important things students can learn in a specific classroom or office, create and hang a poster announcing those goals, and reflect every day on how the day's events promoted—or undermined—such learning. That could make a difference.
- Anyone can spend a week or two consciously analyzing the hidden curriculum embedded in his own classroom or office, or her own school building, to determine what messages are being sent. That could make a difference.

- Anyone can invite colleagues to a brown bag lunch to talk through ideas about what various curricula in the school community are teaching about citizenship—and whether or how it might be modified. That could make a difference.
- Anyone can ask to investigate, or to have a committee formed, to investigate the type, frequency and outcomes of such disciplinary actions as seclusion, restraint or expulsion in a specific school. That could make a difference.
- Anyone can research state opt-out policies as well as state opt-out groups and share the information with interested colleagues and parents. That could make a difference.

While no one can do everything, everyone can do something. Any one of these fairly modest actions could affect a few, or a few thousand, students. Not every idea or innovation will fly, not every goal will be realized, because that's the way of the world. Detours and mistakes are routine elements of every journey. The trick for educators as they work *toward* something better will be not to confuse a detour sign with a stop sign.

The power of one person to spark crucial change has been noted in powerful ways that appear repeatedly in popular culture (and in more than a few email signatures). "The only thing necessary for the triumph of evil is for good men to do nothing" said Edmund Burke.[4] "The journey of a thousand miles begins with a single step," said Lao Tzu. That these observations are commonplace does not make them less true. Waiting for others to make change when you see a clear need for it is a good way to slow down, or get in the way of, the change you would like to see. But oh, dear! We're sounding preachy, aren't we? So we'll stop. You get the idea.

Years of work with young people is a journey equivalent to a life journey of a thousand miles. Our wish for you is that at the end of it, you find that you'd taken a path that led to exactly where you intended to be.

Notes

1. Sutcher, L., Darling-Hammond, L. & Carver-Thomas, D. (2016, September 15). A coming crisis in teaching? Teacher supply, demand, and shortages in the

U.S. Learning Policy Institute. Retrieved from https://learningpolicyinstitute.org/product/coming-crisis-teaching

2. Westervelt, E. and Lonsdorf, K. (2016, October 24). What are the main reasons teachers call it quits? National Public Radio. Retrieved from http://www.npr.org/sections/ed/2016/10/24/495186021/what-are-the-main-reasons-teachers-call-it-quits

3. See "Mission Statement Generator," which offers adverbs, verbs, adjectives, and nouns resembling those often employed by schools at http://cmorse.org/missiongen/

4. While this quote is widely attributed to Burke, we want to acknowledge that attribution has been challenged because a source has not been identified.

Index